ARCHAEOLOGY OF THE ORIGIN
OF THE STATE

Archaeology of the Origin of the State

The Theories

VICENTE LULL AND RAFAEL MICÓ

Translated by
PETER SMITH

OXFORD
UNIVERSITY PRESS

Great Clarendon Street, Oxford OX2 6DP

Oxford University Press is a department of the University of Oxford.
It furthers the University's objective of excellence in research, scholarship,
and education by publishing worldwide in

Oxford New York

Auckland Cape Town Dar es Salaam Hong Kong Karachi
Kuala Lumpur Madrid Melbourne Mexico City Nairobi
New Delhi Shanghai Taipei Toronto

With offices in

Argentina Austria Brazil Chile Czech Republic France Greece
Guatemala Hungary Italy Japan Poland Portugal Singapore
South Korea Switzerland Thailand Turkey Ukraine Vietnam

Oxford is a registered trademark of Oxford University Press
in the UK and in certain other countries

Published in the United States
by Oxford University Press Inc., New York

© Oxford University Press 2011.
This revised English edition has been translated from The original Spanish publication
Arqueología del origen del Estado: las teorias
© 2007 by Vincent Lull and Rafael Micó. Published by Bellaterra Arqueologia.

The moral rights of the authors have been asserted
Database right Oxford University Press (maker)

First published 2011

All rights reserved. No part of this publication may be reproduced,
stored in a retrieval system, or transmitted, in any form or by any means,
without the prior permission in writing of Oxford University Press,
or as expressly permitted by law, or under terms agreed with the appropriate
reprographics rights organization. Enquiries concerning reproduction
outside the scope of the above should be sent to the Rights Department,
Oxford University Press, at the address above

You must not circulate this book in any other binding or cover
and you must impose the same condition on any acquirer

British Library Cataloguing in Publication Data

Data available

Library of Congress Cataloging in Publication Data

Data available

Typeset by SPI Publisher Services, Pondicherry, India
Printed in Great Britain
on acid-free paper by
MPG Books Group, Bodmin and King's Lynn

ISBN 978-0-19-955784-4

3 5 7 9 10 8 6 4 2

To Cristina and Roberto

Contents

Introduction　xi

PART I. THEORIES ABOUT THE STATE

1. The Classical Conception　3
   Plato (428–347 BC)　3
    Social classes in Plato's *Republic*　5
    Forms of government　9
    Conclusion　10
   Aristotle (384–322 BC)　12
    Forms of government　15
    Conclusions　16
   Differences and similarities within the classical conception　17

2. The State according to Christianity　24
   Precedents of Christian political thought　25
   St Thomas of Aquinas (1225–74)　28
   Conclusions　33

3. The Renaissance of the State　36
   Machiavelli (1469–1527)　36
   Conclusions　41

4. The Seventeenth Century: Fear and Property　44
   Thomas Hobbes (1588–1679): the reasonable wolf　45
    Individual and society　49
    Conclusion　52
   John Locke (1632–1704): the instigator of 'human rights'　53
    Conclusion　59

5. The Eighteenth Century: Lights and Shadows in the State　65
   Jean-Jacques Rousseau (1712–78)　67
    Rousseau and political participation　78
    Conclusion　81

6. The Absolute State　86
   Georg Wilhelm Friedrich Hegel (1770–1831)　86
    Hegelian philosophy and his triads　87

The elements of the philosophy of right	89
The State	98
Conclusion: problems with the Hegelian State	102

7. **The Critique of the State in Marx** — 108
   - From idealist humanism to historical materialism — 109
   - The historical conditions of the State: *The German Ideology* — 114
   - The historical conditions of the State: *The Formen* — 117
   - Forms of property and State — 121
   - The future of the State — 124
   - Marxist tradition and the State — 127

8. **Evolutionism and State** — 135
   - Lewis Henry Morgan (1818–81) — 137
     - Savagery — 140
     - Barbarism — 141
     - Civilization — 142
     - The meanings of evolutionary periodization — 143
   - Neo-evolutionism — 148
   - Elman R. Service (1915–96) — 151
     - Bands — 151
     - Tribes — 151
     - Chiefdom — 152
     - Primitive States and archaic civilizations — 152
     - Egalitarian or segmental societies — 153
     - Chiefdom societies — 154
     - Archaic civilization and State — 155
   - Morton H. Fried (1923–86) — 157
     - The egalitarian society — 157
     - Hierarchized or rank societies — 158
     - Stratified societies — 159
     - The State — 160
   - Neo-evolutionism: discussion and assessment — 161
   - Conclusion — 168

PART II. ARCHAEOLOGY OF THE STATE

9. **Archaeology and Research on the State** — 175
   - Definition of the object of study — 176
   - The impact of V. G. Childe (1892–1957) — 180

Processual archaeology and research on the formation of the State	189
Complexity	194
Evolution, typologies, and surveys	197
Empirical regularity and explanation	203
The explanation of change: the reasons for the rise of civilizations	207
Critical remarks	212
Archaeology of the State in post-modern times	215
10. Towards a Marxist Archaeology of the State	227
Notes for archaeological research on the State: theory	230
The production of social life	231
Division of tasks and the social division of production	232
General production and the 'place' of politics	234
The formation of the State	237
The politics of State	241
The state-of-the-world	244
Notes for archaeological research on the State: method	246
11. Epilogue. Theories on the State and the Archaeology of the State: Continuities and Complicity	255
Individual and . . . society?	255
Social relationships	259
Morality, identity, and State	262
Modern archaeology and State	268
References	273
Index	283

Introduction

The objective of this book is to offer a synthesis of the main theories that have been made about what nowadays we define as 'State'; a synthesis that may be useful for anyone undertaking research on societies that have developed that kind of political organization and, above all, on the societies that are conventionally studied by archaeology. It is not by chance, in this respect, that our teaching activity in 'archaeology of the origin of the State' has greatly influenced the writing of this book. The account is not complete, nor for our part could it be; this is a goal of various general works on political science and philosophy.[1] Our interest here lies in summarizing the contributions that, according to our criteria, have influenced most of the forms that the State has taken and which we experience and, above all, understand today. We may be accused of the crime of intentionality in the choice of the different opinions we will examine. We are aware of that. It would be a well-aimed and truthful accusation, we might almost say logical, as, for any political scholar, the choice of discourse is by definition politics itself. A discussion on the State cannot fail to be political, for, if it was not political, it would be nothing.

In the following pages, in the first place we shall embark on a journey around the main stages in the concept of what today we call 'State' with the sole aim of expressing these stages in the authors' own words and situating the topic through a series of definitions and general reflections. This choice is basically a response to the influence we still have on research in archaeology and history in general, even though this influence is sometimes dressed in other terminological gowns. Each author's presentation is based on a brief description of some of their most significant works. We have therefore avoided studying each thinker in totality, a task which would certainly have been beyond our reach and, instead, we have preferred to focus on what we have considered each thinker's most valuable or fecund contributions in connection with the topic in hand. Only Hegel and Marx have been studied in greater detail, especially in order to reflect on the complexity of their proposals (opposing ones, in fact) on the *raison d'être* of the State. It is also worth mentioning that we have reduced the quotations, references, and comments made by other scholars of the authors' works to a minimum. In this sense, we are presenting a very personal analysis of the selected works. In certain cases, however, we could not resist the temptation of questioning the quality or orientation of the political discourse they endorse, despite our original intention of simply showing their more significant components.

These are, in short, theories covering a wide chronological and cultural range, from ancient Greece to contemporary political philosophy. Many of these 'political readings' have taken deep root in the common sense of our age and characterize a clearly Western tradition with its origin in Greek antiquity. We can briefly characterize the classical conception, seen in Plato and Aristotle, by its emphasis on the interest of a collective above strictly individual interests; the Christian viewpoint, by the dominance of the individual subjective perception of *save-yourself* in contrast with the classical collective ideal; and the Renaissance view, singularized in Machiavelli's *The Prince*, for the way it lays bare the strategies of State power and certain material interests that these pursue. The term 'State' itself is born and becomes more widespread precisely at that time.

Out of the three criteria for State listed above, appears the enlightened-liberal perspective, legal tender still in our times, of which several variations are known. The first version stresses the notion of sovereignty as the key to the solution to the problems arising because 'man is a wolf for man'. It commences with the conviction that individuals, in a pre-political natural State, fight against each other permanently, surviving in an environment where only force counts (Hobbes). The unbearable fear of losing one's life is only overcome by establishing a pact which institutes the 'empire of the Law'. Every State and every society is founded on this compulsory covenant, as it is agreed to by those who have no other choice if they want to go on living. Any constitution in force should hold full sovereignty and deserve all possible support, however cruel it may appear to be. Anything is better than returning to the original anarchy and chaos.

The second liberal variation refers to the empirical and, paradoxically, abstract *natural right* of Locke and Rousseau. Both authors founded the State on the assumption of innate individual rights which, by a pact or contract, are ceded to a governmental institution which is thus born precisely at that moment. Again, sovereignty is a

Introduction xiii

key notion, although this time it resides, directly (Rousseau) or indirectly (Locke), with the 'people', understood as the group of individuals holding certain unalienable rights.

The third modern version situates the State fully in the dominion of the Idea. Everything yields to reason and reason sees nothing more rational than belonging to a State. State is reason made matter, reason objectified. This is a metaphysical-rationalist trend (*duty of State*) that Hegel situates in the transformation of the self-consciousness of the spirit.

As a result of the mixture of these three variants and the development of science in the nineteenth century, positivist, and later evolutionist, conceptions of the State were generated, bringing different nuances to the same semantic space. The State was now understood as a historical form which could be analysed by beginning with the recognition and study of pre-State forms of political organization. That it was the best possible form of society was never questioned but, unlike previous proposals, authors tried to shake off the idea of the State as the manifestation of will, either shared by private individuals (contract) or general and metaphysical (ethical idea). Because of this, historical, anthropological, and archaeological studies saw a broad field of research open up, in which we are still working today. In accordance with evolutionism, it is thought that throughout most of its history, the human race has lived within 'simple' societies, that is to say, not in States. However, with increasing frequency since Neolithic times, societies have needed to battle against adverse environmental, demographic, and technological conditions that caused serious problems for the survival of the human groups. This has forced them to seek new forms of organization that would enable them to overcome the crisis; in other words, they were forced to change to adapt and survive, as is the law in all species faced with the continuous filter of natural selection. The institution of the State was precisely a complex adaptive mechanism developed by human societies in response to certain environmental pressures. Politics, an extension of the wider category of 'culture', was to characterize better than anything else the only species that can dispense with the chance of genetic mutation to perpetuate itself successfully.

After the development of evolutionary theory in the nineteenth century, the State is defined as the institution or group of political institutions corresponding to civilized societies. These make up a subgroup within the full range of human variability, and both their appearance and functioning depends on factors that the new social and human sciences must attempt to elucidate. Philosophy is materialized and empirical knowledge is increased by the sciences of anthropology, sociology, historiography and archaeology. The arguments are supported by numerous forms of data until the person of the professional scientist appears. This figure, as a civil servant in the pay of the, generally capitalist, State, usually tends to draft discourses of legitimization and find the opportune data to sanction them.

Timidly looking over Western academia in the twentieth century, yet mobilizing and revolutionary in the social life on five continents, the Marxist conception of the State constitutes the main counter-argument to the previous proposals. Thus, whereas the latter promote discourses legitimizing the existence of the State, Marxism reveals the exploitation and classist socioeconomic reality that the State serves, nourishing segregation and competition, hierarchy and inequality, coercion and exploitation in the hands of a dominant class with a licence to kill. The State is now understood as a political organization rooted in historically determined material conditions. Marxism denies, therefore, that the State is an intrinsic condition of social life, an unavoidable necessity or an ethical aspiration of human reason, and instead, it situates it in the cross hairs of revolutionary objectives that must lead to its extinction once a classless society has been created.

The second part of the book has more specific contents, in that it describes the most influential approaches in the research on the rise and growth of the first States. This part is situated, as may be imagined, within the field of archaeology, the discipline that best defines our training and our profession. Although it is necessary to recognize the accumulated work of innumerable researchers over more than a century, we must comment critically on the premises and methods that, in our opinion, have led to the stagnation currently suffered by the 'state of the question'. Basically two factors contribute to this stagnation. The first is related to the survival of an antiquarian and almost fetishist tradition, closely linked to art history, which obtains an apparently endless source of motifs and resources from archaeology. Monuments in ruins, jewellery, and weapons resized 'spectacularly' by the mass media and thanks to the tourist industry nourish discourses and images which nowadays, just as two centuries ago, are aimed at impressing an audience, lumbering them with some brief message, usually of a reactionary kind, or simply keeping them entertained for a while.

Introduction

The second factor for the stagnation comes from the direction that most official academic research has taken in recent decades. Despite undeniable progress in the analysis of empirical manifestations, processual and post-processual archaeology, which dominates in the countries where most resources are applied to research in the formation of the first States, is constrained by its excessive dependence on other social sciences. Rather than being a tool to produce first-hand knowledge about some crucial moments in our common past, archaeology studying the material remains of the first States is thus restricted to recognizing versions, opinions, and proposals foreign to the materiality being researched. This recognition has been endowed with all the disciplines and formalities belonging to Academia, in such a way that many professionals have adopted ways of working in common, independently of the colour of the interpretation of the State that each one prefers. While these ways of working contributed in their day to overcoming the stagnation of more traditional forms of archaeology, at present they threaten to turn into a dead weight whose inertia we obey without questioning.

Dazzled (although always legitimized) by the fetishism of discovery and regulated by the administrative servitude of the profession, archaeology is accustomed to finding good excuses for postponing a reflection about what it does and why. Please use the modest contribution offered by this book as a step towards constructing and giving meaning to our research.

ACKNOWLEDGEMENTS

To Roberto Risch and Cristina Rihuete Herrada, to whom the book is dedicated. Even if it is only for once, we agree with Aristotle in acknowledging friendship as the greatest social value. The constant support of both and their ever-valuable suggestions and contributions have supported a journey not without its doubts. Obviously, we would like to make clear that they are not responsible for the errors and omissions that the present book may contain.

To María Eugenia Aubet and to Robert Chapman, for their assistance and determination that the book should see the light of day in the best possible condition, and the staff of Oxford University Press responsible for preparing and editing the text, especially Hilary O'Shea. Nor have we forgotten Manuel Lull, who showed great patience in the complex task of revising the Bibliography.

A substantial part of the reflections and proposals expressed in this book were generated in the context of research on the development of the first State society in the Iberian Peninsula, the so-called Argaric Group. Therefore, we would like to acknowledge the support of the bodies that have funded the different projects involved in this research: 'Archaeology of the funerary assemblages in the Argaric Group. Economy, politics and kinship in the prehistoric communities in southeast Spain (2250–1500 BC)' (BHA2003-04546) and 'Archaeology of the Argaric Group. Production and politics in the southeast of the Iberian Peninsula (2250–1500 BC)' (HUM2006-04610/HIST), both supported by the Spanish Ministry of Education and Science, and the Mediterranean Social Archaeo-ecological Research Group, backed by the General Department for Research of the Catalan Government (2009SGR 778).

NOTE

1. For anyone interested in learning about these topics it may also be useful to read some general books about the theory and history of political ideas. The following can be mentioned as accessible to the general reader: N. Bobbio (1987); G. H. Sabine (1937); D. Thomson, ed. (1966); J. Touchard (1996); F. Vallespín, ed. (1990).

Part I

Theories about the State

1

The Classical Conception

PLATO (428–347 BC)

In the Greek world, the 'city government', the notion that we would translate today as 'State', was determined by two opposing ideological positions: as an expression of justice and as an instrument of power. Despite this, they both shared the same premises. The first is that State and society had arisen simultaneously and the second that the State was at once both order and orderliness, whether this was desired or imposed.

The ideal of the Greek *polis*, as a place of harmony between collective and individual life, gave absolute priority to the social situation, as a requisite of identity, with the capability of granting autonomy to individuals and groups of individuals; the very criterion of being fully human was found in that belonging. Individuals *were*, as long they were ascribed to their cultural, economic, political, and social community. The *polis*, as a tie or link or, in any case, autarchic identity, provided the Athenians, Corinthians, or Spartans with something to hold on to; *the* specific place and support in that world that we now call Hellenic.

The different social and territorial collectives gave plenitude to the individual. Among these collectives, belonging to the *polis* was the only exact and effective criterion that equalled *human being* with *citizen*. The *polis*, as the place where human beings could realize themselves, was only occupied with full guarantees by a minority of men and a few women, who were included in the privileged classes, with recognized ancestral roots. Thus, the harmony of the *polis* was maintained by forbidding the largest sectors of society to take part in that sphere.

For nearly all the philosophical schools in classical antiquity, the State was the fairest form of social organization. It was thought and upheld that the State expressed an order inspired by Justice and Goodness. Nonetheless, it was a point of debate whether some types of States were fairer than others, but in any case, they all tended towards the same point. Justice was held up as the foundation articulating social relationships; the most desired State would be one which aspired to the best adjustment of social relationships within the *polis*. The level of Justice obtained was therefore that which granted legitimacy to a State. This level was measured by a foreseen *plan* whose aim was social Good. But, for whom?

The sophists spoke out against this conception held by the majority. They considered that the State was the form of organization wanted by the most powerful, and therefore the best way to ensure injustice. To do Evil brought greater profits and pleasure and was far easier than to be virtuous, whereas to do Good was arduous and extremely difficult.[1]

The dialogue between Socrates and Thrasymachus presented by Plato in the *Republic*[2] is an important text, reflecting on the nature of power and the State, on the link between reality and our abstractions and above all, about the exploitation of others under the assumption of our idea of Good. The sophists' starting point that justice and the law, as the fulfilment of the former, depended on who held authority led to the conclusion that justice was whatever was *most beneficial to the strongest*.

> THRASYMACHUS: And that what has power in any given country is the government?
> SOCRATES: Yes.
> THRASYMACHUS: Now, each government passes laws with a view to its own advantage: a democracy makes democratic laws, a dictatorship makes dictatorial laws, and so on and so forth. In doing so, each government makes it clear that what is right and moral for its subjects is what is to its own advantage; and each government punishes anyone who deviates from what is advantageous to itself as if he were a criminal and a wrongdoer. So, Socrates, this is what I claim morality is: it is the same in every country, and that is what is to the advantage of the current government. Now, of course it's the current government which has power, and the consequence of this, as anyone who thinks

about the matter correctly can work out, is that morality is everywhere the same – the advantage of the stronger party.[3]

This is one of the first descriptions of the State as the representation of a social being in conflict, consisting of opposing interests that only force could choose between. All social orders used force to impose their interests in the field of politics.[4]

These are the theories that Plato fights against with ardour. In a sequential chain of rising abstractions, Plato established dialectical formulae that would have great fortune later and in which the State, revealed by the knowledge of the wise and *above* reality, comprehends and discerns Good, and is seen to able to establish the role of what is 'just'. Inversely, and in a descending order, the State is applied to itself as the most comprehensive road of *men* towards Good, and in turn becomes the compulsory aim of all who wish to live in harmony.

Plato refers to an Order determined by Good. All Order and Justice come from Good. Therefore, the true State should be one that avoids ignorance and its partner, anarchy, at all costs, and should have Good as its main aim, concluding, in a perfect, universal and social loop, which ends where it began, in those *who decide* Good.

Social classes in Plato's *Republic*

Returning to pragmatism for an instant, Plato does not hesitate to profess that the aim of the State is to hold power, attend to the exterior, and take charge in the interior of material things, labour, economy, and social order. To achieve this objective, Plato outlines the project of an ideal State, whose population would be structured in three segments or layers with clearly differentiated social and intellective aims. The first layer, from which the leaders of the State would be taken, would be formed by magistrates, who are both rulers and philosophers. The only solution for the problems of any State and the human race is that its rulers should be the best, in other words, philosophers devoted to the contemplation of knowledge[5] and the search for goodness. The idea of Good is something that only philosophers are familiar with:

SOCRATES: Well, what I'm saying is that it's goodness which gives the things we know their truth and makes it possible for people to have knowledge. It is responsible for knowledge and truth and you should think of it as being within the intelligible realm, but you shouldn't identify it with knowledge and truth, otherwise you'll be wrong: for all their value, it is even more valuable. In the other realm, it is right to regard light and sight as resembling the sun, but not to identify either of them with the sun; so in this realm it is right to regard knowledge and truth as resembling goodness, but not to identify either of them with goodness, which should be rated even more highly.[6]

Wise men are those for whom material things are not an object of covetousness. They are the only people who, through their knowledge of true reason and dialectic,[7] can guide society towards Goodness[8] by establishing and safeguarding the appropriate order and justice for this aim. Government will be 'good' only when its ruler is 'a man who combines the knowledge of good with that of beauty and morality'.[9] Above all, the philosopher should control the management of society. One of their powers is illuminating: choosing at birth to which social layer the new child should be ascribed. The fable said that the gods made those who were destined to govern out of gold, the defenders of the State or warriors out of silver, and the workers and craftsmen who had to provide clothes, shelter, and food for everyone out of iron and bronze. Therefore, it was the magistrates' task to determine what metal each child's soul was made of, and hence assign the child to the function most suited to his or her nature.[10] It is significant that Plato considered it possible for women to have access to the first layer, although he believed in the general inferiority of women,[11] and only valued or accepted those possessing qualities analogous to those of men.

The second layer is formed by the guardian-warriors, destined to watch over and maintain the security of the State. They should form a small, well-trained group, and had to follow a very strict education programme to avoid their becoming tyrants or protectors of tyrants. Meticulous care should be taken in their training, because occasionally some of them could reach the layer of the magistrates.

Plato gives us instructions about the particularities of their education, which should be guided and directed towards the ideas of Good and Truth. He proposes that they should be told fables and stories showing the gods as beings who only perform good, fair, and true deeds. Their instruction must avoid sentimental and emotional literature, and should include a certain type of gymnastics and music. The demand that the same tasks and training be applied to both women and men is again a revolutionary proposition for his time.[12]

The class of guardian-warriors consists of men, women, and their sons and daughters, allowing cohabitation between men and a community in the children's education.[13] Their reproduction was regulated by the State:[14] 'a woman can serve the community by producing children between the ages of twenty and forty, a man by fathering children from when he passes his peak as a runner until the age of fifty-five'.[15] The sons and daughters would be held in common. Between seven and ten months after the union, the warriors would consider all the children who are born as sons or daughters, and, among themselves, these would be brothers and sisters.

This is the class which is typified in greatest detail in Plato's *Republic*, as it forms a social category, the army, capable of upsetting the State and sowing injustice. Details are also given of the kind of life the guardians should lead to avoid their becoming protectors of masters and tyrants. To ensure this did not occur, they were not allowed to own more than a small individual property. Their home and larder could not be closed to anyone. Moreover, the food they needed would be provided by citizens in reward for their services, so that they had no surplus or lack of anything.[16]

The third and final social layer is formed by the peasants who had to provide the means of subsistence, and the craftsmen and people who received a salary for their labour ('mercenaries'). All these were responsible for covering basic social needs by a full-time occupation in the essential tasks of producing society's material necessities. According to Plato's plan, it is obvious that none of these could ever rule the State as, we can recall, only philosophers have rational access to the knowledge of Good and therefore, only they can guarantee a just social order that will tend towards that aim. The remaining citizens, warriors, and producers should possess the virtue of *temperance*, which is simply recognizing the authority of the rulers, not from fear but from the conviction that the rulers are the most capable of the task intellectually and that their decisions will always be guided by the pursuit of the common good and never for private profit. Only the ignorant would act against order, justice, and good.

The social order devised by Plato is structured by a carefully planned division of labour. Each person holds a social position depending on the combination of innate aptitudes (soul made of gold, silver, or bronze and iron) and guided education (choice of fables and musical compositions in agreement with ideas of virtue, temperance, etc., inspiring the State). Therefore, the Republic would not be based on principles of inheritance, where by the practice of certain occupations was passed down from father to son.

However, a contradiction can be seen between the respect for precepts typical of a caste system (the children of each group should learn from the earliest possible age)[17] and a derivation of his concept of Justice, according to which it is just that each person should do what it is in his or her nature to do best. This implies unrestricted recruitment when covering the number of individuals needed for any given occupation; that is, that in principle all individuals are potentially suitable for holding any position in society. This only depends (as Plato puts the words in Socrates' mouth) on the composition of their soul, in other words, on their innate aptitudes and skills, and not on considerations of hereditary wealth or caste endogamy. Thus, what Socrates proposes in book V of the *Republic* is contrary to the fore-mentioned regulations, as he suggests precisely a kind of group endogamy in it.

Plato's social planning of the State creates, in effect, a hierarchy which grants greater value to certain functions. It is always supposed that the rules of behaviour proposed by a small group of guardians and magistrates will be correct and will produce benefits for the rest of society. This implicitly means that greater primacy will be given to the military and governing sectors than to peasants and craftsmen. This is indicated explicitly in brief exchanges, such as:

> 'And what about the rest of the citizen body? Will the guardians be the best?'
> 'By far the best.'[18]

or when recommending that a soldier who 'deserts or discards his weapons or does anything cowardly like that be made an artisan or a farmer'.[19]

In principle, however, the State does not contemplate the regulation of financial inequality. The existence of inequalities in wealth is not denied (the existence of rich and poor is occasionally referred to),[20] but these should not exist among the classes or castes of guardians and magistrates. Both constitute a kind of civil service whose minimum basic needs will be met by the social body, and who are forbidden the possession of sources of private wealth. Thus, the possibility of growing richer or poorer appears to be restricted to the sector of the 'mercenaries' (craftsmen, farmers, and merchants), although this question, like nearly every aspect of this sector, is little worthy of Plato's attention.

Forms of government

The *Republic* describes the project of a future State, but also deals with the analysis and assessment of existing States. Plato believes that the finest form of government, the most 'good' and therefore the most just, is the aristocratic State. The other forms of government, such as timocracy, oligarchy, democracy, and tyranny arise as a degeneration of this form, that is, from bad to worse. Despite this, rebellion can never be justified in the State, as it is the only weapon that can cause its downfall. Chapter VIII of the *Republic* describes the characteristics of these forms of State. Thus, aristocracy is a State governed by the best. Timocracy is the government of the ambitious who believe themselves to be superior because they are good huntsmen, sportsmen, or soldiers and who are, in the end, men of action, who own properties and get rich in secret. Oligarchy represents the government of a small group of wealthy citizens who hold power. In democracy there are neither criteria, nor ideals of law and order, as truth itself is not believed in, only subjective personal appetites, depending on who governs the city. It is only the ideal form of government in appearance, where no one is in command, with no coercion, where equality is shared out equally. Tyranny is the degeneration of democracy and arises when freedom concludes in licentiousness and the people need a leader to settle internal conflicts produced by private desires and selfishness.

Plato exercised great influence later in both philosophy and politics. His political proposals, the first systematic reflections of their kind, are still valid to a large extent today. Plato is the first defender of the State as the only rational and real form of living in society. Although he believes that not all States are good, the solution is to transform them according to new formulae devised by reason. The State, as a rational order oriented by the idea of Good, will tend towards it in a dialectical process of knowledge that will enable social happiness to be reached. This desire is not strange in the context that Plato lived in. Greece in the fourth century BC was a world in upheaval, shaken by frequent conflicts among cities and within them. The traditional *polis* was in crisis and about to be swallowed up by larger political entities. The empires of Philip of Macedonia and Alexander the Great would bring about that transition.

Conclusion

Plato proposed a 'revolution from above'; taking place when the son of a king or ruler of a State might be a 'philosopher' and from his position apply the rules inspiring the ideal State, outlined by Socrates in the course of his dialogues with different speakers. From this start, it was thought the advantages and success that would result from the materialization of those precepts would cause the example to spread to other States.[21]

The *Republic* expresses general consent in the face of inequality based on wisdom, and the recognition of an authority to be obeyed with temperance. The division of tasks and responsibilities in the context of Plato's *Republic* is the fairest and most appropriate, as each person takes his or her place according to the scheme set out by the most suitable (the philosophers) who take into account the innate qualities of each and reinforce them by a correct education. In this way, the social role assigned to everyone results in the best for all, as it guarantees harmony within an order that pursues Good.

Plato harmonizes the idea of Good with the established forms of the political community, afterwards adding to it the value of knowledge and reason, in such a way that Good does not appear paradoxical: a Good that acts and is fortified as the ideology of Good.

When any idea is shared by a group it turns into ideology. The ideology forms and defines the place of the shared ideas. They originate in reflections on a certain social practice and are rooted in the material conditions which make that practice possible. Ideologies seek reasons to legitimize those roots or to subvert them. Therefore, ideologies always imply opposite conceptions about social good. Thus, unfortunately for the Platonic ideal, Good for some usually involves Evil for others. Good is not an absolute that transcends historical or situational conditions. Ideologies are ways of thinking that originate in the world and act in it, owing to certain conditions that support them. Consequently, ideologies only count if they are put into practice, and they are only put into practice when the conditions are appropriate. The important thing is what is done or achieved with the ideologies, not the representation or the opinion of what is good or needs to be done. Plato, in his *Republic*, offered a utopian model of a social order which was never really implanted because materially, it was not in anybody's interest to put it into practice.

The assumptions that Plato started with are questionable and in any case even paradoxical. In the first place, the belief that the gathering of many men originated what we call the State to help each other mutually, equates the notion of State with the notion of society, confusing government with any kind of social relationship. This assumption presupposes a further point: individuality as the starting point of community. The impotence of a single man to be self-sufficient as regards his requirements and needs pushed him to live in society.[22] This starting point of a subjective and individualist conscience even assimilates the art of government with the profession of a doctor or ship's captain, introducing the conviction that all rulers do not pursue their own benefit,[23] but that of their subjects, and that governments always pursue the common interest.

Freedom itself has a conditioned name and the right adjectives to enjoy it. We are not free to do what we wish; our limits are marked by material conditions. In Plato's society, as in our own, the space of 'freedom' was what the owners of material conditions wished to assign in order to increase their own space. In both societies, the poor cannot 'freely' decide to cease to be so; whereas in the *polis* they were refused citizenship, now the freedom proclaimed in the Constitutions can neither avoid nor hide the production of social misery. If the wealth of the poor, together with their real freedom, means the poverty of the rich, the latter will impede it with their full arsenal of violence.

Plato is a true member of the late *polis*; for him morality is 'doing one's own job and not intruding elsewhere',[24] an unambiguous duty for a collective that recognizes its status and aims to progress in the order of the social demands of a community which knows its place in the world. Moral principles are thus established in social precepts (temperance, justice, virtue, etc.) that presage the political context Hegel was to grant them later. With them and the idea of reasonable Good as aims, Plato aspired to overcome the corrupt forms of government he knew in his time.

ARISTOTLE (384–322 BC)

Aristotle's *Politics*[25] differs in its methods and certain objectives from Plato's *Republic*. Aristotle analyses what *is*, in this case the political constitutions of his time, and only tangentially suggests what *should be*. His first goal, therefore, is not to devise a recipe for an ideal world, but to extract practical teachings through the observation of what exists.

In the terrain of politics, the first thing that strikes the attention is the explanation of the differences between the various groups making up the community. Aristotle settles the matter in a clear and decisive way by reverting to natural determination: a man may be a ruler if he has organizational abilities and a subject if he is able to work with his body.[26] Males are granted authority and power of leadership as they are superior to females, whereas these are governed and, despite possessing deliberative capacity, are without authority.[27] Male children also possess deliberative capacity, but in an imperfect form. Therefore, mature males are more apt than immature youths. People are slaves when they are capable of belonging to another, as they are lacking in deliberative faculty and, although they share reason (they recognize it), they do not possess it (animals are not aware of reason).[28] In their uses, animals and slaves are similar (they provide what is needed by the body). Regarding justice, platonic temperance is equally subject to the self-determination of a naturalized being.

> Justice is thought by them to be, and is, equality, not for all however, but only for equals. And inequality is thought to be, and is, justice; neither is this for all, but only for unequals.[29]

Therefore, the starting point is fixed in that things are 'naturally'. The first of these is that human beings are by nature social animals, as no individual is 'sufficient for himself'.[30] However, this notion of original nature that should establish a pristine idea of *community* above the intentions and desires of individuals comes up against numerous affirmations based on another opposite conviction that says that people *choose* to live together. The union between men and women is necessary for social life, and also friendship is equally necessary for the *choice* of the common life already mentioned.

The minimum organizational unit in society is the *oikos* (the household). A collection of houses forms a village, which prefigures in turn the city or perfect community, formed by the union of several villages. The *oikos* is made up of slaves and free individuals whose functions are those of master (patriarch or owner), the wife and mother, and finally the art of acquiring property.[31] Household and property are closely linked and form the material basis of citizenship. For Aristotle, revolutions arise precisely as conflicts over property and can only be avoided through education and laws. 'The beginning of reform is not so much to equalize property as to train the nobler sort of natures not to desire more, and to prevent the lower from getting more; that is to say, they must be kept down but not ill-treated.[32] This sentence is the defence of a certain unmovable and stable *status quo*, and a moral sanction of the excesses that disturb the ideal of order and dominion.

For Aristotle, citizens are those people who have the right to take part in the deliberative or judicial administration of the State.[33] This participation is the essence of political science, 'the greatest good and in the highest degree',[34] and of Law, which is 'reason unaffected by desire'.[35] Politics and Reason with no selfish interests combine with Virtue as the fundamental notions for delivering Justice. The use of these notions is reminiscent of Plato, although we should not deceive ourselves on this topic, as Aristotle puts the absolutes in context. Thus, justice consists of what is in the common interest[36] and this is everything that may lead to happiness. For Aristotle, if a happy life is one that is followed according to virtue, 'and that virtue is a mean, then the life that is in a mean, must be the best'.[37] Therefore, as 'in all states there are three elements: one is very rich, another very poor, and a third in a mean', it is necessary to increase the role of the citizens in the middle class.[38]

Happiness and a harmonious regime are synonyms of the same goal, the citizens' wishes. This aspiration of all citizens for what is good for them and for their city is accompanied by an intense battery of precepts and ethic and moral sentences that try to convince politically about what is needed in order to live in society: 'mankind do not acquire or preserve virtue by the help of external goods, but external goods by the help of virtue';[39] 'happiness, whether consisting in pleasure or virtue, or both, is more often found with those who are most highly cultivated in their mind and in their character';[40] 'external goods come of themselves, and chance is the author of them, but no one is just or temperate by or through chance';[41] 'the happy state . . . cannot act without doing right actions and neither individual nor state can do right actions without virtue and wisdom'.[42]

Aristotle's idealistic position does not leave any room for doubt: 'the greatest opposition is confessedly that of virtue and vice; next comes that of wealth and poverty; and there are other antagonistic elements greater or less...'.[43] First: the idea, the notion, the abstract noun, the subjective reality; later: the substance, matter, objective reality. This does not mean that it is not preferable for spiritual virtues and material conditions to go hand in hand: 'the best life, both for individuals and states, is the life of virtue, when virtue has *external goods enough* for the performance of good actions'[44] (our italics).

Modern readers may be surprised by how up to date Aristotle's thinking is, or equally, how old and out of date our way of thinking is. Just as in the present time, the citizenship Aristotle refers to is constructed beforehand or prearranged. Only a few can enter it if they have a certain level of resources, and respect the conditions laid down by the city. In this point, Aristotle does not need the subterfuge of modern-day politics, when universal rights are declared knowing full well that they can never be exercised with full guarantees. In an example without precedents, laying bare the reality of politics, he tells us 'citizens must not lead the life of mechanics or tradesmen... neither must they be husbandmen, since leisure is necessary for the development of both virtue and the performance of political duties'.[45] Thus, government will be taken over by people who are able to live a life of leisure and, among these, those who tend towards the happy medium: it is natural that there are rich and poor; the question is to avoid the imbalance between them reaching a level which could threaten the government of the city.

The treatment Aristotle gives to the education of the young is highly relevant. In principle he seems progressive and ahead of his time when he proposes that education should be the same for all the citizens and consequently regulated by law and not private.[46] However, it later becomes clear that the education he refers to follows strict and exclusive aims for a small group of inhabitants of the city, the citizens, to whom he sends messages like the following:

> 'Any occupation, art or science, which makes the body or soul or mind of the freeman less fit for the practice or exercise of virtue is vulgar; wherefore we call those arts vulgar which tend to deform the body, and likewise all paid employments, for they absorb and degrade the mind.'[47]

Leisure appears again as the basis of a citizen's life; first it allows him to have access to an exclusive education, and later to take the reins of the city. Leisure is thus 'the first principle of all action... is better than occupation and is its end'.[48] Surprisingly, he does not value in the same way the possibilities of leisure in the lower classes of society, when he laments that 'the laziest are shepherds, who lead an idle life, and get their subsistence without trouble from tame animals'.[49] In conclusion, it is not the type of activity that determines people's aptitudes, but their 'nature'.[50]

Forms of government

Aristotle prefers some forms of government, which he calls *true*, over others he describes as *perverted*, although he does not rule them out completely. True forms of government are monarchy, or government by a single person who watches over common interests; aristocracy, government by a few who desire the best for the city and its inhabitants; and a republic or *politeia*, when those who are armed rule in favour of the common good. Among the perverted forms, in other words, those which do not aim to achieve the best for the community, he distinguishes tyranny, a monarchy in the interests of the sovereign; oligarchy, formed by a few aristocrats who only work exclusively in the interests of the wealthy; and democracy, a perversion of a republic which follows the interests of the poor.

Political changes and the instability of regimes come about because of the typical forms of corruption existing in each kind of government. However, Aristotle assumes that the aim of every State is to maintain itself and, in this respect, he gives some useful advice on how to achieve this. In any case, he expresses his preference for a constitution based on a middle class of responsible citizens, economically self-sufficient and who respect the basic principle which consists of 'making sure that the number of people who are in favour of the regime is always greater than that of those who are not in favour'. Even so, what seems to be a symbiosis between the aristocratic principle (the position of ruler is not at the reach of everyone) and democracy (the majority have their weight in the maintenance of political order) soon vanishes, as, for Aristotle, the best form of government is in the end a monarchy occupied by men of outstanding virtue.[51]

Conclusions

Unlike Plato's *Republic*, Aristotle does not attempt to draw up a detailed plan of a future ideal government. He begins with what he knows and analyses it, sanctioning it in many cases by its very right of existence, that is, by 'nature'. Aristotle gives pragmatic advice about the achievement of a happy city, in contrast with the ideal city of Plato. He is particularly concerned with practical questions, such as the geographical location of the city, its climate and size, its architecture or industry. He also refers to the best conditions for biological reproduction, a matter that Plato had discussed previously, and has no doubts about entering into all kinds of details on the topic.[52] The legislator should take into account such aspects as 'women should marry when they are about eighteen years of age and men at seven and thirty; then they are in the prime of life and the decline in the powers of both will coincide'.[53] He orders that no defective child should be raised and forbids having children beyond certain age limits, which in the man he fixes at about fifty-five. He also stipulates the conjugal union should take place in winter and proposes limiting the number of children and aborting if this number is in danger of being passed. He condemns adultery, even ordering the loss of civic privileges.[54]

The citizens, a group of men with the ability to deliberate (legislate, rule, and decide), administer justice, make war and lead worship, should not be excessively wealthy, but sufficiently to allow them leisure time, which is the basis of a virtuous political life, that is, of a life that tends towards Good and Happiness for the city. Obviously, this involves a population of slaves, craftsmen, peasants, merchants, and women who are producers and who guarantee the citizens' leisure. In summary, Aristotle proposes the model of a *polis* ruled by a sufficiently large group of land-owners and men of leisure, the only ones with the right to be called citizens. It is in the extent that this group achieves the happy medium (in the wealth of its members and in the prudence of their decisions) that the key to success lies and the survival of the political constitution they shared.

In a certain sense, Aristotle's *Politics* is a precedent of *The Prince*, as its final books include a series of instructions for the conservation of political regimes, tyranny included, although as we have noted, he prefers a monarchy ruled by virtuous men. It is therefore not only a text with exclusively theoretical or erudite intentions, but it also provides elements of 'political technology' aimed at the people who might have access to it. These, again, were none other than the citizens of the dominant Greek and Macedonian classes, in this case led by the expansionist monarchy of Philip and his son Alexander.

Aristotle does not develop a theory to explain the diversity of political constitutions, but focuses on classifying the known forms of civilized coexistence, defining types and sub-types and illustrating them with the available information in his time. The only attempts to explain the existing situations are based unfailingly on a series of basic ideas that are justified 'by nature': 1) man is a social animal who lives in communities, preferably in cities; 2) men are superior to women and children; and 3) some men are destined to rule and others to obey. These fixed 'natural' principles, combined with two dynamic factors, the search for Happiness through Justice and Good, and the ups and downs of political contingency, enable an understanding of the many forms of government he had knowledge of.

Aristotle starts with a determinate ideology and according to it he puts forward principles closely related with the material conditions of his time, based on patriarchal dominance and slavery. His text has the virtue of showing us, in all its harshness, the fundaments of participation in government. This participation is articulated around belonging to *citizenship* and the *political rights* this status conveyed. However, the position of citizen was far from being universal. Aristotle conceived the State as an 'association for the good life', based on the family and community of land-owners. In fact, as we have already reiterated, the only people who can be citizens are those whose social and economic position allows them to benefit from the exploitation of slave labour and domestic servitude. This reality, shown by Aristotle for ancient Greece, should represent a permanent invitation to reflection on the exercise of government in any place and at any historical time, including our own time in a modern parliamentary democracy.

DIFFERENCES AND SIMILARITIES WITHIN THE CLASSICAL CONCEPTION

Plato and Aristotle are still compulsory reference points for political analysis, mainly because together they posed a wide range of crucial questions about relationships in and among human groups, which are still valid today. Not only this, they also articulated answers from different points of view that, one way or another, have satisfied and continue to satisfy the expectations or the ways of viewing and approaching social life for many people. Without them it would be difficult to understand how later proposals were generated, following in succession until the conceptual instruments available to us today were formed.

Apparently, Plato did not include in his reflection what we would call the empirical analysis of the politics of his time. In reality, he must have carried this out, and as he was not satisfied with the diagnostic, saw the need to produce a change. The goal was a fair and orderly society, ruled by the idea of Good. An ideal society administered by philosophers-magistrates who, despite having obtained wisdom through the exercise of rational dialectic, replaced social dialectic with harmony programmed by a few and accepted with temperance by the rest. In the *Republic*, Plato pursued an absolute, a Good as a shared ethic imperative; a social ideal that required specialization accepted consciously and willingly by the different layers in society; the advent of a just society through the shared faith in a series of principles.[55]

In contrast, Aristotle explicitly includes the analysis of certain forms of government, classifies them in types and grants them 'naturalization papers' without stopping too long to draw up a theory of their existence and their process of development. From this point onwards, he is content to give a series of advice and recommendations, aimed at the pragmatic goal of social happiness that, as perhaps he knew, only occasionally was worthy of the effort of its identification with the attributes of an ideal Good. Aristotle sought a real conciliation instead of a utopia: in his words, a Constitution that protected the poor from the abuse of the rich and the rich from the expropriation of the poor—to express it another way, a society dominated by a land-owning middle class that moderated the conflicts between rich and poor, constituted its counterbalance, and brought stability to political order. In short, he sought a happy society established by agreements of coexistence, with certain precedents in the history of the Greek *polis*.[56]

Plato and Aristotle developed schemes of political evolution that followed a descending order from the best and fairest forms of government to their most degenerate versions. They defined types based on a series of characteristics related with political elements

The Classical Conception

(who held power and sometimes why they held it, and how they used it) and they illustrated them profusely (at least Aristotle did). Many of the labels used and the definitions accompanying them (aristocracy, oligarchy, democracy, tyranny) are still fully valid today as accurate syntheses for political relations that can be proven in practice. Both philosophers considered the transition between one form of government and the other, indicating that this often took place for reasons of the moral kind (corruption, weaknesses in virtue, fissures and adversities of the regimes). There is no doubt that they were discontent with the social order of their times and sought a future that would overcome the disadvantages they saw in the present. However, despite both Plato and Aristotle pursuing the project of a better society, their wishes did not come true by any means. The establishment of a platonic republic failed during the attempt made in Syracuse under the rule of Dionysus, meanwhile some years later, the moderate *polis* of Aristotle was overcome by Alexander's empire and later by the Hellenistic kingdoms. Perhaps both proposals failed to attend to the analysis of the material conditions that, in the end, usually re-determine idealist political desires.

The idealism in Plato and Aristotle cannot be mistaken by their different nuances. It is more evident in Plato, as the world (the substance) is ruled by the Idea. In Aristotle, idealism is shown by attributing the right to govern to virtuous land-owners; a virtue that is based on a pre-fixed idea, however 'natural' it is presented as. Platonic and Aristotelian thought, with its emphasis on the ideas of Good, Order, Justice, and Happiness, explains what it wants to explain by references to itself, through arguments biased by interests and full of circularity. In this way, they are not arguments and explanation as such, but rather a kind of illustration supporting a metaphysical 'truth' constructed in advance and which is not questioned at any moment. To affirm that something is 'by nature' is a tautology and a value judgement: a tautology because it sanctions what it is because it is; a value judgement because it assigns a positive rating to what is natural. They are fundaments full of arbitrariness and moral connotations. Based on them, the classical Greek writers developed arguments and theories to explain phenomena in the physical world or to solve and programme moral, ethical, religious, political, and social questions without realizing that their reasoned, and often reasonable, conclusions had their origin in initial fundamentals closely connected with the common sense of their time or, rather, with the sector of society to which they belonged. They rarely examined in detail what the process of constructing the knowledge they valued as Good or Just had been or where these pompous, supposedly universal, concepts came from and under which conditions they could be introduced, received, and applied. Although the world of the *polis* was the first to question the conclusions of reason with no correlation in the reality of the physical world, and the first to demand a genuine applicability of sociological principles in the social world (sociopolitical philosophies instead of theologies), it neglected, in the fullest sense of the word, the instrumental methodology or practice that should be derived from reasoned thought. This aspect remained in the hands of techniques and experimentation, whose process of development is rarely related to the place of production of philosophical theories and, instead, more frequently to the pragmatic needs of subsistence or the material correlates of political domination.

NOTES

1. This account will be guided by the *Republic*. We have used the edition published in the series of Oxford World's Classics, translated by Robin Waterfield (1998), and the page numbers given in the notes refer to this version.

    GLAUCON: self-discipline and morality may be commendable, but are also difficult and troublesome, whereas self-indulgence and immorality are enjoyable and easily gained, and it's only in people's minds and in convention that they are contemptible. (*Republic*, 52.)

2. *Republic*, 16–43.
3. *Republic*, 19.
4. These are the origins of Nietzschean positions in politics (later translated to knowledge). This perspective agrees with Marxism in the existence of profound differences in interests in class society, but disagrees in the causes that produce these interests. For Marxism they are rooted in groups occupying dissymmetrical positions in the organization of material production (production relationships), whereas for Thrasymachus and other sophists, the reasons lie in the exercise or not of political power (the *power* that we shall see in recent liberal texts together with concepts such as 'status' or 'prestige'), power which is gained, conserved or lost through ethical, moral, psychological, religious, or purely violent factors.

5. *Republic*, 193.
6. *Republic*, 236.
7. It may be an intelligible theme, but sight can be said to reflect it, when, as we were saying, it sets about looking at actual creatures, at the heavenly bodies themselves, and finally at the sun itself. Just as in this case, a person ends up at the supreme point of the visible realm, so the summit of the intelligible realm is reached when, by means of dialectic and without relying on anything perceptible, a person perseveres in using rational argument to approach the true reality of things until he has grasped with his intellect the reality of goodness itself. (*Republic*, 264.)
8. The search for goodness is connected with the topic of Platonic idealist epistemology and the allegory of the cave. See *Republic*, 240–5.
9. *Republic*, 201.
10. *Republic*, 119.
11. SOCRATES: 'Therefore, my friend, there's no administrative job in a community which belongs to a woman *qua* woman, or to a man *qua* man,' I said. 'Innate qualities have been distributed equally between the two sexes, and women can join in every occupation just as much as men, although they are the weaker sex in all respects.' (*Republic*, 167.)
12. It is stated that it is necessary to train women for war and treat them like men (*Republic*, 163), and that the only difference between the sexes is that 'females bear offspring and males mount females'. (*Republic*, 166).
13. *Republic*, 171–2.
14. This task was controlled secretly by the magistrates, who by lies and tricks would procure that the most outstanding individuals of each sex would mate most often.
15. *Republic*, 175.
16. *Republic*, 179.
17. *Republic*, 183–4.
18. *Republic*, 169.
19. *Republic*, 184.
20. *Republic*, 181.
21. *Republic*, 219–26.
22. *Republic*, 59.
23. SOCRATES: No one in any other kind of authority either, in his capacity as ruler, considers or enjoins his own advantage, but the advantage of his subject, the person for whom he practices his expertise. Everything he says and everything he does is said and done with this aim in mind

and with regard to what is advantageous to and appropriate for this person. (*Republic*, 25.)

24. A sentence put in Socrates' mouth (*Republic*, 140). Immorality would be precisely the intrusion in the functions of others within the State. Each individual should remain within the limits of their class: those who work for a living (farmers and craftsmen), the guardians, and the auxiliaries. (*Republic*, 142).
25. We have used the translation by Benjamin Jowett, available online at <http://socserv.mcmaster.ca/econ/ugcm/3ll3/aristotle/Politics.pdf>. *Politics* has been published in Oxford World's Classics.
26. *Politics*, book 1, part II.
27. *Politics*, book 1, part V.
28. *Politics*, book 1, part XIII.
29. *Politics*, book 3, part IX.
30. *Politics*, book 1, part II.
31. The main economic activity is agriculture. Other productive activities to be considered are animal husbandry, hunting, and fishing, as well as piracy. The art of getting wealth, especially the retail trade, is clearly differentiated and defined as the acquisition of 'money without limit'. Wealth-getting activities include trade and usury, paid work and the exploitation on non-subsistence natural resources such as wood or minerals. This activity is censured by Aristotle ('it is unnatural, and a mode by which men gain from one another'); he abhors usury, as money only procures more money, and not those things for which it was invented. (*Politics*, book 1, parts VIII–XI).
32. *Politics*, book 2, part VII.
33. Aristotle defines the city-state as a body of citizens sufficing for the purposes of life (*Politics*, book 3, part I) and also as a community of free men. (*Politics*, book 3, part VI).
34. *Politics*, book 3, part XII.
35. *Politics*, book 3, part XVI.
36. *Politics*, book 3, part XII.
37. *Politics*, book 4, part XI.
38. *Politics*, book 4, parts XI–XII.
39. *Politics*, book 7, part I.
40. ibid.
41. ibid.
42. ibid.
43. *Politics*, book 5, part III.
44. *Politics*, book 7, part I.
45. *Politics*, book 7, part IX.

46. *Politics*, book 7, part XIV.
47. *Politics*, book 8, part II.
48. *Politics*, book 8, part III.
49. *Politics*, book 1, part VIII.
50. 'The art of war is a natural art of acquisition, for the art of acquisition includes hunting, an art which we ought to practice against wild beasts and against men who, though intended by nature to be governed, will not submit, for war of such a kind is naturally just.' (*Politics*, book 1, part VIII).
51. *Politics*, book 3, part XVIII.
52. *Politics*, book 7, parts XV–XVI.
53. *Politics*, book 7, part XVI.
54. ibid.
55. The utopian proposals given in the *Republic* were modified in some of Plato's later dialogues, to be precise in *The Statesman* and *Laws*, possibly as a consequence of the Syracusian experience. Thus, in *The Statesman*, instead of proposing a regulated structure of all society as a way to achieve a good government, he defends the figure of the 'outstanding ruler, gifted with skill'; that man 'gifted with knowledge' capable of *ruling* correctly the collectives making up the *polis*; that man who by purifying, favouring, and in conclusion, improving the city, makes it happier. This shift towards what could be termed political pragmatism, distances his views from the spirit of the *Republic* and opens similar perspectives to those of Aristotle.
56. In Athens in 411 BC, the hoplite citizens, i.e. those who could afford weapons and did not need to receive a wage from the State to follow politics, brought down the 400 oligarchs in the context of the war against Sparta. They then founded the Constitution of the Five Thousand, which granted a leading role to the middle classes. However, this political order was ephemeral, and soon shifted towards more democratic positions.

2

The State according to Christianity

In classical antiquity, the State was the institution guaranteeing order and justice, the two requirements to achieve social happiness. The differences between Platonic and Aristotelian aspirations were minimal, as they shared an interest in ensuring a comfortable, happy life, or if you prefer, orderly and just for all those who were equal, that is, the few free men with the financial capability to be so. In Western society, reflection on the State was born out of a theoretical and apologetic need of the dominant class, who constructed a sectarian and interventionist building, whose doors were closed to a productive majority, forced to remain at the mercy of the elements. The construction of this exclusive building commenced in Greece, by resorting to a lie: the inferiority or incapability, by nature, of women, slaves, and craftsmen to participate in the government of the community in which they lived.

Even so, the virtue of this point of view lay in the express recognition of social segmentation in groups or classes, which contributed to maintaining the State itself. All had a role in this, unequal and unjust as it may be, yet necessarily interrelated and therefore collective, in a *social state of things*. Far from vindicating individuals as autonomous and sovereign beings, the class dominating this State invoked the particular collective calling itself 'citizenry' in its search for the best way ahead for what it thought of as *its* city.

The political panorama in Europe clearly changed in the fourth century AD, producing a clear division between the realms of the collective, the private, and the individual. The philosophy of the Christian State, from the formulation by Augustine of Hippo to that by Thomas of Aquinas in the thirteenth century, produced a mutation in Western thought that moved politics towards a doctrinal ideology which gave importance to the individual over any private or universal expression, whether it be a class or a nation, caste or interest group, aspects that would shift towards areas of sublimation of the practices of coexistence. Ethics and morals were reduced to discourses of submission and charity, enabling the political sphere to be filled with a doctrine of faith characterized by the habitual appeal to Providence. The Christian Church, properly said, is a different institution to any political State. It forms a kind of para-State or trans-State institution, but one which, curiously, claims for itself the control and opinion about the moral and ethic basis of States. In order to rule the spiritual affairs of mankind independently of political institutions, it establishes a material force which through its action supports or ignores States at its convenience.

PRECEDENTS OF CHRISTIAN POLITICAL THOUGHT

In appearance the main reference point is the central figure of the doctrine, Jesus, or if you prefer, the version of his teachings after they had been steadily refined and finally made official in the course of the various councils held in late antiquity. However, many of the social conceptions of the first Christians were not very different from those held by stoic pagans and, later, Neo-Platonists. Furthermore, certain attributes and slogans were even rescued from old forgotten *spiritual* traditions, such as Mithraism. Nonetheless, we are not interested here in the history of religious discourse, but in its components and implications in the field of politics. These, in a nutshell, can be summarized in four aspects: belief in the providential government of the world, the obligation of submitting to divine law, the requirement to be just, and the premise that all men are equal in the eyes of God.

Christ's teachings, according to the gospels chosen by the Church in the composition of the New Testament, were conflictive for the Jewish society of His time. They involved a solid criticism of hypocrisy and announced the end of human law, by proclaiming an apocalyptical end of History, the end of Time. These teachings contained a highly conflictive message: relinquish your earthly possessions and embrace the Truth through conversion, before the End of the World.

These moral instructions, however, did not make up what we could call a real political programme. In fact, they foresee the end of politics, because the Kingdom of Good News *is not of this world*. Each of us carries inside us, in our spirit, this new world, the Kingdom of God, but its coming will not take place until the end of Time; until after death. Even so, two elements can already be seen which formed basic pillars of the later political doctrine of the Church: obedience and submission as virtues of individual behaviour. Jesus admitted the submission to earthly powers which, as they are *of this world*, are of no concern to the true and primordial relationship of the individual soul with God. 'Render therefore unto Caesar the things which are Caesar's; and unto God the things that are God's' (Matthew: 22, 21) is the famous sentence signifying believers should accept the worldly powers of the status quo.[1]

In principle, as explained above, the gospels do not contain organized political thought, as the affairs of the earthly community are radically different from heavenly and spiritual matters, which should be the priorities for a Christian. However, the attitude of Christianity towards politics began to take consistency in the writings of Paul of Tarsus, who held the opposite view to Jesus' lack of concern for the things of this world. With Paul a change occurs from 'My kingdom is not of this world' to 'The kingdoms of this world are of God'.[2] This opened the door to the active participation of believers in the political sphere, and presented the invitation for later doctrinal development. However, the direction of the involvement that Paul proposed did not break with the indications of Jesus, as it lay in the same line of submission to power:

> Let every soul be subject unto the higher powers. For there is no power but of God: the powers that be are ordained of God.
>
> Whosoever therefore resisteth the power, resisteth the ordinance of God: and they that resist shall receive to themselves damnation.
>
> For rulers are not a terror to good works, but to the evil. Wilt thou then not be afraid of the power? do that which is good, and thou shalt have praise of the same:
>
> For he is the minister of God to thee for good. But if thou do that which is evil, be afraid; for he beareth not the sword in vain: for he is the minister of God, a revenger to execute wrath upon him that doeth evil.
>
> (Romans: 13, 1–4)

Probably, Paul, or what Paul signified, was the response to the anarchical tendencies of the first Christian communities. Faced with this situation, he called for order and clamoured for social peace and the maintenance of the contemporary relationships of obedience which, as in classical Greece, upheld a patriarchal social structure and slavery. Obedience to imperial political orders and the practice of charity formed the main attitudes encouraged by early Christian policies, under the general command that obedience is a duty imposed by God.

Although this is not the place to describe the vicissitudes suffered by Christianity in its origins, it should be recalled that the first Christian churches took in mostly slaves and the poor, and that upper-class Christians could cushion their participation in political life and in the imperial cult by *feeling* that they owed faith to an authority whom they believed to be superior. Perhaps these factors help to explain why the Roman State thought at certain times that Christianity was a source of instability or sedition and, therefore, an object of persecution. In any case, in the year 313, the Milan Edict authorized the Christian cult. Constantine proclaimed Christianity the official religion of the Empire, although he maintained tolerance towards paganism.

From this time onwards, the relationship between State and religion made the Christians change their attitude towards the State, and the State towards its justification. In this respect, the work of Augustine of Hippo (354–430), especially *The City of God*, is regarded as one of the fundaments of the doctrine that enabled the medieval Church to absorb the right of the State, or in other words, to endow the Church with the right to influence or guide governments.

Augustine is important in Christian political thought as he was the first to stress the differences between the political State and the Church, granting moral authority to the latter and claiming at the same time that, as the sole repository of Jesus' message, it should *govern* indirectly and thus be the inspiration of customs and laws. A very well-aimed desire: the State should be morally subordinate to the Church. In metaphorical terms, Augustine speaks of the existence of two cities: the earthly City of Man or civil society, the society of the body, of sin and evil, and the City of God, which is the heavenly Christian Church and the community of believers, in this world and in the future. Only in the latter is it possible to attain peace, justice, and the triumph of good.

The Augustinian arguments in political theory can be summarized in the following axiom: God is the source of all earthly power, although God does not designate specific political regimes. This axiom allows him, in the first place, to affirm the absolute power of God over all political affairs. In the second place, to escape from any close commitment with one or other political regime, a link that could involve risks for the survival of the Church in the case of eventual changes in the political sphere. Thus, the Church was situated above governments: in a place where it was needed to coat them with moral legitimacy, but safe from the ups and downs they might suffer. This has been, and still is, the position that the European Catholic Church has been careful to maintain for itself over the centuries, without abandoning the circles of government and power in many States.

Despite the overall advantages of this attitude, the loyalty and obedience of Christians thus became divided between two governments. Divine government was the more important and was above political right and the State; not opposing it but strengthening it. However, for many Christians it has been very hard to commune with the decisions of certain governments. Thus, harmonizing both loyalties has been a great source of tension, and has conditioned the generation of other proposals from the realm of Christian thought. Claiming to be the light and, at the same time, the switch that turns it on, is by no means an easy task to justify.

ST THOMAS OF AQUINAS (1225–74)

The thought of Thomas of Aquinas is basically influenced by Augustine of Hippo, but also to a large extent by Aristotle, from whom he takes the requirement that the State should begin with economic, social, and political autarchy. He held great influence over later Christian thought, and like Augustine, he was canonized.

At the time that Thomas of Aquinas lived, during the crusades, religion galvanized social forces and the material and political power of Rome was highly significant. In this context, great rivalry arose between the papacy and European States. In these, the model of an aristocratic State headed by a *primus inter pares* began to change, and in its place gathered strength the centripetal trend towards greater centralization of power. Thomas's work is an allegation in favour of papal primacy and against the independence of secular power.

The works we shall examine here are *On Kingship* (*De Regno*, 1265–7)[3] and occasionally *Summa Theologica* (1267–74), especially the parts referring to law,[4] where certain assertions in the former work are touched upon. *On Kingship* is divided into two books, and makes frequent use of quotations from the Bible to illustrate or support arguments, as well as metaphors of society as a living organism needing the coordination of its parts in order to fulfil its aims. On other occasions, Thomas substitutes the metaphor of the organism for the metaphor of a ship needing a steersman or captain to bring the ship safely to port for the benefit of all (common good and happiness); in other cases he uses the metaphor of the flock and the shepherd. It is also worth noting the sporadic mention of examples taken from antiquity, mainly from the history of Rome.

At the start of this book, Thomas Aquinas describes fundaments, based on which the *raison d'être* of the State should be understood. In the first place he points out that man is naturally a social and political being. Man, unlike animals, possesses reason, the instrument used to satisfy his needs. However, a single, isolated individual's reason does not suffice for his survival. To achieve this, we need to live together. The community provides *the* context for mutual help, and makes it possible for groups of individuals to take charge of various aspects that are useful for the rest, such as the different professions, tasks and occupations. It is a starting point taken from Aristotle; none other than the premise of the social character of men, due to the insufficiency of a single individual to subsist by his own means alone.

The social character of human beings takes us to another point concerning the organization of social life itself which, according to Thomas, requires the existence of a ruling authority: the State. Not living in a State or not aspiring to do so is a sign of anarchy and living like an animal:

> For when there are many men together and each one is looking after his own interest, the multitude would be broken up and scattered unless there were also an agency to take care of what appertains to the commonweal... With this in mind, Solomon says: '*Where there is no governor, the people shall fall*'.[5]

A significant paradox is soon noted in Thomas's discourse: if it is natural for men to live in society, why would they want to be scattered? Why must someone be responsible for stopping the dispersal of society, when from their nature they would not do that? There is no other answer than that of the justification, ignoring any paradox, of the natural need for leadership, in this case of the king. The chain therefore reaches the point of affirming that the State is the consequence of man's nature. Consequently, as this comes from God, all human laws will emanate from Him.

Once it has been formed, the State has three goals. The first is to procure a sufficient supply of the things needed to live (food and shelter); the second, to defend society from the attacks of external enemies;[6] and, finally, the third and most important, ensure that earthly life guides souls towards eternal salvation.

> Yet through virtuous living man is further ordained to a higher end, which consists in the enjoyment of God... Consequently, since society must have the same end as the individual man, it is not the ultimate end of an assembled multitude to live virtuously, but through virtuous living to attain to the possession of God.[7]

The total happiness of a human being is achieved, therefore, with the contemplation of God after the salvation of the soul. The State, as an instrument for good government, is an essential means to reach this objective. In order to succeed in the practical, ethical, and transcendental missions it has been given, the State makes use of laws: thus from the four preceding articles, the definition of law may be gathered; and it is nothing else than an ordinance of reason for the common good, made by him who has care of the community, and promulgated.[8] Laws should promote and guarantee social unity which, for Thomas Aquinas, is synonymous with peace.[9] Laws should overcome the internal and external impediments that stand in the way of perfect life in society, such as variations in the vigour of men, the ups and downs of life that make it difficult to act correctly and uniformly, the wickedness of desires or wars arising from external dangers.[10]

However, are any kinds of government better prepared than others to make more appropriate laws? For Thomas, like Augustine, all authority comes from God, but it is individuals who must choose the form of government. In his opinion there are three just forms of government: kingship, aristocracy, and *polity*, in which authority should be in the hands of men who are known for their virtue and wisdom. In contrast with these, he places three corrupt forms:

tyranny, oligarchy, and democracy (demagogy in *Summa Theologica*).[11] Finally, he expresses his preference for a monarchic government,[12] giving as reason that social union is achieved more easily if one person rules than if many do, and in addition, the model of one-person rule is the same as the divine model.[13]

Thomas has now succeeded in one of his aims: the defence of kingship. The king is a minister of God on Earth, and is in charge of ruling God's creation in a similar way to the divine model.

However, the justification of monarchy was not his main aim. Thomas did not propose a model of absolute monarchy, but subordinates it to a higher power. It is important to stress that the ethical goal of the king should consist of obtaining the eternal salvation of his subjects, ruling so that they lead a virtuous life, one which will put them in the position of entering God's kingdom. Yet, according to this, it is deduced that all kings must in turn be subjects of priests and, above all, of the chief priest, the Pope,[14] as the Church is the sole authority in the knowledge of the law of God,[15] according to which kings must legislate and rule. Therefore, Thomas is on the side of Rome in its dispute with European kings over the control of the political affairs of Christendom. Kings are responsible for leading their subjects to the universal good, and therefore happiness, through good government complying with divine principles. Kings are God's servants in the task of guiding men towards a higher life, and are subordinate to the Church in its role as the privileged interpreter of divine will.

We have thus presented the main thread of Thomas Aquinas's political philosophy, but his discourse contains other lines of interest. Having demonstrated that kingship is the best form of government, Thomas goes on to stress the dangers of tyranny and warns that the first king should be chosen among the men least probable to fall into it.[16] However, what can be done if it should finally become established? Here, a compliant side of Thomas Aquinas appears: 'it is more expedient to tolerate the milder tyranny for a while than, by acting against the tyrant, to become involved in many perils more grievous than the tyranny itself'.[17] This is before showing himself as conservative as Paul when he states that, in the case of a strong tyranny: 'Peter admonishes us to be reverently subject to our masters, *not only to the good and gentle but also the forward*: "For if one who suffers unjustly bear his trouble for conscience' sake, this is grace"'.[18]

In reality, he argues that tyranny is both a divine punishment for a society's sins and the way this society can redeem itself. Tyranny is thus an indirect tool in the hands of Providence with which the subjects can reach virtue. God is always found behind any event (Divine Providence and Omnipotence), when it is positive, as a reward, and when it is negative, as a punishment.

> But to deserve to secure this benefit from God, the people must desist from sin, for it is *by divine permission that wicked men receive power to rule as a punishment for sin.*[19]
>
> Hence God permits tyrants to get into power to punish the sins of the subjects... So God does not permit tyrants to reign a long time, but after the storm brought on the people through these tyrants, He restores tranquillity by casting them down.[20]

In *Summa Theologica*, however, he proposes the possibility of changing that submissive attitude towards laws, more precisely, towards unjust laws. These include those that he calls contrary to human good and divine good. This is the only glimmer of possibility that Thomas Aquinas grants to non-observance of the law and, therefore, rebellion. However, it does not escape ecclesiastic tutelage, the faithful representation on Earth of divine omnipotence. It is worth recalling the entire passage, because in its 'exact ambiguity' it provides the keys to the arguments used later by the Church to explain its support or opposition to different political regimes, as it suited it:

> laws may be unjust in two ways: first, by being contrary to human good, through being opposed to the things mentioned above—either in respect of the end, as when an authority imposes on his subjects burdensome laws, conducive, not to the common good, but rather to his own cupidity or vainglory—or in respect of the author, as when a man makes a law that goes beyond the power committed to him—or in respect of the form, as when burdens are imposed unequally on the community, although with a view to the common good. The like are acts of violence rather than laws; because, as Augustine says, 'a law that is not just, seems to be no law at all.' Wherefore such laws do not bind in conscience, except perhaps in order to avoid scandal or disturbance, for which cause a man should even yield his right... Secondly, laws may be unjust through being opposed to the Divine good: such are the laws of tyrants inducing to idolatry, or to anything else contrary to the Divine law: and laws of this kind must nowise be observed, because, as stated in Acts 5:29, 'we ought to obey God rather than man.'[21]

Regarding the king, what prize does he deserve? Earthly honour and glory are very ephemeral rewards, although earned by many 'labours and anxieties',[22] but they are not recommended because with them, the aim is to show off before other men, which is a sign of hypocrisy. Together with this, he denounces riches and pleasure, as they involve plundering from the people.[23] The true and worthy reward is the eternal reward coming from God, as the king is only His minister. This will be the prize for a reign which has made his subjects happy.[24]

In addition, the happiness reached by kings, coming from God, is much greater than that achieved by ordinary men, as 'that is indeed signal virtue by which a man can guide not only himself but others'.[25] That is to say, it is harder to rule one's self and rule, than only to be ruled; consequently, the reward for the former should match their greater merit.[26] With this, Thomas also suggests that the punishment for kings who do not rule correctly will be proportionately greater too.[27]

CONCLUSIONS

The key words in the politics of Thomas Aquinas are obedience and submission to God in all directions: people towards God, people towards the sovereign as the minister of God, and the sovereign towards the Church as the interpreter of divine law. This political discourse offered by the metaphysical theologian is everywhere and justifies everything in order to inculcate the 'slave morality' typical of Christianity. That which accepts and endures adversity and suffering for the greater glory of God—in other words, that which trades material suffering for promises of redemption.

The double morals of sharing the feelings of the oppressed, while justifying the power of the oppressors by considering it a metaphor of God's kingdom on Earth, construct an interpretation of reality that, in the last resort, only heeds and obeys the Pope as the true, and not metaphorical, vicar of God. Thomas conjugates the Augustinian City of God and City of Man with an omnipotent Church, to which everyone, both humble and mighty, must request consent for any social initiative. It is an earthly political philosophy, which reasons with the heights of Heaven as the grounds for obedience to the State and which immobilizes the subject-believer under the terrible threat of the punishment that he will receive before death by the ruler's sword and, after dying, from God for all eternity. The line initiated by Paul thus succeeds in building a para-State institution which, with Thomas Aquinas, assumes the authority of controlling certain States, without discrediting its foundations by doing so.

This section dedicated to the political philosophy of Christianity is by no means a summary of ideas that are no longer in vogue. Nearly eight centuries later, the Catholic Church remains a highly hierarchical collective, with its own earthly State, the Vatican. In the other States where it is installed, despite many of their constitutions declaring them to be non-confessional States, it maintains the aspiration of setting itself up as the moral arbitrator of political actions. Agreeing, as usual, with the interests of the dominating classes, in States like Spain the Church forms a para-State power of great importance. Its influence not only derives from the authority of the gospels. It enjoys tax benefits, administers its own abundant properties within the capitalist system, and plays a significant role in the fields of education and the health service. In fact, some of its members, belonging to organizations like Opus Dei or the 'Legionnaires of Christ', rise to occupy high positions of responsibility in the government. From its message of submission and obedience to the power of the capitalist State, the Church defends the most reactionary policies in favour of the maintenance of patriarchal relationships within the family and the sanctification of salaried labour within the capitalist form of production.

Religious obscurantism, whatever form it takes, is currently expanding. On one hand, presidents of the United States believe they have been conferred with divine authority and political parties vindicate Western Christian tradition in the draft of the European Union Charter of Fundamental Rights. On the other hand, in response to the brutality of fundamentalist standard bearers of Christianity, other fundamentalists, Islamic or of any other religion, act in a similar way. Meanwhile, the field is enlarging for television preachers, sects, and numerous esoteric trends. The development of capitalism, and its brutal frontierless globalization, requires subordination and ignorance more than ever, and it appears it is able to generate these even in the people who react against it.

NOTES

1. Frederick William I, founder of the military and bureaucratic Prussian State, revised this political principle in the eighteenth century when he said: 'The soul is of God; the rest belongs to me'.
2. Touchard (1996: 89).
3. Here we use the translation by Gerald B. Phelan, revised by I. Th. Eschmann, O.P., published by the Pontifical Institute of Mediaeval Studies (Canada, 1949). The page numbers cited here refer to the edition reprinted in 2000.
4. We have used the English translation of *Summa Theologica*, translated by the Fathers of the English Dominican Province (1947), available online at <http//www.sacred-texts.com/chr/aquinas/summa/index.htm>.
5. *On Kingship*, 5–6. Our italics here and in the other quotations.
6. *On Kingship*, 65–6.
7. *On Kingship*, 60.
8. *Summa Theologica*, question 90, article 4.
9. *On Kingship*, 11.
10. *On Kingship*, 66–7.
11. *On Kingship*, 13.
12. In *Summa Theologica* he considers it better if power is shared more: he is still in favour of a king, but advocates that magistrates and other offices should be elected by the people; so he is proposing a mixture between monarchy, aristocracy, and democracy. This is pointed out by Robles and Chueca in the introduction to the Spanish edition of *On Kingship* (*La Monarquía*, Tecnos, Madrid, 1995).
13. *On Kingship*, 12. On the advantage of one-person government, also see pp. 15–16 and 21–3 in the same book, where he points out that a pluralist regime is more likely to end in tyranny, the worst of governments (see below).
14. *On Kingship*, 62.
15. *On Kingship*, 64.
16. *On Kingship*, 24.
17. ibid.
18. *On Kingship*, 26.
19. *On Kingship*, 29.
20. *On Kingship*, 48.
21. *Summa Theologica*, question 96, article 4.
22. *On Kingship*, 30.
23. *On Kingship*, 33.
24. *On Kingship*, 34–6.
25. *On Kingship*, 39.
26. *On Kingship*, 40.
27. *On Kingship*, 50.

3

The Renaissance of the State

MACHIAVELLI (1469-1527)

By the late fifteenth century, the Papacy had lost momentum in its goal of guiding the earthly government of Christendom. Throughout the late Middle Ages, across Europe, States had begun to consolidate around dynasties which centralized, substituted, or controlled the local powers of feudal tradition: the nobles, the church, and the cities. The kings were no longer the *primus inter pares* of feudal aristocracies, as they were invested with power, which became increasingly absolute, by the nobility and the rising merchant-bourgeoisie who considered this strategy the best way to maintain their traditional privileges and establish new ones. It was a period of great economic growth and the birth of new fortunes as a consequence of the expansion of production and trade, and also of the plundering of the New World. In this situation, European States, locked in combat for hegemony, pragmatically adopted the combination of a strong government at home and an aggressive one abroad.

'Renaissance humanism', the term by which we know the intellectual movement of the period, secularized political philosophy. Although references to deity did not by any means disappear from political thought, the question of government began to be approached as a specific, strictly human, business. Politics again became civil and in that way was forged the concept of the sovereign as the source of all power. New winds blew in unison with those of the Reformation, the movement by which religious ideas were shaped to the new foundations of socio-economic power. The defence of a new relationship with God, in a religiosity at last without any intermediates, implied, like the secularization of political thought, a serious questioning of the world-view professed by the Catholic hierarchy.

Machiavelli lived in a convulsed and brilliant time. He held official posts in the Florentine Republic, although he could not aspire to those of ambassador or governor as his once reputable family had come down in the world. His political career continued until momentary vicissitudes in his city removed him from public life in 1513. He was the first author to give a mature and realistic idea of the State, which he considered a purely human institution and therefore with no metaphysical basis. He wrote two main works that dealt mainly with politics, one of them practical, *The Prince* (1513), which is the one that interests us here,[1] and another strictly theoretical one entitled *Discourse on the First Ten Books of Titus Livy* (1513–18).

Machiavelli was not concerned with a philosophical State, but with his own city, his own land, and his own times: the Florence whose government was disputed alternately between a council of wealthy and prominent citizens and the lineage of the Medicis. Belonging to a republican tradition, he obtained a post in the Chancery a few years after the installation of the Republic, following the expulsion of the Medicis in 1494. When these returned to power in 1512, they dissolved the Republican government and banished Machiavelli. After that time, until his death, he spent his time intensively on intellectual and literary activity. He wrote *The Prince* in 1513, in an attempt to win the favour of the Medicis, which he indeed obtained some years after, but to a fragile and modest extent. The new fall of the Medicis in 1527 and the rise of the Republicans put him once more on the losing side. He became ill and died shortly afterwards.

Machiavelli's aim consisted of proposing a practical political doctrine, based on and supported by the reality of historical events.[2] We could define *The Prince* as a guide about how to achieve, execute, and preserve political power. In its pages he describes all kinds of situations in which this power is put to use and suggests the appropriate solutions for the attainment of the ultimate goal, which is none other than that of keeping power. This is the supreme *end that justifies all means*, means which are here profusely described, analysed, and illustrated with examples taken from Machiavelli's Italy (Republics like Venice, Genoa, and Florence, the Papacy, and the foreign powers that were present, like France and Aragon) and also from antiquity (Sparta, Athens, the Greek cities in the south of Italy, Rome, and Persia). All these cases are used to expound on the different problems involved in the exercise of power, the right and wrong decisions that can be made, and finally and decisively, what teachings may be drawn from it. It is necessary to be a part of the world in order to observe it, to study its trajectory and decide what to do and how to make the desire of power a reality, by avoiding tensions skilfully, by banishing crimes against property and by relying on ideals if it is opportune to do so to avoid losing control of the State.

Machiavelli's interlocutor is the 'New Prince', the supreme leader of a State who has acquired this position without the need for a law of hereditary succession; an individual who has conquered power thanks to his virtue. However, here 'virtue' does not have the meaning attributed to it in Greek antiquity or by Christianity, consisting of doing 'good' by obeying the laws of the *polis* or of God. For Machiavelli, virtue is the capability to carry out strategies aimed at obtaining and holding on to political power successfully. It is therefore an eminently pragmatic quality, and whether or not it is possessed will vary depending on a certain result. In order to achieve it, it is necessary to understand the real workings of human affairs (of 'human nature' we might say), which forces us to reappraise and question the proposals on the topic made by ethics and religion. Unlike the traditional doctrine on the matter, Machiavelli affirms that humans are *not* good by nature, in fact quite the contrary. Human beings are moved strictly by selfish interests and are more concerned with their own lives and property than with promoting lofty virtues and sentiments such as love, friendship, loyalty, or goodness:

> For one can generally say this of men: they are ungrateful, fickle, simulators and deceivers, avoiders of danger, and greedy for gain. While you work for their benefit they are completely yours, offering you their blood, their property, their lives and their sons, as I said above, when the need to do so is far away. But when it draws nearer to you, they turn away.[3]

If any doubts remain about Machiavelli's view of the human condition, it suffices to recall such proverbial sentences as: 'men forget the death of their father more quickly than the loss of their patrimony'.[4]

The first lesson the Prince must learn from this ontology of the human condition is to forget the need to follow ethic precepts that, as we have just pointed out, nobody respects in reality: 'A man who wishes to profess goodness at all times will come to ruin among so many who are not good. Therefore, it is necessary for a prince who wishes to maintain himself to learn how not to be good, and to use this knowledge or not to use it according to necessity'.[5] Machiavelli's political pragmatism has no use for ethical reference points when these are not appropriate for maintaining the control of the State. Thus, all ethics are eluded if they are declared above the reason of State; references to any natural human rights are ignored, in the same way as later modern thought, and any moral axiology is equally neglected, as had been the norm since classical antiquity. The usual behaviour of the ruler consisted of drawing the multitude towards his interests, winning men over, or overriding them. His virtue lay precisely in his ability to do this.

In order to conquer a State, it was necessary to possess the good will of the inhabitants, as well as military force. In order to preserve what has recently been conquered, he advises wiping out the previous lineage, leaving local laws unaltered, not increasing taxation, and moving the official residence to the conquered land to be able to control it from near at hand.[6] There should be no doubts about using violence if in this way the subjects can be made to respect the obligations they have with the Prince: 'Therefore, a prince must not worry about the infamy of being considered cruel when it is a matter of keeping his subjects united and loyal'.[7] Physical force should be regarded as another instrument to be used to attain the oft-repeated objective. A valuable and effective instrument which should not be abandoned for fear of being criticized for it: 'From this arises an argument: whether it is better to be loved than to be feared, or the contrary. The answer is that one would like to be both one and the other. But since it is difficult to be both together, it is much safer to be feared than to be loved, when one of the two must be lacking'.[8] However, to use a system of terror habitually would be a serious political error, as people will always attempt to free themselves from tyranny. The intelligent prince will use cruelty in a calculated way, try to ensure that it is 'well-used',[9] and combine it with all kinds of pretences. Regarding the qualities that people generally assign to all good rulers, such as 'greatness, spirit, dignity, and strength',[10] or generosity and piety, the conclusion is clear: if they really are practised, the inconveniences and the costs they involve should fall upon others.[11] In any case, the main thing is that the Prince is seen to have them; that is, he should procure that the appearance takes the place of reality.

> Therefore, it is not necessary for a prince to possess all of the above-mentioned qualities, but it is very necessary for him to appear to possess them. Furthermore, I shall dare to assert this: that having them and always observing them is harmful, but appearing to observe them is useful: for instance, to appear merciful, faithful, humane, trustworthy, religious, and to be so; but with his mind disposed in such a way that, should it become necessary not to be so; he will be able and know how to change to the opposite.[12]

There is a reason why it is so important to maintain certain appearances: most men only know what the Prince is like from what they see of him, and the few who really know and might oppose him would not dare to go against the opinion of the majority.[13]

The verdict on the Prince's 'goodness' or 'wickedness' should not depend on an assessment of his actions simply by taking one or another ethic code as the criteria, instead, this verdict should only be based on the observation of whether or not his acts have allowed him to hold on to government. In this way, Machiavelli scandalizes when he remarks that a tyrant is as good a prince as any other and that his worth as a ruler will be measured according to the length of time that he succeeds in remaining the head of State. Any means is potentially valid to perpetuate command; remember that the end justifies them. It will be the Prince who makes the right or wrong decisions in the choice and application of these means. Only if he keeps power will he be 'good' and establish legitimacy;[14] if not, he will have failed. Nothing should stop him achieving his goal, although to do this he should be careful to apply the correct portions of cruelty and appearance, strength and cunning, according to a calculated strategy. This will be the test of his 'virtue'.

Machiavelli defends the radical secularization of politics, a proposal that is even more outstanding for being made at a time dominated ideologically and intellectually by Christianity and the influence of the classics. The goals of government are not the same as those of religion. In fact, this becomes an instrument of the Prince to be used for his ends, and he should not hesitate before any action that might go against Christian morality (murder, brutality, lies ...). Everything will be well-used if it achieves its end, because as Machiavelli himself says, 'a wise ruler, therefore, cannot and should not keep his word when such an observance would be to his disadvantage, and when the reasons that caused him to make a promise are removed'.[15] In order to hold on to power, the Prince may be forced to 'act against his faith, against charity, against humanity and against religion'.[16]

CONCLUSIONS

Machiavelli does not propose any ideas about what should be done in politics depending on any transcendental ethical imperative ('good', 'happiness', 'eternal salvation', etc.), but instead he brutally describes what he observes and offers a work full of tactics that were successful in other times and places. Thus he distances himself from the philosophical tradition that established a certain ethical ideal conduct as the criteria with which to measure whether political actions are right or wrong. Everything happens here, in the world: means, strategies, and results, which, in the end, are all that matter. In order to hold on to the State, classical ethical considerations are forgotten and subsumed in the praxis of power. All that remains is to explain as clearly as possible what it is successful rulers do, removing any moral assessment from their obligations and any thought of goodness from their acts, and draw a lesson from it.

Since 1559, when Pope Paul VI included it in the index of books forbidden by the Church, *The Prince* has been the topic of much comment and debate. Many philosophers and rulers, from Descartes and Hegel to Napoleon Bonaparte,[17] have expressed their opinions about Machiavelli's work. The 'clash' of opinions occurs in the meeting of two philosophies with opposing views in the way they understand politics: one based on the realism of what is done, and the other on the idealistic wish of what should be done. It was to Machiavelli's credit that he set the groundwork for this discussion to take place and to remain valid until the present time. However, more merit-worthy was his contribution to instituting a view of history focused on the analysis of social acts and their consequences, identically and exclusively social. If we limit ourselves to this field, it is difficult not to agree with Machiavelli when he affirms the amorality of power, as later history has provided and unceasingly continues to provide examples of behaviour that without doubt would receive the approval of the Florentine author and his admired Cesare Borgia.

Another of the reasons for the secular interest awoken by *The Prince* was suggested by Rousseau, who was surprised to discover that Machiavelli, while pretending to give lessons to princes, in fact gave some very important ones to the people. Hence, by giving advice about how to achieve and preserve the power of the State, teachings beyond any ethical or moral humanistic consideration, one may begin to doubt whether the text is a handbook for absolutist princes or, on the contrary, a rare testimony to the normal workings of State power, acting as a warning to their subjects. In other words, Machiavelli shows the true methods of princes, and by extension, all forms of instituted political power, and thus provides clues on what to expect in all relationships with rulers. Therefore, two readings can be made: of the reactionary Machiavelli who encourages and advises absolute power above any possible ethical or moral scruples, and of the progressive Machiavelli who reveals the amoral nature of power to the public and makes the mechanisms by which power acts available to social understanding so that it might be fought against more effectively.

NOTES

1. The English translation of *The Prince* being used is by Peter Bondanella, published in Oxford World's Classics (2005), and the page numbers given here refer to that edition.
2. 'But since my intention is to write something useful for anyone who understands it, it seemed more suitable for me to search after the effectual truth of the matter rather than its imagined one' (*The Prince*, 53).
3. *The Prince*, 58.
4. ibid.
5. *The Prince*, 53.
6. *The Prince*, chapter III.
7. *The Prince*, 57.
8. *The Prince*, 57–8.
9. *The Prince*, 33.
10. *The Prince*, 63.
11. It is important to be generous, but with the money of one's enemies, as 'of what is not yours or your subjects, you can be a more generous donor' (*The Prince*, 56).
12. *The Prince*, 61.
13. *The Prince*, 62.

14. 'Therefore, let a prince conquer and maintain the state, and his methods will always be judged honourable and praised by all. For ordinary people are always taken in by appearance and by the outcome of an event. And in the world there are only ordinary people' (*The Prince*, 62).
15. *The Prince*, 60.
16. *The Prince*, 61.
17. In this respect it is worth mentioning the *Anti-Machiavel* by Frederick II of Prussia, written before he came to the throne and published anonymously in Holland in 1740. Despite this juvenile critique, the long reign of the king is an exemplary case of how to put Machiavelli's principles into practice. In this sense, he perpetuated and increased his power to the point of being given the name Frederick 'the Great'.

4

The Seventeenth Century: Fear and Property

During the seventeenth century, mercantilism and proto-industrialization contributed decisively to the establishment of capitalist forms of production. In Europe, the economic and political weight shifted from the Mediterranean towards the north and west, where England, France, and the Netherlands disputed hegemony. The vanguard of thought moved in the same direction. The old southern centres of Renaissance learning were slowly substituted by the philosophies of modernity, under the cover of the spectacular development of experimental sciences and mathematics.

The secularization of thought now dominates political philosophy. The absolute monarchies gave substance to strong, centralist, and protectionist policies at home, and expansionist abroad. Absolutism gave strength, meaning, and space to an incipient capitalism which, in time, would destroy its progenitor. The defenders of absolutism favoured the success of its future destroyers, who, bearing the standard of innovative republican ideas and nationalist patriotism, were to shape different ideologies of 'freedom', which would become symbols of the struggle against dynastic privileges.

The main political theories would bring out the counterpoints that questioned them: from the monarchic privileges by divine right would come the arguments in favour of the idea of social equality, without pausing to analyse the role of the real conditions that supported both concepts. In this way, the pathway of politics as we know it today began: a field inhabited by forms of conscience that supposedly force the forms of coexistence to respect certain ethical and moral considerations. We are witness to the rise and establishment of bourgeois conscience, capable of writing the most beautiful pages on human liberty, whilst denying the majority the food they need to live.

THOMAS HOBBES (1588-1679): THE REASONABLE WOLF

Hobbes was a clergyman's son and, because of that, benefited from his position at the top of the English establishment. It allowed him to learn the customs and ways to make contacts in that privileged world and, at the same time, to become a famed intellectual who knew Galileo personally, to study classical literature in depth, and be first the tutor and then the secretary of the Earl of Devonshire. England was going through a period of crisis and confrontation between the Crown and Parliament. Although economic reasons were at the bottom of the political disagreements at the time of Cromwell, the dispute was coloured by religious doctrine and also opened doors for political reflections, whose main arguments still form the framework for debate today.

For many political theoreticians, the roots of modern democracy were sketched out in Hobbes' work, whose influence can easily be traced in the thinkers who followed him, from Locke to Hegel, taking in Rousseau and finally arriving at Marx. Unlike Machiavelli's political proposal, derived directly from the praxis by which power was expressed, preserved, and imparted, Hobbes found the fuel of social order in a psychology *avant la lettre* that sought its foundations in biology. The human species is understood as matter in movement. Some men collide with others. Hobbes begins with the individual as a precise physiological entity who has the obligation of remaining alive (a trend that represents Good), faced with the mechanisms or circumstances that might lead to his death or extinction. These could be physical, as the victim of conflicting interests and impulses, or intellectual, by imprisoning his reason. The individual is the centre of his political theory, while social relationships occupy a secondary position, whose main *raison d'être* lies in providing the citizens with security.

His most important political work is *Leviathan, The Matter, Forme and Power of a Common Wealth Ecclesiasticall and Civil* (1651).[1] The term 'Leviathan', a metaphor for the State, designates a kind of artificial super-man built by everyone together, a 'mortal god' with the faculty of guaranteeing peace and exorcising the fear that characterized human relationships in their original and natural state, marked by violence amongst individuals. His work is that of a philosopher who calls himself the brother of fear and who firmly defends policies aimed at finishing with the natural impulses of men, which usually lead them to ruin. He would like to change them for a powerful and effective social reason, capable of asserting itself on these impulses and dispelling internal and external wars. In short, he vindicates a strong political State over private and individual egoism.

In the original, pre-State, and pre-political condition, all human beings were guided solely by considerations connected with their own security and survival. The desire for security and the desire for power both lie in the same continuum, as the latter is simply the aspiration of guaranteeing security permanently by dispelling in advance any possible aggression. All men were equal,[2] not because any constitution said it should be so, but because they were all subject to the same passions, distrusted all others, and only relied on their own strength and ingenuity to survive in a world in which the principle that 'Man is a wolf for Man' found its clearest meaning. In the state of nature, the life of human beings was 'solitary, poor, nasty, brutish and short'.[3] They were continually exposed to danger, ever in fear of being killed. There was no law common to all, but a situation of permanent conflict, a war of every man against every man.[4] In such a context, however, nothing could be thought unfair: 'Where there is no common Power, there is no Law: where no Law, no Injustice'.[5] The only law, 'the law of nature', was an extension of the instinct for survival, which granted everyone the freedom to use whatever means they could in order to save their life.

Under these conditions, dominated by unceasing conflict, equality did not by any means imply freedom. Since individuals spent their lives trying to survive, any property was only temporary and depended on the individual strength of who held it. Therefore, no unions that might be classified as social could exist: 'if any two men desire the same thing, which nevertheless they cannot both enjoy, they become enemies; and in the way to their End, (which is principally their owne conservation, and sometimes their delectation only), endeavour to destroy, or subdue one another'.[6] 'In the nature of man, we find three principall causes of quarrel. First, Competition; Secondly, Diffidence; Thirdly, Glory'.[7] Life and property were under a constant threat and the only law was war.

The way that succeeded in leaving the oppressive state of nature behind was built thanks to the use of reason, of a reason that explains, summarizes, and subsumes the truly human condition in understanding. Reason made it possible to analyse the world, understand and imagine procedures that would create a new world. Hobbes does not proceed by using induction as did the sciences that were appearing in his time, but by understanding reason as a mechanism for calculation and foresight, oriented in this case at the search for a formula that would guarantee individual security. The basic precept of reason, which Hobbes assimilates as the fundamental law of nature, says that 'every man, ought to endeavour Peace, as farre as he has hope of obtaining it'.[8] If this were not possible, he may always refer back to the law of nature, according to which anything goes in order to survive. However, a second law of nature, derived from the first, points out that 'a man be willing, when others are so too... to lay down this right to all things; and be contented with so much liberty against other men, as he would allow other men against himselfe'.[9] In other words, reason advises individuals to make pacts. Through these pacts, men transferred their rights, especially the use of force to defend themselves, to a sovereign power, to which they submitted themselves. In this way they created the civil State, the Leviathan.

> And in him consisteth the Essence of the Common-wealth; which (to define it,) is 'One Person, of whose Acts a great Multitude, by mutuall Covenants one with another, have made themselves every one the Author, to the end he may use the strength and means of them all, as he shall think expedient, for their Peace and Common Defence...'[10]

It wasn't that individuals welcomed giving up the satisfaction of their natural appetites and passions, but reason made them choose to pact, as this solution enabled them to avoid greater evils, precisely the evils that surrounded them everywhere in the state of nature. The civil State was understood as a necessary instrument, as it removed from coexistence the risk of losing one's life. The pact among the men that founded the State, transformed individuals into subjects and, by doing so, created society. The State was given civil laws ('artificial chains' in Hobbes' words)[11] and, above all, the necessary strength to enforce them, for without this they would be worthless pieces of paper. Security and peace were achieved through fear of punishment, a useful and necessary punishment that only the Leviathan-State was qualified and authorized to decide and execute.

The covenant Hobbes alludes to is a key part of his political theory and most of those that followed it. In this case it is based on the permanent and consented cession of all or part of the natural rights of the individual, basically that of self-defence, to a higher power. In short, individuals freely submitted to a strong power that would guarantee life by keeping peace. The desires of all were reduced to a single will.

In a certain way, Hobbes' arguments favoured the legitimizing discourse of the absolutist monarchies, at that time being questioned by the political aspirations of new and forceful bourgeois classes, as they rejected any attempt at rebellion against established power. Despite this, the theory of the compact does not necessarily presuppose in itself an instrument to justify the absolute power of the monarch, and it is also susceptible to imply arguments that will lead to opposite conclusions. If, for Hobbes, the pact granted absolute power to the government (at that time, the monarchy, defended as the most useful system to achieve social peace), for other thinkers, as we shall see, the contract did not imply such an attribution. Consequently, despite being a central argument in Hobbes, the compact was subordinate to a higher concept, that of sovereignty. In fact, the differences between Hobbes and other philosophers lie mostly in their different attitudes in deciding what part of sovereignty is ceded by individuals when government is established, and whether or not this cession is reversible.

The compact founded sovereignty on two fundamental attributes: the absolute being and the indivisible being.[12] For Hobbes, the terms of the choice in the field of politics are posed between absolute sovereign power and anarchy. From this point of view, the differences between forms of government are only variations in the numbers of representatives who hold the sovereignty: one in a monarchy, all in a democracy and several in an aristocracy.[13] However, in any of these cases, the sovereign power is still absolute. In consequence, the main question is not centred on classifying the forms of government as good or bad, but in determining whether existing governments hold (absolute) sovereign power or not. Hobbes maintains that there are no objective criteria for distinguishing a good king from a tyrant, or an aristocrat from an oligarch. All distinctions are subjective verdicts based on opinion; that is, criteria based on passion and not on reason: 'For they that are discontented under Monarchy call it Tyranny, and they that are displeased with Aristocracy call it Oligarchy: so also, they that find themselves grieved under a Democracy call it Anarchy'.[14] There are no differences between good and bad princes, but between princes and no princes, between who is and who is not, in condition to exercise sovereign power.[15]

Hobbes decisively opposes any reduction in sovereignty. In this sense, he criticizes both the philosophies that supported the separation of powers within the State (which, however, would end up triumphant in future enlightened and liberal programmes) and any type of conduct subordinated to considerations different from the supreme duty to be rendered to the State, such as, for example the interior 'conscience' or obedience to the Pope: if the sovereign power is divided it is no longer sovereign. And if a sovereign power cannot continue and ceases to be, that would mean returning to a situation of war of all against all; 'the confusion of a disunited Multitude'.[16] If nothing is able to enforce the law, the law of nature will prevail once more and each one is free to do whatever they like and can, and as a result the calamities that were the original scourge of mankind will return.

Hobbes does not deny natural and divine laws. However, he also affirms that they are not like civil laws, because they cannot be enforced by a common power, as they are not compulsory externally but only in our conscience. Therefore, if a subject does not keep the positive laws, he can be made to do so, whereas if the sovereign does not respect natural or divine laws, no one can force him and punish him.[17] Absolute power should have no limits, as that would put the health and survival of the State at risk. Once the State has been instituted, the field of public relationships absorbs the private field, and so the freedom of each individual only has meaning within the framework of what the sovereign has predetermined.[18] Not even religion stands above the sovereign's power. He has the faculty of ordering the creed that best suits his subjects, as well as authorizing the way of transmitting it and performing worship. The Church does not constitute or represent a source of authority to which civil power should yield. Quite the opposite: clergymen are other servants of the State, equal in status with any civil servant.[19]

Individual and society

Hobbes distances himself from the Aristotelian tradition, as for him, humans are not social beings by nature. Neither are they integrated within a 'perfect community', ordered hierarchically by God, as

Christianity proposes. In seventeenth-century Europe, the relationships of power and exploitation require a different type of legitimization. Human beings are recognized by individuality and regarded as subjects capable of deciding and guiding their conditions of life, and this requires a new explanation of the reasons that guide human coexistence and the role played by political organizations.

Hobbes' arguments are supported by two premises: one, an ontology of the individual as a selfish and competitive being and, the other, the aspiration of the individual for a secure life.[20] The community is reduced to a mere chorus for the sake of the satisfaction of this need, and is understood as a conscious device that brings private interests together. Cooperation has no meaning if it does not produce benefits for its members, who are individuals in isolation. The individual is the substance of the human condition, while society only supports the necessary relationships for the survival of private entities when they decide it rationally. Society becomes a means for the individual; it is a fabrication of the individual through the covenant (consent); it is a rational invention of individual thinking minds in search of its usefulness. Even so, Hobbes' individualism is more attenuated than in later philosophers like Locke, owing to the central role that sovereign power takes in his theory. Once this power is instituted, individuals do not hold on to the slightest part of sovereignty and not even to the innate 'freedom' which later centuries agreed to attribute them. Their lives are conceived according to the course marked out by civil laws, and there is no break between the sovereign's will and their private will. Therefore, Hobbes condemns any thought that encourages individual conscience as a criterion to guide behaviour (what is known as 'acting according to your conscience') or the individual feeling of the absolute property of goods,[21] as this only leads to reducing sovereign power, without which the property itself would not be possible.

Today, the primacy of the individual over the collective has converted individualism into the substrate of all the dominant ideologies to the point of turning itself into a meta-ideology. From the figure of the political, religious, or sporting leader, to ways of thinking that extol the *person* as a subjective entity, the measure of all things, and personal development as the goal of social relationships, individualism has become one of the main distinguishing features of the ideology of bourgeois society. These reasons encourage that myth of the indomitable subjectivity of the individual and 'if you want it, you can do it', even though these arguments only end in irrationalities which, undoubtedly, would annoy those who see each individual as a bearer of the precious asset of reason.

Whether it be in the seventeenth or the twenty-first century, these proposals presuppose an ontology of the human being that surrenders the social being to supposedly self-sufficient and autonomous individuals. Accepting that society does not exist except as the sum of pure individualities which fully define what it is to be human, is based on a series of ideological-religious prejudices and superstitions that have claimed from time immemorial that all human skills, including language, come from a place beyond the human condition and not from social materiality itself. Thus it has been enunciated since the biblical 'I am who I am'. In this way are exalted those who compete for their primacy, the heroes, the 'great men', the individuals most gifted, both for competition (victory in the social struggle) and for recognition (prestige or glory due to the public acknowledgement of their virtue).

On the contrary, society always comes before the individuals, it goes beyond them and it comprises them. The individual comes from it and is formed in it from *two* in the fertilization, from a *woman* in the gestation and from the *multitude* in the rearing and education, until finally, social relationships decide at each historical moment what the criteria of the human condition are, whether or not they are individualized. Therefore, the state of nature imagined by Hobbes, formed by selfish male figures with no history, could never have existed. Hobbes himself must have realized it when, in reference to parents' role in the education of their children, he remarks that 'the Fathers of families, when by instituting a Common-wealth, they resigned that absolute Power, yet it was never intended, they should lose the honour due unto them for their education'.[22] To say that the family existed in the state of nature contradicts the characterization of that state as a pre-political situation, as the family establishes alliances and presupposes a legal framework where these are possible. Deconstructing Hobbes' text, we would suggest that the *bellum omnium contra omnes* fought by selfish males is not so much a pre-condition of a social situation as a fully social product.

The fact that Hobbes, and so many after him, decide to hide and disregard both women and descendants and the relationships that any human community is bound to weave, whilst on the other hand giving primacy to a male individualist conscience, can only be understood in terms of a patriarchal ideology created to justify and defend certain forms of property, including that of certain men over women and their sons and daughters. The myth that in the beginning all men were autonomous and autarchic is a subterfuge aimed at legitimizing material pretensions of dominance and property, as it naturalizes an arrival point (the decision-making power of men), by placing it as the starting point (the pre-social world). Upon these ideological precedents, in the Modern Age in Europe, the ancestral idea of the individual was reformulated; it took on androcentric tones and was positioned in the middle of a political philosophy which ranked individual equal with 'citizen', precisely where it most suited bourgeois labour law.

Conclusion

Hobbes' basic law is the law of survival: men will try to survive at the expense of others. In the lack of any type of control or regulations, men will destroy one another in a situation dominated by fear. Only the institution of an absolute power is capable of bringing the peace that will guarantee survival and banish fear. For this reason, political power, the State, is an artifice, a Leviathan which, in a certain way, is contrary to human nature.

Hobbes justifies the absolute power of the State because it contributes to individuals' security. The search for security moved individuals to abandon the state of nature, through voluntary and rational submission to a common power that is so strong that it prevents the anarchic use of private force. The supreme good that an individual's will is devoted to is life. This maxim never loses its validity. He defends absolutism in terms of the supreme interest of individuals, the preservation of their life. He thus achieves its legitimization by referring to the *usefulness* of absolute power. References to Providence or Goodness are left behind. The secular pragmatic field opened up by Machiavelli, among others, is widened and strengthened.

In Hobbes can be seen a logical opposition that lasted until modern liberalism. On the one hand, he states that individuals and groups of different kinds develop socially useful work and functions, regulated by a government for the good of everyone, within a legal framework that makes a community out of the group. However, on the other hand, he believes that society is made up of essentially selfish individuals who only support a common political power to protect themselves from other egoists. It is a philosophy that in another direction will opportunely serve the interests of liberalism, by its defence of individuals with their own unique natural interests, and a vision of the community as an instrument of private desires of happiness.

JOHN LOCKE (1632–1704): THE INSTIGATOR OF 'HUMAN RIGHTS'[23]

The fundamental question that Locke tries to answer is centred on the sources of political power, a power that consists of the right to pass laws to regulate and protect property, and the possibility of using the forces of the State to enforce obedience to these laws, simply in the interest of public well-being.[24] In his essay he combines considerations in the Christian tradition and proposals within the scope of the emerging bourgeois philosophy. Thus, Locke defines natural law as an expression of divine will, in allusion to all those rights inherent in the human condition which remain valid in any situation, whether in the original state of nature or in, as we shall see, the later civil government. These rights are universal and inalienable; no one can take them away. Therefore, Locke uses a natural and theological foundation precisely to undermine the doctrine, also theological, of the divine right of monarchs, which was the justification for the absolute power of the European monarchies in the *Ancien Régime*. At the same time, Locke was the first to demonstrate the central role of private property in the development of modern society and, hence, of the (bourgeois) State. His intention was to draw up a pragmatic political model which granted sovereignty to individuals to the detriment of dynastic arbitrariness. His proposal, more moderate and less coherent than the one defended in Leviathan, has, in practice, enjoyed much greater repercussion, as it directly influenced the American Constitution, and a number of European magna cartas in the nineteenth century. Its echoes are still sounding loudly in the political discourse of the liberal parliamentary democracies of today.

For Locke, the law corresponding to the natural state, the original situation when individuals were not subject to any government, does not emerge from innate characteristics in human beings, but coincides with divine commands and is recognized empirically through an individual reason. Natural and individual law harmonize when the latter seeks the preservation of human beings themselves and pursues happiness. The basic precept is that nobody can harm another (nor himself, naturally) in his liberty, health, limb, or goods.[25] When this happens, the injured person may claim a punishment, as the transgressor has shown that he has no use of reason or justice. Because of that, he has stepped outside natural law by declaring war on other humans and deserves a fair punishment, which may be administered by anyone who has acknowledged the transgression.[26] However, unlike Hobbes, Locke imagines a state of primitive nature that was not dominated by violence, but by mutual help and respect for the principles of natural law. In this situation there is equality as regards power and jurisdiction,[27] and it may arise when there are men living together according to reason, but without a common superior on earth with authority to judge between them.[28]

Locke argues that property is the most important individual natural right and the one that would have greatest weight in relation with the constitution of political power. Instituting a tradition with enormous influence in political economy, he places the origin of property in the work that all perform in the state of nature. As all men possess the property of their own person, the labour of their body and the work of their hands should also be theirs. By investing this labour in nature, they add something of their own to it and, in consequence, its fruits become their property.[29] Thus, he emphasizes that only work confers the right to property by adding value to uncultivated land. In the earliest times, everyone would invest time in common land and, without harming other individuals, would obtain from it what they needed to cover their basic needs.

As we can see, for Locke work is not a social activity, but an individual faculty granting the right to owning the obtained product; it is therefore the work of individuals in isolation who work part of a land that is communal in the original situation of the state of nature. No society as such existed yet; only series of individuals apparently without any links between them. In fact, the definition of what is common land clearly shows Locke's presupposition: common land is that which is not worked by any man, and not that which an assembly of individuals have agreed to declare as common. Locke assumes that in the state of nature a model of individual autarchy existed, in which everyone obtained what they needed to live by working the land; in which individual property is limited to what each person could use or consume; in which bartering was limited to providing for subsistence, and in which, in short, no large accumulations of wealth or serious inequalities existed.

However, the situation changed with the appearance of money: 'some lasting thing that men might keep without spoiling, and that by mutual consent men would take in exchange for the truly useful, but perishable supports of life'.[30] Money opened up the possibility of increasing wealth, exchanging goods, and also of putting a value on work, the origin of all property, as merchandise. It is worth pointing out that, thanks to this theoretical justification put forward by Locke, salaried employment began to be recognized as part of the economy, breaking with Aristotelian thought which had dominated until then, and which had included paid work within the acquisition of wealth, an activity that was unworthy of any citizen with full rights (see above). However, Locke did not explain why the introduction of money was advantageous and necessary, and neither does he include it within his later argumentation about the foundation of civil society. The only thing he retains is the individual character of property as the fruit of individual labour and the need to safeguard it.

How and why did the transition from the state of nature to civil society occur? He begins by pointing out that the first human society was formed by man and woman as spouses. From this arose the society of parents and children, and later, that of masters and servants. For Locke, conjugal society was a voluntary compact consisting chiefly in carnal union and its aim: procreation, as well as mutual support and a joint interest in raising a family.[31] However, civil society involves a qualitative change. We saw that according to natural law, any man had the right to defend his life, his liberty, and his possessions, and to punish any harm to this right. Political society will preserve the defence of those rights, but will differ substantially in the way of achieving it:

> because no political society can be, nor subsist, without having in itself the power to preserve the property, and in order thereunto, punish the offences of all those of that society; there, and there only is political society, where every one of the members hath quitted this natural power, resigned it up into the hands of the community... And thus all private judgment of every particular member being excluded, the

community comes to be umpire, by settled standing rules, indifferent, and the same to all parties; and by men having authority from the community, for the execution of those rules, decides all the differences that may happen between any members of that society concerning any matter of right.[32]

We should note the importance of the concept of individuals 'quitting' the rights of the defence of property and freedom as the key to understanding the origins of civil society. Certain parallels can be seen with other contemporary authors. For Locke, as for Hobbes, the pact is consented voluntarily. For both, also, the State is a useful solution that suits the majority of individual interests. However, whereas for Hobbes the factor that triggered the pact leading to the foundation of the State was the fear reigning in a situation of war of all against all, typical of the state of nature, for Locke it was due to a concatenation of less precise factors, if not to say contradictory ones. He ventures the idea that the growth of the population in some places meant that land became scarce and this led to the establishment of the first agreements about the boundaries of the communities.[33] Then, the true foundation of civil society would take place when each individual renounced his natural rights; putting them in the hands of the community, which could better protect and preserve these natural rights: life, liberty, and, above all, property, which ultimately was the supreme reason for the union of men to form States.[34] It is this act, in these conditions, that grants legitimacy to governments, and from this point onwards the individuals must be prepared to obey the will of the majority translated into laws.[35] A political society is one in which people live together forming a single body, with a common sanctioned law and with a legal structure able to settle disputes and punish offenders.[36] In this way, civil society or the State has two basic powers, legislative and juridical-executive, both aimed at defending property and the natural rights of the individuals who consented to forming a civil association.[37]

In an attempt at reconstructing the formation of civil societies historically, Locke reiterates the initial transition between the family organization and the constitution of the first monarchies as an unforced consequence of the continuity of paternal affection and care. He remarks that because of factors such as the need for military leadership, the government of society was taken over by a single man, within a climate of mutual trust. It is thus a kind of Golden

Seventeenth Century: Fear and Property 57

Age which, unfortunately, ended when 'ambition and luxury' of later times made princes dissociate their own interests from the common good.[38] Thus, Locke explains the creation of despotic and tyrannical governments by alluding to factors of a psychological kind, such as the lust for power, ambition, and flattery, among others.

Locke bases all legality in the *people*, understood as the association of individuals who one day consented to forming a civil society. Laws should be promulgated by individuals elected by the people and should not try to take away the individuals' natural rights: 'Legislative power, in the utmost bounds of it, is limited to the public good of the society'.[39] Because of the inalienability and non-expiry of the innate rights founded in natural law, people will always hold sovereignty. In this respect Locke is significantly different from Hobbes, as for the latter, the concession of natural rights to the State is complete and for perpetuity. In contrast, for Locke, individuals' innate rights are still inalienable, and thus no one, not even the prince, can take them away. Sovereignty and legitimacy are always due to the precepts of natural law and its beneficiaries, the union of individuals designated as the people. Consequently, the people will always be in possession of the legitimacy to change the government if this 'is corrupted' and ceases to guarantee the rights that protect life, liberty, and property. In political matter, the source of Law and the sole judge is the people.[40]

From this viewpoint, absolute power is an attack on the natural rights of individuals. Anyone who tries to get another man into his absolute power puts himself in a state of war with this man, as in this way he is attempting to enslave him by taking away his natural freedom as the first step before taking away everything.[41] In this moment, it is legitimate for the people to take the necessary actions to correct this situation:

> for no man or society of men, having a power to deliver up their preservation, or consequently the means of it, to the absolute will and arbitrary dominion of another; when ever any one shall go about to bring them into such a slavish condition, they will always have a right to preserve, what they have not a power to part with; and to rid themselves of those, who invade this fundamental, sacred, and unalterable law of self-preservation, for which they entered into society.[42]

In cases such as these, he speaks openly of armed struggle: 'In all states and conditions, the true remedy of force without authority, is to oppose force to it'.[43] However, in chapter XIV ('Of Prerogative'),

Locke contemplates the licence for working outside the established law: 'This power to act according to discretion, for the public good, without the prescription of the law, and sometimes even against it, is that which is called prerogative',[44] and although in chapter XIX he reviews the ways in which it is licit and legitimate to dissolve an existing government and once again stresses the sovereignty of the people and justifies all actions taken against absolutist abuses, the prerogative still questions the inalienable natural rights of the people and is a recurrent resort in the constitutions of modern States.

In the final chapters of his essay, Locke shows his pragmatism in certain political matters in civil society[45] and concludes his essay without returning to the premises about it or the institution that sustains them. This first and central place from which civil society arises, and which later nourishes it, is the family. According to his reasoning, family comes before civil society. Consequently, it *manifests* itself in the state of nature. This positioning involves a contradiction, as for Locke the basic cell in the state of nature was the individual, and not the union of a man, a woman, and their offspring (a family). Hence, the ontological individualism which Locke used to explain the origin of property through work is put into question; we should bear in mind that for Locke, any man could work a piece of uncultivated common land and thus obtain the property of the products that would guarantee his subsistence, but he neglected to mention the fact that as well as some land, a man should also count on the support of a woman.

The precepts of natural law are also applicable to the approach of paternal power. In consonance with the natural right of individual liberty, the parents (father and mother) are unable to submit their children to their will, once they have come of age. The parents' rights are circumscribed to their obligation of maintaining, educating, raising, and protecting their children while they are under age. The parents must use their intelligence and their reason (the fundaments to understand natural law) to guide their children while they are still incapable of using such faculties.[46] When children come of age, they are supposed to have acquired these and, from that time, natural law will be the same for all.

However, he acknowledges that parents possess an instrument with which to tie their children to obedience: the power of deciding on whom to bestow their estates, that is to say, *inheritance*.[47] It is paradoxical that Locke does not question this, as it is an attack on the children's liberty, in that it acts as a mechanism by which parents can impose their will, thus infringing natural law (see below).

Conclusion

Locke's role as an inspirer of political liberalism can be summarized in his defence of a human condition possessing, in a state of equality, a series of inalienable rights referring to the preservation of life, liberty, and private property. The owner of these rights is the individual, the pillar supporting liberal political and sociological thought. In fact, the birth of society is the fruit of a compact, of a covenant made between free and rational individuals, conscious of their rights and who, with this decision, seek to improve their ability to defend and guarantee these rights. In addition, as he considers this initial agreement, made by certain groups of individuals occupying a certain territory, to be inviolable,[48] he makes possible the nationalist school of thought which came after his time and which has been reconciled so well with the principles of political liberalism.

We must note Locke's indignation with the prerogatives of European absolute monarchs in the question of the defence of individual property, almost certainly in response to arbitrary requisitions and the creation of taxes whenever the king wanted. In this respect, Locke not only sides with the bourgeoisie, but also with the nobility and small land-owning farmers who might be victims of the absolute monarch's looting. In short, he defends the interests of all the propertied classes, except the dynastic sector.

The resort to individual, universal, and inalienable natural rights is Locke's argumentative weapon in the struggle against absolutism, and situates him as one of the greatest exponents of *ius naturale*. It might be said that the proclamation of a natural law is similar in its form to the modern defence of the so-called 'human rights'. In both cases, the reasoning rests on a basic premise: if there is an unchanging nucleus in individual human nature, not dependent on any particular time or place, community life should always respect certain minimum conditions of 'good government' that will safeguard individual interests in society. In other words, there should be certain basic rules of good behaviour and good government that no one can ignore with impunity. These are moral rights and duties, previous to and above judicial Law and which no government should infringe if they do not want to place themselves against natural law, and consequently lose their legitimacy.

Two main points that do not easily go together arise, however, out of Locke's approach. The first of these is about the family. We mentioned above that Locke 'naturalizes' the family, although this might be considered the first truly political institution. This supra-individual grouping is previous to civil society, and its existence in the state of nature questions the leading role of the individual in the formation of society and civil government.

The second controversial point has to do with the origin of property. According to natural law, individual labour is the source of property. If this is so, why does the custom of inheritance contradict it, as it allows the assignation of possessions to certain individuals even though they do not come directly from their labour? Inheritance is additionally the only way that parents have to injure their children's right to individual freedom once they have come of age. Why, then, does Locke never question this institution in any depth? Such a critique would also be useful to question even further the privileges of absolute monarchies, whose *raison d'être* and continuance depends entirely on the hereditary transmission of wealth, prebends, and titles. However, he makes no critique in these terms, perhaps because a reason outside the arguments of his political theory intervenes, a reason coming from a discourse that is different from the one enunciated in his work. This discourse is the extreme defence of private property, one of whose pillars consists precisely of arrangements for inheritance.

The defence of property is one of Locke's *leitmotivs*. This defence should be ensured by explicit laws and by an executive capable of enforcing them. 'For the good of the people', that is, everything that contributes towards the tranquillity of the owners of property, is the final yardstick of the acceptability and legitimacy of government. In any case, it is not 'natural law' but the use of money as the universal equivalent of goods and labour which alters the initial state of equality and social peace, although the origin of this mercantile system is left unexplained. In Locke, the 'people' is a solid entity, formed by the union of *private property-owners*. If we accept this definition, it is clear that everyone is a property-owner, as everyone obtains products with their labour. However, Locke never considers the causes of the inequalities in wealth that existed and continued to exist, nor, of course, their possible effects on the forms of government. The only

Seventeenth Century: Fear and Property 61

references made in this respect occur when he deals with the origin of money, within a poor series of arguments (see above). In this sense, by resorting to psychological factors (ambition, some princes' lust for absolute power) to explain later deviations from the initial Golden Age, Locke situates himself in the line of classical authors, for whom ethic-moral virtues and defects lead men towards certain political and economic attitudes. The origins of their wealth or poverty either remain unstudied and taken as given, or are explained as the consequence of their moral inclinations.

In our opinion, Locke did not conceive the social world as the product of the labour of a whole community, but regarded the individual as the leading actor in relationships and always saw property-owners behind everything. The definition of labour as the connection between the autonomous individual and nature, and as the origin of property, explains some commonplaces in reactionary thought that have continued until the present time. From this point of view, differences in wealth are due to differences in attitude, so that industrious people are rich whereas the lazy, foolish, or handicapped usually end up in poverty. Thus, the State has the mission of safeguarding property and the lives of its owners. This approach ignores the social character of production. It is as if each individual started from scratch, and on coming of age with full use of his faculties, set to work to obtain property. Obviously, this argument hides the real role of original dissymmetry, and implies a naturalization of the differences in wealth, when their origin is of a socio-economic kind. This directly favours the wealthy, who are attributed virtues that rarely come from labour, and more frequently from hereditary privileges. The role of the State proposed by Locke consists of watching over the principle of the conservation and aspiration to happiness of property-owners. The natural order of things sketched out by Locke does not provide an explanation of the inevitability of the State, but is used to justify property-owners' rights against, on one hand the pretensions of those who are not, and on the other hand, the arbitrary decisions of a special owner: the absolute king.

The reproduction of social life is the result of general collective production and not the result of autonomous individual initiatives. This assertion is valid, from the formation of the individuals themselves to any of their participations in labour processes enabling the material reproduction of a whole community. If the totality of wealth accumulated by a single person was exclusively the fruit of individual labour, there would be no initial inequalities, as the duration of a 'day's work' required to produce the desired goods is the same for all members of society.

Locke does not find a solution to the problems between property and labour or between individual, family, and society. This is paradoxical for a critic of innatism, a thinker who proposed, before his time, the fluidity and transformation of things and thoughts, of changes and transformations in society and human beings, and who did not accept that dynamic actions could be supplanted by static concepts. Perhaps his concern did not reach those places and this made him fall in the paradox of proposing the existence of innate unmovable rights, owing to his preoccupation with putting limits on absolute power and its impunity.

Locke is known as the precursor of 'human rights' that do not depend on any particular material situation, and at the same time he takes on the role of the unfortunate instigator of their infringement (as in, for example, inheritance, the power of the husband and of the property owner, and the disturbing 'prerogatives' of government). The model of society he desired must have given hope to many people in those times. Even so, it was burdened by a heavy patriarchal and oligarchic-democratic load, according to which power fell upon the *owners* of the conditions and means of production and subsistence. The importance of Locke's proposal lies in having succeeded in placing owners' 'natural rights' above any other social or individual interest. Logically, their protection became the main *raison d'être* of liberal States.

NOTES

1. An edition is available in Oxford World's Classics.
2. 'Nature hath made men so equall, in the faculties of body, and mind' (*Leviathan*, part I, chapter XIII).
3. *Leviathan*, part I, chapter XIII.
4. ibid.
5. ibid.
6. ibid.
7. ibid.
8. *Leviathan*, part I, chapter XIV.
9. ibid.

Seventeenth Century: Fear and Property 63

10. *Leviathan*, part II, chapter XVII.
11. *Leviathan*, part II, chapter XXI.
12. Bobbio (1987: 95).
13. *Leviathan*, part II, chapter XIX.
14. ibid.
15. Bobbio (1987: 95–107).
16. *Leviathan*, part II, chapter XVIII.
17. Bobbio (1987: 95–107).
18. *Leviathan*, part II, chapter XXI.
19. *Leviathan*, part II, chapter XXXI.
20. In the preliminary study of a Spanish edition of Hobbes' work, Tierno (1991: x) summarizes the core of Hobbes' philosophy: 'Man is essentially a selfish animal, and the first and main formula of selfishness is survival' (E. Tierno; 'Estudio preliminar', in T. Hobbes, *Del ciudadano y Leviatán*, Editorial Tecnos, Madrid, pp. IX–XVI).
21. *Leviathan*, part II, chapter XXIV.
22. *Leviathan*, part II, chapter XXX.
23. Our interest is centred on his observations in the *Second Treatise of Government. An Essay concerning the true original extent and end of Civil Government*, first published in 1690.
24. *Second Treatise*, chapter I, section 3.
25. *Second Treatise*, chapter II, section 6.
26. *Second Treatise*, chapter II, section 8.
27. *Second Treatise*, chapter II, section 4.
28. *Second Treatise*, chapter III, section 19.
29. *Second Treatise*, chapter V, sections 27–30.
30. *Second Treatise*, chapter V, section 47.
31. *Second Treatise*, chapter VII, sections 78–9. Despite the voluntary nature of the pact between husband and wife, Locke establishes the family hierarchy and its limits based on different reasons:

    But the husband and wife, though they have but one common concern [raising their children], yet having different understandings, will unavoidably sometimes have different wills too; it therefore being necessary that the last determination, i.e. the rule, should be placed somewhere; it naturally falls to the man's share, as the abler and the stronger. But this reaching but to the things of their common interest and property, leaves the wife in the full and free possession of what by contract is her peculiar right, and gives the husband no more power over her life than she has over his. (*Second Treatise*, chapter VII, section 82)

32. *Second Treatise*, chapter VII, section 87.
33. *Second Treatise*, chapter V, section 38 (see also chapter VIII, section 95).

34. In later chapters this defence is omnipresent, and he even denies the right to property through conquest apart from the immediate reparations to be paid by the conquered (*Second Treatise*, chapter XVI, sections 175–7).
35. *Second Treatise*, chapter VIII, sections 95–7.
36. *Second Treatise*, chapter VII, section 87.
37. *Second Treatise*, chapter VII, section 88.
38. *Second Treatise*, chapter VIII, section 111.
39. *Second Treatise*, chapter XI, section 135.
40. *Second Treatise*, chapter XIV, section 168.
41. *Second Treatise*, chapter III, section 17, and also chapter IV, section 23.
42. *Second Treatise*, chapter XIII, section 149.
43. *Second Treatise*, chapter XIII, section 155.
44. *Second Treatise*, chapter XIV, section 160.
45. In chapter XVI he deals with conquest and the reasons that advise against submitting the conquered country to slavery. Chapters XVII and XVIII provide a discourse on usurpation and tyranny, respectively. Finally, chapter XIX examines the ways in which the dissolution of government is considered legitimate.
46. *Second Treatise*, chapter VI, sections 58–9.
47. *Second Treatise*, chapter VI, section 72.
48. See chapter XVI, dedicated to conquest, where he forbids enslaving the conquered.

5

The Eighteenth Century: Lights and Shadows in the State

The eighteenth century is known as the Century of Lights. The Enlightenment is recognized as a revolutionary time in which Western European bourgeoisie believed it could radically oppose monarchic privileges of feudal origin and, at the same time, question superstition, arbitrariness, and ancient customs. The bourgeois intellectual revolution wished to restore the universe of reason and place this at the crossroads of social decisions. It aimed to bring down the classist world of the Ancien Régime and in its place establish a realistic and rational social constitution, with the idea of extolling the agreement of general will.

It was human reason which, by the firm steps of science, would enable a true knowledge of the world and society to be reached. The project of the Enlightenment promised progress and the emancipation of mankind. On the one hand, scientific and technical development would provide the material means that human beings needed to achieve their well-being. On the other, the triumph of the values of Liberty, Equality, and Fraternity, the ethico-moral means of production, would put societies on the road towards happiness; at last a *universal* happiness which the whole human race would have the right to.

The absolutist order and its prerogatives were smashed to pieces with the imposition of bourgeois economic policies: freedom to trade and make contracts, legal protection of individual private property and the constitution of a State formed by the citizens, to guarantee internal law and order and capable of imposing its will abroad. Frontiers would be opened not only for trade and the annexation of territory, but also for the political expansion of the bourgeoisie, who would gradually colonize neighbouring aristocratic worlds, drawing them into the new capitalist order.

As we have seen in previous chapters, the thesis of a *social contract*, necessary to lead from a state of nature to a political community, had been in vogue since the seventeenth century, thanks to Hobbes and Locke, among other thinkers. Both agreed on the existence of that natural state, previous to the appearance of the State, although they differed in some nuances. Hobbes began with a belief in the selfishness and the natural evilness of man, and drew a picture of a state of nature dominated by a war of all against all. To put a permanent end to conflict and guarantee individuals' security arose the Leviathan, an artifice to control evil mankind, unsociable by nature, but which needed to form associations to avoid greater evils. This pact required the renunciation of the individual right to self-defence by violent means, which was deposited in the hands of a third party, the sovereign. The latter, in turn, was not a party to the contract, and therefore was not tied or obliged to his subjects in any way. The State that was born in this way, whether it took a monarchic, aristocratic, or democratic form, would enjoy absolute power as a result of the concentration of sovereignty.

Locke, in contrast, began with the idea of the equality of the origin of human beings and, above all, a series of innate rights which should take care of any individual at all times and places. When the conditions of life in the primitive state of nature became hard, individuals sealed a pact which established the State, also called civil society. Its main aim lay in guaranteeing life, liberty, and, above all, the property of the contracting parties. The latter, unlike in Hobbes' proposal, never lost their sovereignty. Thus, they always preserved the legitimacy to bring down any corrupt government, that is to say, one which had ceased to safeguard the laws that the people wanted and which worked in the interests and benefit of a small number of individuals.

J.-J. Rousseau, the author whom this chapter is about, put forward a new proposal based on the arguments made by previous philosophers. His political philosophy took the ideology of the contract to radical extremes and became an important source of influence for future theories of society.

JEAN-JACQUES ROUSSEAU (1712–78)

Rousseau wrote two main works on the topic that interests us and which we will examine here. The first is the *Discours sur l'origine et les fondemonts de l'inégalité parmi les hommes*, written in 1755,[1] and the second is *Du Contrat Social*, in 1762. We shall be guided in our explanation by the argumentation in the first work, where he proposes a course that could be described as sequential or historic, from the state of nature to civil society, and we shall add some diagnostic elements from *The Social Contract*, especially in reference to the description of the state of nature and the later nature of the State.

Rousseau's political notion is the opposite of Hobbes', and in contrast, coincides in many points with that of Locke, although he radicalizes the goodness of human beings in the natural state. He even suggests that the political State should return human beings to their original good-natured and virtuous state, as man is not only equal to his fellow creatures (we are all equal by birth) but we are born free and we are, by nature, peaceful and virtuous.

Problems arise with the coexistence and cooperation that occur in society. Human beings are born free; no one is more powerful than any other by nature, but life in society has put most people in chains. The situation should change through a new form of association, agreed to by consensus, which defends and protects persons and their property with all the *common force*, and in such a way that no one loses their freedom.

As we shall see in the following pages, the nature of the social contract proposed by Rousseau never leaves the reins of the community in the hands of the government. It is all for one, where that one is the *general will*, the people united in assembly. Unlike what happens in the state of nature, in the civil State justice takes the place of instinct, duty the place of physical appetite, and reason the place of inclinations: 'What man loses by the social contract is his natural liberty and an unlimited right to everything he tries to get and succeeds in getting; what he gains is civil liberty and the proprietorship of all he possesses'.[2] Civil liberty is none other than obedience to what people themselves have prescribed.

The *Discourse on the Origin of the Inequality of Man* begins with an exhortation to the leaders of the Republic of Geneva, in which some of the traits anticipating his political posture can already be noted. He declares his preference for a moderate democratic government where the right to pass the laws drawn up by the magistrates corresponds to the people and where citizens meeting in assembly can decide about legal, judicial, and government matters. Thus, he places himself against the absolutism that was still dominant in the Europe of his times.

We may highlight some points and themes in the preface of the book that are later developed at greater length. In the first place, we may stress his vision of a descendent, degenerative evolution in the sense of a human history commencing with an initial 'Golden Age', comparable with the state of nature, in which: 'every advance made by the human species removes it still farther from its primitive state'.[3] For Rousseau, the increasing degeneration runs parallel with the development of social life and the empire of reason over the senses.[4] Just as domestication degenerates wild animals (they lose strength, vigour, and bravery), civil life produces the same effect in humans: 'as he becomes sociable and a slave, he grows weak, timid and servile; his effeminate way of life totally enervates his strength and courage'.[5] Once again a negative and degenerative opinion about the history of mankind.

In the second place, he stresses that, although men are, by nature, equal to one another, the changes that have been introduced in their history have not occurred homogeneously, and therefore there are men who 'continued a longer time in their original condition'.[6] In this way, he opened a pathway to research into the human past based on contemporary social forms, along which anthropology travelled in the nineteenth century.

The mention of equality should not deceive us, as women are excluded from politics, despite the good words that Rousseau offers them before whisking away the possibility of any social right:

> Amiable and virtuous daughters of Geneva, it will be always the lot of your sex to govern ours. Happy are we, so long as your chaste influence, solely exercised within the limits of conjugal union, is exerted only for the glory of the State and the happiness of the public.... What man can be such a barbarian as to resist the voice of honour and reason, coming from the lips of an affectionate wife?... It is your task to perpetuate, by your insinuating influence and your innocent and amiable rule, a respect for the laws of the State, and harmony among the citizens....
> Continue, therefore, always to be what you are, the chaste guardians of our morals, and the sweet security for our peace, exerting on every

occasion the privileges of the heart and of nature, in the interests of duty and virtue.[7]

The last phrase is especially revealing: woman as the depositary of all that is sentimental and natural, should put these qualities, in the field of private coexistence (the conjugal home), to the service of responsibilities that are typically masculine: the duty and virtue that citizens should possess and put in practice for the government and good of the Republic. In fact, the Rousseaunian perspective is essentially male: the 'man' in the state of nature and in the transition to civil life is a man understood as a *male individual*, not mankind in general.

Rousseau acknowledges two forms of *inequality* in the human species, ignoring of course the inequality between sexes, as for him, that is so natural as to become invisible. The first form is *natural or physical*, and consists of differences in age, health, strength, and qualities of the spirit. The second is *moral or political*; it depends on a convention and is established with the consent of men. It is expressed in the privileges that some enjoy to the prejudice of others (being wealthier, more honoured, more powerful, etc.).[8] Convention is one of the basic points in his whole reasoning: as no one possesses a natural authority over his fellow men and as force creates no rights, only conventions remain as the basis of legitimate authority.[9]

We should highlight the importance of this last aspect, as it establishes the foundations for all explanations of human inequality based on causes of a juridical-political kind. This is so because, by situating causality within convention, he also situates it within human will. However, we should warn that a wide range of variations are opened in this field. Those that are nearest to liberalism will affirm that people always decide according to a common desire that pursues a general good. Nevertheless, other versions will emphasize the weight of private will and how this can be imposed upon the rest of society. In this case, we find ourselves amongst common proposals in the anarchist tradition and in idealist modalities of Marxism. Curiously, and as perhaps only happens among great thinkers, in Rousseau we shall find elements and intuitions that cover this whole field of possibilities.

The *Discourse* is centred precisely on the second type of inequalities that we have just mentioned above; why was nature submitted to the law? To answer this, it is necessary to go back to the state of nature. However, Rousseau approaches this research from a different viewpoint from that of Hobbes or Locke, as we have already pointed out. For Rousseau, these thinkers have tackled the question wrongly when they characterized the natural state with the qualities corresponding to civil society (authority of the strongest, when authority and government were concepts that did not exist; preservation of what belongs to each person, when the word 'belong' held no meaning, etc.).[10] In this way he was able to criticize Hobbes,[11] by noting that the need to satisfy numerous human passions cannot be proposed as a cause to explain leaving the state of nature.

Following the tradition of seventeenth- and eighteenth-century treatises, the first part of the *Discourse* is a sketch of the typical form of life in the natural human state. Rousseau announces that the characteristics of human beings in the state of nature have to be studied, as there lie the real, original foundations of society. This research is the key to the present and the future, since 'as long as we are ignorant of the natural man, it is in vain for us to attempt to determine either the law originally prescribed to him, or that which is best adapted to his constitution'.[12] The aim is to determine the true human needs and establish the fundamental principles of their duties, which is essential knowledge for human will to agree to submit to laws, while fully aware of the reason.

In the state of nature, men live dispersed, with the sole assistance of their skills and their body. We can suppose that life in nature produces healthy and vigorous bodies, where the only limitations are wounds and age.[13] Men live in proximity to danger, but possess the means to defend themselves. Males and females would unite fortuitously as they met each other. Rousseau also breaks with the philosophical tradition, going from Aristotle to Locke, when he proposes that man is not gifted with reason by nature and so this does not make him different from animals. The essential characteristic of human behaviour would be man's free will, which allows him to act as a 'free agent' in the world.

He puts forward two principles previous to reason from which all the rules of natural law can be derived: the interest in one's own *welfare* and preservation and, in second place, the repugnance felt on seeing another being suffer pain or death,[14] that is to say, *compassion*.[15] Therefore, at the outset it is not necessary to include the principle of *sociability* in the explanation of human fundaments. Here can be glimpsed one of the features of enlightened-liberal thought: once again the ontological individualism that we noted in previous philosophers.

The notion of *sociability* does not appear in the characterization of the state of nature, since for Rousseau, men lived in isolation in a kind of self-sufficiency. There could not have been any moral relationship or interpersonal duties; men could be neither good nor bad, possess neither vices nor virtues.[16] The feeling of *compassion*, as it calls us to help those who suffer unthinkingly, occupies the place of laws, customs, and virtues in the natural state.[17]

Regarding the question of morality, Rousseau points to the human capability of choosing, that is, the liberty of will as a specifically human trait, very different from instinct, and also the faculty of improvement. In contrast with these virtues, he recalls the desires of men living in the state of nature, which bear no relation with those of men empowered by the use of reason, as the only good things they know of are food, a female, and sleep, and the only evils they fear are pain and hunger.[18]

As regards the sentiment of love, he distinguishes the physical desire of sexual union from the moral aspect or love. For the savage, love is inconceivable, as he cannot consider concepts such as merit, beauty, regularity, proportion, etc. For the natural man, 'every woman equally answers his purpose'.[19] A manifestation of his andro-centrism is underlined persistently: 'It is easy to see that the moral part of love is a fictitious feeling, born of social usage, and enhanced by the women with much care and cleverness, to establish their empire, and put in power the sex which ought to obey'.[20]

Rousseau continues describing the state of nature and relates the first revolution characterized by the invention of simple stone tools and hut-construction, with the establishment and differentiation of families and the introduction of a 'kind of property'.[21] He has just introduced the family surreptitiously and, with no apparent cause, uses the family unit to force a qualitative change in contrast with a previous situation in which men lived dispersed from one another, and he said nothing of women and their children. The family, understood as the husband and wife, parents and children, living under one roof,[22] was characterized as the starting point of the feelings of conjugal love and of paternal love. With the family, *another* way of life was produced: 'The women became more sedentary, and accustomed themselves to mind the hut and their children, while the men went abroad in search of their common subsistence'.[23] The links between children and their parents were broken when they came of age. As the first law of human nature is to take care of one's own preservation, and also as we are all born free, it can be deduced that on coming of age, each person could choose the best way to preserve himself. Everyone then becomes 'his own master'.[24]

Little by little, leisure time was used to create comforts and superfluous needs, which was assessed in negative terms, as these comforts weaken and make the body dependent.[25] With sedentarism, men come together, they unite in groups, and 'at length in every country arises a distinct nation, united in character and manners, not by regulations or laws, but by uniformity of life and food, and the common influence of climate'.[26] This also favoured the appearance of a common language.[27] In addition, they took the first steps towards the emergence of public esteem in the context of the amusements of song and dance (the search for consideration and prestige), which was the first step towards inequality and vice, as they favoured the rise of vanity, contempt, shame, and envy.[28]

With this natural background, inequality is still far from making an appearance, as there are no means in the state for one man to make another obey him: 'what ties of dependence could there be among men without possessions?'.[29] Any attempt to dominate and enslave[30] another man would only end with the latter's escape.

> as the bonds of servitude are formed merely by the mutual dependence of men on one another and the reciprocal needs that unite them, it is impossible to make any man a slave, unless he be first reduced to a situation in which he cannot do without the help of others: and, since such a situation does not exist in a state of nature, every one is there his own master, and the law of the strongest is of no effect.[31]

Rousseau explains the division of labour by stating: 'Metallurgy and agriculture were the two arts which produced this great revolution',[32] because from that moment one man began to stand in need of the help of another. This origin for the *division of labour* was to be maintained in several Marxist and evolutionist approaches to the emergence of social hierarchies and the State.

Cultivation of the land meant that it had to be divided up, leading to *property*, and the first rules of justice. In Rousseau, as in Locke, the origin of property is in *labour*, understood as an individual activity which produces things that become one's own. In this context, natural individual differences in various capabilities (strength, ingenuity, wit, and skill) were the cause of differences in property, to the extent that the application of these qualities in work resulted in an increase in productivity and production for those people who possessed them. Thus, 'while both laboured equally, the one gained a great deal by his work, while the other could hardly support himself'.[33]

The development of the arts, inequality in fortune, uses and abuses, etc., are unleashed from this point on. In this development, there are motivations of the characteriological or psychological type, again in agreement with the whole tradition of classical ethico-politics. Thus, *insatiable ambition*, and the *thirst of raising one's fortune* above that of others, inspire *jealousy* and the *desire of profiting* at the expense of others.[34] In this respect, once the wealthy knew the *pleasure of command* 'they disdained all others'.[35] In short, men became avaricious, ambitious, and evil, and 'the new-born state of society thus gave rise to a horrible state of war'.[36]

The importance of this kind of psychological motivation had been made clear when Rousseau, in a famous passage, explained the beginning of inequalities. In it, he connects property with inequality, taking the origin of property back to an evil act of will that did not receive the opportune reaction from the will of those who were ignorant of the future danger that it involved.

> The first man who, having enclosed a piece of ground, bethought himself of saying *This is mine*, and found people simple enough to believe him, was the real founder of civil society. From how many crimes, wars and murders, from how many horrors and misfortunes might not any one have saved mankind, by pulling up the stakes, or filling up the ditch, and crying to his fellows, 'Beware of listening to this impostor; you are undone if you once forget that the fruits of the earth belong to us all, and the earth itself to nobody.'[37]

However it happened, this state of war that set rich against poor was unbearable for both sides. Thus, the rich conceived 'the profoundest plan that ever entered the mind of man: this was to employ in his favour the forces of those who attacked him, to make allies of his adversaries, to inspire them with different maxims, and to give them other institutions as favourable to himself as the law of nature was unfavourable'.[38] They proposed a union, apparently aimed at safeguarding the weak from oppression and making safe the property of all: the institution of the rules of justice and a supreme power that governed according to the laws. For Rousseau, this was the origin of society and laws, although in his opinion it

> bound new fetters on the poor, and gave new powers to the rich; which irretrievably destroyed natural liberty, eternally fixed the law of property and inequality, converted clever usurpation into unalterable right, and, for the advantage of a few ambitious individuals, subjected all mankind to perpetual labour, slavery and wretchedness.[39]

For the origin of inequality, he established several successive periods: 1) establishment of laws and the right of property (authorization of the state between rich and poor); 2) institution of magistracy (distinction between powerful and weak); and 3) conversion of legitimate into arbitrary power (existence of master and slave).[40] In this last stage, a new state of nature is reached, different from the first and the result of an excess of corruption in which only the law of the strongest prevailed.[41]

Up to this point, Rousseau had sketched out a social and political evolution in which a series of material factors carried a great deal of weight. To be exact, we are referring to the effects of the adoption of metallurgy and agriculture as activities that lead to the origin of property and, after that, the emergence of inequalities in wealth. However, we have also noted that psychological factors had been present since the very start of inequality, apparently as the consequence of the demands of public recognition. Towards the end of his essay, Rousseau reaffirms a type of causality that we can describe as clearly idealistic. He establishes four main kinds of inequalities present in all societies: depending on riches, nobility or rank, power, and personal merit.[42] According to Rousseau, personal qualities are the origin of all the others and 'wealth is the one to which they are all reduced in the end'.[43]

> I could explain how much this universal desire for reputation, honours, and advancement, which inflames us all, exercises and holds up to comparison our faculties and powers; how it excites and multiplies our passions, and, by creating universal competition and rivalry, or rather enmity, among men, occasions numberless failures, successes and disturbances of all kinds by making so many aspirants run the same course.[44]

In this last part of the *Discourse* he criticizes the governments which use power in an arbitrary way (absolutist regimes), questioning the key premises in monarchic arguments such as: the institution of absolutist rule that uses the protection of the subjects as a pretext,[45] the right of one country to conquer another,[46] and paternal authority as the foundation of the absolute right of kings.[47]

Finally, Rousseau, taking up again the stratagem of the wealthy to create civil society through a pact that formally united the people and the elected leaders in the observance of certain laws (which involved the union of their wills in a single will and the peaceful enjoyment of each one's property), defended the idea that this contract cannot be irrevocable.[48]

Some years later, in *The Social Contract*, Rousseau approaches civil society from a different viewpoint from that in the *Discourse*. In that work he had respected a sequential discourse of the transition to civil society beginning with the primitive state of nature. Many of the concepts and categories used ('savages', sedentarism, division of labour, agriculture, etc.) are a century in advance of evolutionist theories and still today are worthy of attention. However, in *The Social Contract* Rousseau abandons diachronic history and pays greater attention to the definition of the two opposite situations: state of nature and civil society. He also abandons, as we shall see, the causal force of inequalities in property when he explains the rise of government and the law, taking on a more integrationist position, in the line followed by Locke.

According to Rousseau, a time comes when living in the state of nature becomes no longer viable. He does not give any particular reasons for this, apart from a point when the obstacles in the way of their preservation overpower the resistance that each individual can offer separately.[49] Under these conditions, men can only unite and use the strengths they possess by common agreement, which necessarily requires the cooperation of many. However, how can they cooperate, without compromising their force and liberty, the chief instruments of their self-preservation? The issue is expressed in a formulation that has become a classic:

'The problem is to find a form of association which will defend and protect with the whole common force the person and goods of each associate, and in which each, while uniting himself with all, may still obey himself alone, and remain as free as before.' This is the fundamental problem of which *The Social Contract* provides the solution.[50]

The social contract should involve the advantage resulting from abandoning an uncertain, precarious natural life, dependent on a sole individual strength, in favour of a more secure life, guaranteed by a mutual right that creates an invincible force. The individual is consigned to the State and this protects him constantly.[51] Nevertheless, it is absurd to think that someone surrenders or submits for nothing. If anyone or a whole country does so, they are mad, and madness creates no right. In any case, even if they did, this act would not be binding on their children, which would impede the perpetuation of the dominion.[52] Rousseau states that he is against the law of the strongest. 'To yield to force is an act of necessity, not of will';[53] therefore it does not create right. Force is not the same as law, and we are only obliged to obey legitimate powers.[54] If a man submits successively to a series of men acting in isolation, even if they were many men, they would still be acts performed by an individual. In the case of a whole people submitting to a king, Rousseau points out that, although this submission is a civil act which implies public deliberation, it is necessary to go back to the prior act by which the people became a people as such, for that is the true foundation of society.[55] The foundational convention and its objectives must be renewed. At the time of the pact, everyone submits totally to the community in the act which constitutes the *general will*. The general will is institutionalized in the State as a means agreed upon by a consensus to pursue a common good or interest. In this act, the individual personality of each contracting party disappears and a moral and collective body is born, made up of as many members as the *assembly* contains votes.[56] The assembly, as the place of the expression of the general will, is precisely where the source of all legitimacy and sovereignty resides. There can be no representatives or intermediaries of the general will, which must act by the word of mouth of all its members in reunion. As soon as a master exists, no longer is there a sovereign.[57] In this point, Rousseau is the champion of full, direct democracy, one which mistrusts parliaments. Marxism and anarchism will take up this idea and include it in their emancipation programmes.

One of the tasks of the assembly is to pass laws. Laws are necessary to tie together rights and duties in civil society. A *law* is an act of the general will which regulates a matter affecting it as a whole. Hence, it can be understood that no one is above the law (not even the king, because the king is a member of society) and neither can the law be unjust, as no one is unjust with themselves. The order of a chief or the decree of a king are not acts of sovereignty, they are not laws, but acts of magistracy. The author of a law should be the *people* (the general will).

Therefore, the demands the social body makes of an individual always have a cause and should be satisfied immediately by the person concerned. The commitments binding to the social body are compulsory because they are mutual: they come from all and they apply to all, according to the common good that all pursue. The social compact thus establishes a general equality, as everyone binds themselves to it in the same conditions and enjoys the same rights.[58]

The contract pursues the preservation of all, but on occasions it involves risks and losses. If, for the sake of the continuity of the State, it is necessary that someone must die, the person has to die, because thanks to the State this person has lived safely up to this point;[59] the justification is expressed in the following example: 'it is in order that we may not fall victims to an assassin that we consent to die if we ourselves turn assassins'.[60]

The person who commits a crime breaks the pact and places himself in a state of war with respect to the general will and deserves to be punished. Rousseau considers the death penalty, although he recommends a restrictive use. In the line of Thomas More (*Utopia*), Rousseau points out that 'There is not a single ill-doer who could not be turned to some good', specifying that 'The State has no right to put to death, even for the sake of making an example, any one whom it can leave alive without danger'.[61]

For Rousseau, there are no good and bad forms of government, only more or less suitable ones. In general, he believes that democracy is most appropriate for small states, aristocracy for medium-sized ones and monarchy for the largest states. Of the different forms of government that originate due to greater or lesser differences among individuals at the time of instituting the contract, Rousseau prefers democracy,[62] although he doubts that this has ever existed and has little faith in it ever happening in the future: 'Were there a people of gods, their government would be democratic. So perfect a government is not for men'.[63]

We should emphasize here that Rousseau distinguishes between forms of government and source of sovereignty or power. For him, all these forms of government may occur, provided that the people decide what type of government they would like. Rousseau also shows his sympathies towards aristocracy: however, that kind of aristocracy whose members have been elected, and in the same way he seconds Plato on the benefits of a *government of the wise*: 'it is the best and most natural arrangement that the wisest should govern the many, when it is assured that they will govern for its profit, and not for their own'.[64]

Finally, monarchy arouses certain apprehensions, since despite being the form that mobilizes the greatest strength and appears the most agile in decision-taking, it is also the most prone to use its strength for objectives other than that of 'public happiness'.[65]

Rousseau and political participation

The *Discourse* defended the idea that will, exercised in a certain situation of material development, was in the origin of property and that property was the cause of inequality: all this within a degenerative view of human history. Later, the *Social Contract* granted a charter to the individual, showed his needs, and set out his politics of general will and the social solutions that mutual agreement can afford.

Rousseau lies at the origin of several trends without fully characterizing any of them. He earned the respect of Kant and Hegel, and therefore can be considered one of the sources of contemporary idealism. Nevertheless, he questions the economic conditions that produce social dissymmetry, an aspect that materialism would sympathize with. In addition, he condemns the historical development of states as the cause of all social evils, which is an announcement of future anarchist postures. By postulating that moral and political inequality is contrary to natural law and adopting a critical position with respect to property, he opens the door for proposals of more egalitarian ways of life. This is an apparently progressive proposal which is paradoxically based on an involutionist route—that is, returning to a past stage and ignoring new material conditions. Rousseau's political offer was for a return to the past, a nostalgic search for ways of life nearer the state of nature and the initial times of the social contract. A return that embraced the myth of the good savage and the longing for a society formed by small land-owners in assembly and, of course, their important and yet almost invisible families. To achieve this he demands, as would any anarchism, a new act of will, this time

Eighteenth Century: Lights and Shadows 79

a positive one, to counteract that other ill-fated act of will that caused the expulsion from Paradise.

For all these ideas, Rousseau suffered persistent persecution. On occasions, he expressed himself with a bluntness similar to that of later thinkers like Marx.

> I could prove that, if we have a few rich and powerful men on the pinnacle of fortune and grandeur, while the crowd grovels in want and obscurity, it is because the former prize what they enjoy only in so far as others are destitute of it; and because, without changing their condition, they would cease to be happy the moment the people ceased to be wretched.[66]

In *The Social Contract*, Rousseau describes a state of nature that was left behind when men agreed to provide themselves with laws and to form a civil society. Individuals were joined together by a common interest in the preservation of all and with that aim they established rights and duties after each one entered the community in an act that shaped the general will (assembly).

Hobbes spoke of forcible conquest and of the strength of absolute sovereignty. Locke spoke of overcoming the force with force if the sovereignty broke natural law. Rousseau appealed to the strength of legitimacy. For him, the author of the law should be the people in assembly (the general will), as the most important and fundamental thing is not the force but legitimate power, that is, one which is based on an agreement. Legitimacy provides the only licit force with which to stop the individual will when this goes against the general one. In short, in order to enforce the law it is necessary to possess that legitimate force that appears when general will grants the political body a sovereign power aimed at the common good and which has its origin in a general agreement. The State protects the individual permanently, because the individual has devoted himself to the State and is an active participant in it. It is the citizen who gives legitimacy to the State and not the other way round.

In book III of the *Contract*, Rousseau sketches out his conception, contrary to the system of representative democracy, in favour of a system of direct democracy. The formation of the general will requires each citizen to express his opinion only on what he understands, avoiding the existence of factions or political parties that capitalize on differences in individual will and reduce them to supposedly general interests. The general will, as it only acts 'when the people is assembled',[67] implies a demand for a constant renewal of the original pact through frequent meetings of the general assembly. Thus, it is not enough for the people to have given their approval to a civil State at the start, by sanctioning a body of laws. The assembly of the people should take place in a fixed and periodical way, as well as in any unforeseen circumstances that might arise.[68] In these assemblies, the executive power of the government is suspended and all citizens are absolutely equal in terms of representation.[69] 'The moment a people allows itself to be represented, it is no longer free: it no longer exists'.[70] This precept is a radical defence of the effective involvement of all citizens in public affairs in order for the State to progress successfully: 'Every law the people has not ratified in person is null and void – is, in fact, not a law'.[71] The general will of the people 'does not admit of representation: it is either the same, or other; there is no intermediate possibility. The deputies of the people, therefore, are not and cannot be its representatives: they are merely its stewards'.[72]

For Rousseau's social project, the greatest good that the legislative system should tend towards is the achievement of liberty and equality. It should tend towards equalizing power and wealth in a world where all have the same rights and duties. However, these encouraging words do not entail any great alternatives in social policies. Thus, he does not advocate equal fortunes as a way to achieve the cited aim of emancipation, but only dares to recommend that no citizen should be 'poor enough to be forced to sell himself: which implies, on the part of the great, moderation in goods and position, and, on the side of the common sort, moderation in avarice and covetousness'.[73] As regards power, he simply expresses a wish: that it is not used over and above the limits marked by law. In order to achieve these goals, Rousseau's idealism again resorts to ethics: individual will under the form of 'moderation' of one and another will make it possible to reach an approximate middle way, and it is thought that this form is the least prone to social conflict. This position is reminiscent of Greek antiquity, when Aristotle proposed in *Politics* a model of a city dominated by a just middle way. In both cases, the ideal society would be ruled by a large group of male land-owners. However, while Aristotle could still observe examples of what he was preaching, the same ideal was for Rousseau a utopian discourse.

Regarding the *raison d'être* of the government of the State, Rousseau warned that it was only a commission created by and subordinate to the people, who are at all times the source of sovereignty. Legislative power can only belong to the people, while the executive power is an agent who puts public force into action according to the directives of the general will. The will of government must agree with the general will, that is to say, with the law.

> What then is government? An intermediate body set up between the subjects and the Sovereign, to secure their mutual correspondence, charged with the execution of the laws and the maintenance of liberty, both civil and political.
>
> The members of this body are called magistrates or kings, that is to say governors, and the whole body bears the name prince. . . . I call then government, or supreme administration, the legitimate exercise of the executive power, and prince or magistrate the man or the body entrusted with that administration.[74]

Finally, we can point out an interesting aspect regarding the later foundations of nationalist doctrines. Rousseau noted that the exact legislation of each State should be modified depending on local situations and the inhabitants' character. Hence, it can be understood that there is no perfect legislation in absolute terms, only legislations adapted to the people who enacted them[75] and who, of course, are always able to revoke them or change them. This political discourse emphasizes particularities and identities, and provides arguments for an academic discourse that might attempt to investigate them with particularist and relativist parameters.

According to Rousseau, ambition, corruption, vile interests, or 'secret motives', all motives of an ethical kind, make it inevitable that sooner or later governments tend to try to oppress the people. In this moment, states enter into decadence and fall.[76] The social contract that built them is thus broken and the cycle can start again.

Conclusion

Rousseau proposes 'it was so and so it should be', and uses natural right as an ethical reference point in order to criticize the existing political systems and believe in others to come in the future. At the same time, he rejected the politics of his age and looked towards the past through the reasons of his time. This past nourishes an ideal featuring an association of small agrarian land-owners that is patriarchal, in assembly, and pre-capitalist, with the Greek *polis* as a model. For Rousseau, like most of his contemporary liberal theoreticians, the government is no more than a commission acting on behalf of and subordinate to the people, who form the source of sovereignty. In this respect, the Prince's will must concord with the general will, which is the law.[77] However, the main difference between Rousseau and other theoreticians of natural right lies in that, for him, sovereignty should *always* remain in the hands of the people, and that it should be impossible to delegate it to representatives. Ideas such as these would still be revolutionary at the present time.

In his collectivizing proposal, Rousseau stresses the solidarity of ethical values, against a world of monarchic privileges and the avidity for wealth of the nascent capitalism. For him, there is no justification for the loss of political virtues, such as patriotism and solidarity. In a similar way to More, although based on a secular conception, his reference framework is a humanism of mutual respect and affective and effective collaboration among humans. He coincides with other supporters of *ius naturale* in that, if the people are forced to obey against their desires for natural freedom, it will be better to obey because there is no other alternative. However, if they take action to free themselves of the oppression, it will be even better. In this sense, Rousseau's *ius*-naturalism is, as in Locke, a weapon for revolt against established power, which at that time was personified by absolute monarchy, supported by the Christian religion. He therefore stated that Christianity was a serious obstacle to social progress and the liberation of mankind. 'Christianity preaches only servitude and dependence. Its spirit is so favourable to tyranny that it always profits by such a regime. True Christians are made to be slaves, and they know it and do not much mind: this short life counts for too little in their eyes.'[78]

Because of this kind of sentence and criticism, *The Social Contract* was burnt publicly in the city where it was conceived, Geneva, and forbidden and persecuted in many other places. The Church, the powers associated with its interests, and the defenders of rancid absolutism did all they could to make sure its ideas would be forgotten. They did not succeed.

NOTES

1. The translations used here are by G. D. H. Cole, in the public domain, available online at <http://www.constitution.org/jjr/ineq.htm> (*A Discourse on the Origin and Foundation of the Inequality of Mankind*) and <http://www.constituion.org/jjr/socon.htm> (*The Social Contract or Principles of Political Right*).
2. *Social Contract*, book I, chapter 8.
3. *Discourse*, Preface.
4. *Discourse*, part 1.
5. ibid.
6. *Discourse*, Preface.
7. *Discourse*, Dedication.
8. *Discourse*, part 1.
9. *Social Contract*, book I, chapter 4.
10. *Discourse*, part 1.
11. ibid.
12. *Discourse*, Preface.
13. On the contrary, 'we are tempted to believe that, in following the history of civil society, we shall be telling also that of human sickness' (*Discourse*, part 1).
14. *Discourse*, Preface.
15. On this matter, also see *Discourse*, part 1.
16. *Discourse*, part 1.
17. *Discourse*, part 1. Some clear expressions of this natural feeling are 'do to others as you would have them do unto you' or 'Do good to yourself with as little evil as possible to others'.
18. *Discourse*, part 1.
19. ibid.
20. ibid.
21. ibid.
22. 'The most ancient of all societies, and the only one that is natural, is the family' (*Social Contract*, book I, chapter 2).
23. *Discourse*, part 2.
24. *Social Contract*, book I, chapter 2.
25. *Discourse*, part 2.
26. ibid.
27. ibid.
28. ibid.
29. *Discourse*, part 1.
30. In contradiction with Aristotle: 'If then there are slaves by nature, it is because there have been slaves against nature. Force made the first slaves,

and their cowardice perpetuated the condition' (*Social Contract*, book I, chapter 2).
31. *Discourse*, part 1.
32. ibid.
33. ibid.
34. ibid.
35. ibid.
36. ibid.
37. ibid.
38. ibid.
39. ibid.
40. ibid.
41. ibid.
42. ibid.
43. ibid.
44. ihid.
45. ibid.
46. ibid.
47. *Discourse*, part 2. In these points he refers explicitly or implicitly to Locke's book.
48. *Discourse*, part 2.
49. *Social Contract*, book I, chapter 6.
50. ibid.
51. *Social Contract*, book II, chapter 4.
52. *Social Contract*, book I, chapter 4.
53. *Social Contract*, book I, chapter 3.
54. ibid.
55. *Social Contract*, book I, chapter 5.
56. *Social Contract*, book I, chapter 6.
57. *Social Contract*, book II, chapter 1.
58. *Social Contract*, book II, chapter 4.
59. This argument is similar to the one Plato puts in the mouth of Socrates in the dialogue *Crito*, in which Socrates refuses his friend's request to escape from prison and save his life, after receiving the death sentence. Socrates says that by accepting death, as the laws of Athens had prescribed, he was acting in coherence with the respect for them that he had observed and preached all his life. In the dialogue, the laws come alive and in his imagination they speak to Socrates, pointing out that he owes his whole life to them, from his parents' marriage, to his education and his commitment to living in the city.
60. *Social Contract*, book II, chapter 5.
61. ibid.
62. *Discourse*, part 2.

63. *Social Contract*, book III, chapter 4.
64. *Social Contract*, book III, chapter 5.
65. *Social Contract*, book III, chapter 6.
66. *Discourse*, part 2.
67. *Social Contract*, book III, chapter 12.
68. *Social Contract*, book III, chapter 13.
69. *Social Contract*, book III, chapter 14.
70. *Social Contract*, book III, chapter 15.
71. ibid.
72. ibid.
73. *Social Contract*, book II, chapter 11.
74. *Social Contract*, book III, chapter 1.
75. *Social Contract*, book II, chapter 11.
76. *Social Contract*, book III, chapters 10–11.
77. See also *Social Contract*, book III, chapters 17–18, above all chapter 18, from which it is worth extracting a particularly concise fragment:

    the institution of government is not a contract, but a law; that the depositaries of the executive power are not the people's masters, but its officers; that it can set them up and pull them down when it likes; that for them there is no question of contract, but of obedience and that in taking charge of the functions the State imposes on them they are doing no more than fulfilling their duty as citizens, without having the remotest right to argue about the conditions.

78. *Social Contract*, book IV, chapter 8.

6

The Absolute State

GEORG WILHELM FRIEDRICH HEGEL (1770-1831)

Hegel was born in 1770, the same year as Beethoven and Hölderlin, and a year after Napoleon, all representatives of the political and cultural changes that took place in the late eighteenth century. He descended from a family of protestant reverends, with a high social standing, their roots being in the Duchy of Württemberg. In Hegel's time, Germany was a society divided up territorially (the different *Länder* disputed amongst themselves and with the Empire) and ideologically (the rift being between Protestants and Catholics). It still possessed a mainly traditional agricultural economy, with the agrarian resources in the hands of the land-owners, and an incipient industrial sector, unlike what was happening at the same time in France and England. A society that would feel the impact of the political changes taking place in France, but with a different pace and intensity and with opposite effects to those in its neighbouring country.

In the Germany of that time, the political order expressed a profound contradiction between the absolutist reality of the rulers of the different *Länder* and the guilds that protected the private interests of its members and acted as true socializing institutions. Above all these, the Holy Roman Empire, in the hands of the Archduke of Austria, was going through its death throes, until finally collapsing in 1806, shortly before the appearance of the *Phenomenology of the Spirit*.

Hegel appreciated the French Revolution in 1789, despite the horror he felt for the havoc of 1793. Because of this, and perhaps not so paradoxically as is usually thought, he is considered a reactionary ideologist, teacher of the Prussian State and, at the same time, the methodological substrate to the revolutionary ideas of the nineteenth century. It is not unusual for his publications to be occasionally ambiguous. He is capable of defending reactionary institutions, such as primogeniture, in *The Philosophy of Right*, and quite the contrary in an article about the British Reform Bill in 1831, shortly before his death.[1]

He might be considered, to a certain point, an *enlightened man*, and therefore *modern*. The modern project intended human progress and emancipation to be reached through scientific knowledge and the use of reason. The development of science and laws would free people from oppression and suffering. The Enlightenment aimed to put an end to old feudal privileges, the fraud of Providence, fate, and chance. This 'Tribunal of Reason' as Kant called it, assumed the capability of deciding the validity or not of the aims of reaching the truth and justice through science, art, religion, morals, or everyday practices. The Hegelian philosophy had the objective of contributing the *system* and at the same time providing the yardstick to measure the necessary knowledge for the imagined changes to become reality.

Hegelian philosophy and his triads

For Hegel everything is made up of triads, from dialectics itself (be-affirmation, not be-negation, unit-negation of the negation) to philosophy (*logics* or thought in itself, *philosophy of nature* or exteriorized thought and *philosophy of the spirit* or return of the idea to itself). The spirit also is produced and returns in three movements (*subjective*-interior, *objective*-exterior and *absolute* or spirit itself), each one in turn divided into another three: the first, subjective spirit, into *natural soul, consciousness* (of another and of one's self), and *spirit* as will; the second, objective spirit, into *abstract right, morality*, and *ethical system* (social life); and, finally, absolute spirit or subjective–objective dialectic unit, which shows the procedural union between thought and reality, idea and nature, fused in their development. This is the place of the conciliation and expression of the purest manifestations of the spirit: *art, religion*, and *philosophy*.

We find the analysis of *social institutions* in the development of objective spirit (*abstract right, morality*, and *ethical system*), which is outside the subject and in nature without being nature. Abstract right is the expression of the free will of a human being as a person; it is founded in it. It is the very manifestation of the juridical person, as *one* reason. Will is the driving force that obtains three moments outside itself, formed by *property, contract,* and *wrong.*

Property, as the first objective manifestation of will, presupposes the appropriation of the thing in a domain for itself and manifests *private freedom.* Property achieved through the exercise of private will may be required by other desires, the will of others, which demands their development towards the *contract* or conciliation of wills. The third moment, *right in itself* or full right, finally provides the necessary channel to restore the order pre-existing before contractual infringements. This channel collects all the sediments of disputes and confrontations caused by the different objective wills and simultaneously checks and contains them through penalties susceptible of re-establishing judicial order.

Morality is the second part of objective spirit. This now concerns a person as a *subject* involved in rules for a correct life. Morality comprises the motivation for any action and stipulates the realm of what *should be*, characterizing this part just as the *law* characterized the first.

The *ethical system* is the achievement of integration. For Hegel, law and morality are inseparable, in such a way that right is only an ethical expression of liberty, the true essence of life in society. As it integrates *being* and what *should be, person* and *subject,* the ethical system is a manifestation of social life in three aspects: the *family, civic community,* and the *State,* each one developed correspondingly.

For Hegel, the *family* is the *natural* place of a human being. Individuals do not exist in isolation, but are subordinate to that institution which produced, welcomed, and formed them. Families who act among themselves as 'independent concrete persons'[2] show the union above what is united. The family is produced in *marriage* and, through labour, in the *family property,* the two factors that make it possible to achieve the needs of its goal: raising and educating *children* until the unit is broken up in order to form others.

The *civic community* is the second part of social life and is occupied by the *citizen.* It is the *phenomenal* form of the ethical system[3] and shows the totality of social relationships. The command of the citizen over the person and the subject is now clear, as for Hegel, if an individual objective contradicts a general goal, it should be rejected.

The Absolute State

Civic community consists of another three factors. The first is shown by the *wants* of the individuals and the inevitable clash they cause. This situation leads to the formation of a second factor, the *administration of justice*, which avoids conflicts, and a third, the *police and corporations*, whose task is to prevent subversions and annul alterations to the social order. The first factor is developed in turn by *fortune*, *labour*, and *intelligence*, which will attempt to satisfy individual wants. As we have seen, they will not avoid, but rather be the cause of conflicts. Once they arise, they need a second factor, the administration of justice which will promote and produce a *formal right*, an *individual right*, and, finally, *legal activity* which, under the subjective, attentive, and expert eye of the judge, will impose the law correctly and will use the preventive and vigilant institutions of the third factor, the police and corporations, in order to make good the damage caused by private freedom, qualified by nature to break the rules.

The *State* is the full universe of objective spirit; that which *locates* the preceding places, contains them, and merges them. A universe of reason formed to provide harmony amongst individuals and society, as well as private and social freedom, and will. The State is the social substance that has reached awareness of itself and congregates family and civil society within itself. It is a higher form of the joint development of morality and law.

The State, as the absolute goal of life in society, appears in Hegel's eyes as 'the divine will as a present spirit, which unfolds itself in the actual shape of an organized world'.[4] The State is the achievement of liberty and, at the same time, the way of achieving it. It is a structured and constituted State, a State of right following the course and direction of History.

We shall devote the rest of this chapter to examining in greater depth the course outlined briefly above, following the guidelines laid down in *The Elements of the Philosophy of Right*.

The elements of the philosophy of right

Hegel's philosophy is a philosophy of concept, as the identity of meaning and life, idea, and reality. Reason is this precise identity of the differences, and dialectic, which 'does not merely apprehend any phase as a limit and opposite, but produces out of this negative a positive content and result'.[5]

Hegel speaks to us of the philosophy of right as a science. In this way he again shows himself to be a firm defender of the modern, enlightened, and rationalist project, in contrast with the appearance in his time of romantic attitudes which abandoned all rational explanations of the world for free will, the heart, fancy, intuition, caprice, and contingency.[6] For Hegel, these accompanied the most degraded forms of philosophy. From the moment philosophy declares the knowledge of truth as meaningless, it discredits itself and opens the door to the equalization of all thoughts and all matters: the law has the same worth as opinions about it.[7] With the same firmness, he attacks other supposed values of his time, such as the consideration of enthusiasm or of feeling as criteria of what is fair or not.[8] Hegel expresses an unmitigated condemnation of free will and the justifications it attributes to human actions, such as goodwill, kind heartedness, and subjective conviction.[9]

Hegel also attacks the historicism which attempts to 'explain' right through a mere account of the concatenation of previous events (circumstances, 'context', peculiarities). Instead, he prefers to arrive at the elements of right by pure deduction, and draw up a system of universal deductions going beyond empirical erudition.[10]

Hegel shows the direction of all his thought in the following assertion:

> What is rational is real;
> And what is real is rational.[11]

What matters is the knowledge of substance and the eternal in what is temporary and fleeting. 'To apprehend what is is the task of philosophy, because what is is reason'.[12] Thought should provide explanations of feelings and the world. Only rational thought leads to the truth and the world is exteriority as regards the Idea; these are the profoundly rationalist and idealist foundations of Hegel's philosophy.

> To consider anything rationally is not to bring reason to it from the outside, and work it up in this way, but to count it as itself reasonable ... The business of science is simply to bring the specific work of the reason, which is in the thing, to consciousness.[13]

Based on the development of the ideas of will and freedom, the pillars of his edifice, Hegel conceives the sphere of right within what is spiritual, as could be no other way: 'Right in general is something holy, because it is the embodiment of the absolute conception and self-conscious freedom'.[14] His starting point is *will*, which is free and unyielding to anything, nothing determines it; it is within itself and for itself and, as rationality, it always tends towards the universal. In the first place, will contains 'the element of pure indeterminateness or pure doubling of the I back in thought upon itself'. Will is, compared with the real, its negative reality that only refers to itself abstractly, and is in itself, the individual will of an individual.[15]

Hegel explains that there is a first free will which obeys natural instincts and desires, although in this case it is not correct to speak of real freedom. True freedom is reached through thought, when this succeeds in establishing right and an ethical system (laws, the State) in a rational way. As we saw, Hegel confronted individual free will, as for him, individual will should tend towards the universal. As this universal will is rational, all human beings can reach it through thought.

> The will is true and free only as thinking intelligence.... The self-consciousness, which by thought apprehends that itself is essence, and thus puts away from itself the accidental and untrue, constitutes the principle of right, morality, and all forms of ethical observance.[16]

Right is the kingdom of actualized *freedom*.[17] The State will be the most perfect way to achieve freedom and put pure human rational thought into practical reality. Since individuals should practise a universal relational life, to act according to right is no other thing than to obey the laws that have been passed and in that way enjoy this freedom in its universality.

Abstract right

In the first part of his work, Hegel tackles *abstract right* and its development in *property* and the *contract* in order to reach, finally, *wrong*. The main actor in this process is the *person* or the consciousness the individual, in his free will, has of himself. The person is conscious of his finitude and this determination situates him, through reason, in the infinite, universal, and free.[18]

> Personality does not arise till the subject has not merely a general consciousness of himself in some determinate mode of concrete

existence, but rather a consciousness of himself as a completely abstract I, in which all concrete limits and values are negated and declared invalid.... Individuals and peoples have no personality, if they have not reached this pure thought and self-consciousness.[19]

This solid individualist and even nationalist vindication would weaken in other parts of the book (see below). An individual, the essential factor, who will rise above his finitude thanks to reason, and will be recognized as a part of the universal and also of a people, similar to the Fichtean I-us, who should be conscious of themselves to define their personality, of themselves within the universal—in other words, their identity. Accessing this self-consciousness is the first step towards true freedom within the universe of human life; people—self-awareness—identity are expressions beloved of nationalism. We should not forget that, for Hegel, the truly free spirit is one that overcomes mere natural existence and gives himself his own, conscious and truly free existence, and that is where right and legal science begins and where slavery becomes definitively unjust.[20]

In the first instance, Hegel defines right as the existence that freedom gives itself directly.[21] This directness is expressed in the form of *property* or the relationship of a person with himself with regards to the external things he might possess, and *contract* or relationship with property owners. Both lead to *wrong*, which explains the unjust, crime, coercion, punishment, or penalties.

Everything different from the free spirit is external to it, is an impersonal and illegal thing. This thing has its goal in the fact of receiving my will. When my will possesses it, it exercises a right of appropriation and it becomes my property, a private possession.[22] Private property is only subordinate to a superior instance, which is the State. Thus, taking possession of external (natural) things is the origin of property. It may happen thanks to cunning, craft, etc., but in any case, it originates in the moment when there is the free will of appropriation.

The first private property is my own body, the body that my spirit has possessed.[23] Therefore, any violence exercised against my body is violence against me, against my spirit, and against my person as free will, because 'In so far as the I lives, the soul, which conceives and, what is more, is free, is not separated from the body. The body is the outward embodiment of freedom, and in it the I is sensible.'[24]

Private property is, for Hegel, the true expression of the free person and right in itself, an absolute right or absolute right of man above all things ('by means of an agreement a property becomes mine').[25]

The word *property* means the specific attribute, that which defines and is typical of each individual, and also means the possession of an external thing. It is therefore easy to identify the *possession of something* as *something typical* of the human condition. Both meanings merge in the Hegelian discourse and finally form a single entity, as property and use that cannot exist separately. The possessed thing is used to satisfy a need or certain requirement, which is quantitative and comparable in the world of relationships among individuals. Hence property equally presupposes the integrating will of the appropriation of external things.

The sphere of the contract appears when the property of a thing becomes a common agreement between several free wills.[26] The contract involves mutual recognition and affects external individual things. 'Stipulation is already the embodiment of my volition. I have disposed of my property; it has ceased to be mine, and I recognize it as already belonging to another.'[27]

The original establishment of contractual relationships between persons with the aim of safeguarding their body and their properties does not express, for Hegel, the *raison d'être* of the State, unlike the opinion of believers in *ius naturale* such as Locke and Rousseau. For him, the nature of the State must be found in the *ethical system* (below). In contrast, the foundations of right come from property in terms of taking possession of a thing through my free will and the contract between wills.[28] Because of this, right arises from the person and the respect for the relationships between persons. Given that the person is abstract as he extends beyond all the determinations he may *perform*, the right of the person is an abstract right which can only refer to the abstract conceptual identity of persons; a pure, undifferentiated equality. In this place, only free will exists, and this can encounter the will of others as it shows itself and asserts itself in the empirical world through the possession of things.

Nature is the expression of inequality, it is external appearance itself. Things have no rights and, in consequence, they are objects of contract.[29] For Hegel, right originates in the free person, formed in society itself, which has nothing to do with natural situations of no right: natural right is a contradiction. What emancipated society should achieve is 'to limit and sacrifice the arbitrariness and violence of the natural situation'. In contrast, society is based on the relationships between individuals who carry out different tasks that 'in their manifold variety make more pronounced the differences in the development of natural endowments, physical and mental, which were unequal to begin with'[30] (in nature). The division of labour is the cause of inequality among persons. This involves hereditary and personal inequality among individuals and is assumed to be a condition of civil society.

Actual right is an objective manifestation that occurs when it represses any infringement of itself. Its empire is its own permanent re-establishment and to do this, it penalizes and punishes without taking into account the subjective factors of the delinquent. It is the crime or offence which produces the right to force its application. In Hegel's dialectic process, wrong refutes right and the subsequent punishment has the aim of re-establishing the damaged right once more. The fairness of right is the primary position, the idea of Good and Justice; the unfairness of the crime aims to refute both criteria, and finally, the punishment is established to overcome both, which is necessary to restore right in reality. Therefore, the punishment is necessary and, in addition, it recognizes and restores the delinquent as a person (he had ceased to be so when he transgressed against right). Therefore, the punishment also benefits him. It is also clear that the violation that the crime involves exists only as the particular will of the criminal.[31] The crime cannot be repaired by private revenge, as revenge only leads to generating a new injury and 'through this contradiction it becomes an infinite process, the insult being inherited without end from generation to generation'.[32]

Morality

In the second part of his work, Hegel stops to take a look at the second moment of objective spirit, which is defined by morality. The principle of the *moral point of view* is for him 'freedom in its infinite subjectivity'.[33] Morals represent the subjective moment of will. Morality is not, in principle, the opposite of immorality, but the general standpoint on which the subjectivity of will depends.[34] In this section he tackles the question of the *purpose* of voluntary action; in fact, action is defined as the external expression of subjective or moral will.[35]

The Absolute State

The particularity of each act is what Hegel calls 'internal content'. Here exists *intention* and its contents, whose particular goal is my *well-being*. However, this internal content, raised to universality and objectivity, refers to the absolute end of will: *good*. Purpose, when it comes from an intelligent being, does not contain simply individuality but essentially a universal aspect, intention.[36]

Hegel clearly differentiates between, on one hand, purposes related with natural will placed in pre-political environments and, on the other, the universal purpose of intelligent or rational action: well-being or happiness. According to Hegel, in contradiction with the situation in antiquity, in modern times, individuals are given the right to possess a subjective freedom. He recognizes the role of Christianity in the establishment of this right and accepts it as the universal principle that has given a new form to the world.[37] However, the satisfaction of my subjectivity in fact also implies working towards the well-being of others, to be exact, the *well-being of all*, given the universality of rational thought.[38] In this way, the place of *what should be* has been established, the starting point for the rules of correct life in society.

The intention of my well-being cannot justify an unjust act.[39] Nor, as we shall see below as regards citizens and civil society, can it give free rein to the satisfaction of an individual end when it goes against a general end. Hence, the public good, the well-being of the State as universality, takes priority above individual subjectivity. Common good (State) transcends over the individual. Only in cases of extreme danger to individual life can a person resist (right of necessity).[40]

Good constitutes the substance of will. Good is made reality through subjective will.[41] Hegel establishes the *duty* to do good, be just, and observe the well-being of one's self and of all.[42] However, the abstract idea of doing good cannot be translated to the determination of private duties. For this, the ethical system (social life) is necessary, as it gives objective content to the moral conscience which, in itself, is only formal.[43]

> Right and duty, viewed as absolutely reasonable phases of will, are not in essence the particular property of an individual. Nor do they assume the form of perception or any other phase of mere individual sensuous consciousness. They are the universal products of thought, and exist in the form of laws and principles.[44]

We alluded above to this double evaluation of individualism, which is now being criticized. In this section, Hegel clearly positions himself against the foundation of right in the individual and, implicitly, against natural law, as he declares himself to be in favour of universal rationality as the creator of rules for individual behaviour, and conceives laws as the result of a related rational exercise.

The ethical system

The third part of objective spirit is expressed by the ethical system or the idea of freedom which has become the existing world and as the nature of self-consciousness.[45] The ethical principle, or what should be done, becomes a goal through laws and institutions. These provide fixed contents which have an existence above subjective opinion and whim.[46] Both form ethical substance and provide authority and absolute power.[47] Furthermore, social forces are not foreign to the individual, whose spirit takes them as his own being.[48]

Ethical determinations are duties for the individual, *binding* on his will.[49] Apparently, this duty may seem to be a limitation on the subjectivity or abstract freedom of the individual, determining his undetermined good capriciously. However, individuals find their *liberation* in duties.[50] Virtue is ethics reflected in the individual character, the adaptation of the individual to the duties of the relationships to which the individual belongs (virtue). Ethics determines what a virtuous man should do in society.[51]

Right and duty are united in the identity between universal and private will; by means of the ethical system human beings have rights in so far they have duties, and duties in so far they have rights.[52] This concept is objectified in two fundamental aspects: the *family* or direct, natural, ethical spirit; and *civic community*, or association of members as independent individuals in a universality which has an internal order, with a legal constitution as a means of security for people and property, and an external order for their private interests as State.[53]

The family finds its determination in affection (love). In addition, by belonging to a family, the persons are aware of their individuality as members of that family.[54] Families consist of the following three aspects. First, as a direct concept, *marriage*, which keeps the species alive ('external unity') and where self-consciousness of the unity of the sexes is transformed into spiritual or self-conscious love ('internal unity'),[55] a point which Hegel considers highly important.

Marriage begins in the consent of two individuals to form a single person, abandoning the natural personality of each one. Marriage is also an *ethical duty*. It receives the consent of the respective families and also of the community.[56] Hegel does not give marriage the character of a contract,[57] as he situates it in an undefined 'nirvana', distinct from private egoisms that do require a contract. In the development of marriage there is only room for love, unity (monogamy), and indissolubility.

The role of men and women is different. Men carry out the substantial part of their lives in the State, science, battle, and labour, and should be at the head of the family.[58] Women have their full substantive place in the family and in piety.[59] This extreme defence of monogamy is presupposed as one of the absolute principles supporting the ethical life of a community.[60]

Secondly, Hegel refers to *family property*. He compares the institution of marriage with the origin of property[61] and describes the family means as its external existence, owner of goods, and in charge of its care.[62] The husband, as head of the family, is expected to go out and earn its living, care for its needs, and administer the family means.[63]

Thirdly, we find the objective of the *education of the children and also the dissolution of the family* in connection with inheritance.[64] Children have the right to be supported and educated with the common family means. In the family, children are educated and brought up with discipline so that one day they will be self-dependent and acquire a free personality, able to leave the natural unity of the family.[65] With the dissolution of the family, understood as the death of the father, the testament should attempt to maintain the family, avoiding unreasonable bequests that might compromise the continuity of the surviving members.

In the transition from the family to the civic community, owing to the principle of personality, the family is dissolved within a plurality of families who behave mutually like independent concrete persons.[66] Thus, the people and the nation emerge as extensions of the family. Both have a common natural origin.[67] Civic community is society understood as a system of universal multilateral dependence, 'a system which interweaves the subsistence, happiness, and rights of the individual with the subsistence, happiness, and right of all ... This system we may in the first instance call the external State, the State which satisfies one's needs, and meets the requirements of the understanding'.[68]

Civic community is also made up of three phases. Hegel calls the first one *the System of Wants*, and this involves the satisfaction of the individual's needs through his work and also through the work and the satisfaction of all others' needs.[69] The social basis, as the reciprocal determination between individuals, is founded on labour as the way to satisfy these needs.[70] The development of the division of labour, the origin of social inequality as we have already seen, is now claimed to be the driving force behind its contrary: organic solidarity, although in Hegel's case it is a type of solidarity with a liberal concept in which personal and private pleasure and satisfactions will contribute towards achieving a collective equilibrium. This is so because he trusts that what is good for me will be good for the rest, an unfortunate emulation of an idyllic division of labour in which the enjoyment of a few produces the enjoyment of the others.[71] However, the possibility of sharing universal means is conditioned by private capital and particular skills which, together with multiple contingent circumstances, create inequality, differences, and dissymmetry that are manifested in classes.[72]

The second moment in the civic community is the Administration of Justice, or protection of property through universal laws according to which judgements can be made. This administration is in charge of seeing that general freedom, belonging to all, dominates in reality by laws established objectively by formal right, individual right, and the concrete activity of judges and magistrates. The administration of justice curbs the problems generated by individual freedom stepping out of the legitimate line of right. Hegel regards this moment as the instant of prevention and reparation. Given that the law does not function without conflicts, it is realized when it deals with them for the care of a private interest in so far as it is a common interest. In order to maintain the pre-established order, it resorts to the police and the corporation,[73] which make up a third moment of uninterrupted guarantee for the security of people and property.[74]

The State

The definitive part of objective spirit is the *State*: 'The state is the realized ethical idea or ethical spirit. It is the will which manifests itself, makes itself clear and visible, substantiates itself. It is the will which thinks and knows itself, and carries out what it knows, and in

The Absolute State

so far as it knows'.[75] The State is a rational realization; in fact the ultimate end of all rationality. In the State, individual self-consciousness is raised to universality and the unity thus established is 'its own motive and absolute end. In this end freedom attains its highest right'.[76]

The highest duty of any individual is to be a member of a State.[77] This position again disagrees with natural law, for which the State is an institution at the service of and depending on the interests of the individuals who amongst themselves agree to form it. For Hegel, the individual forms part of the State as a duty, as only by forming part of a State does an individual possess objectivity, truth, and an ethical status, and can lead a universal life.[78] The differences with Rousseau and Locke are clear: for Hegel, the State is *not* founded on the coincidence of private wills in their search for a direct and material goal (security in life and individual properties). In Hegel's opinion, the State is founded on an act of reason, a reason thought out individually but in which, so far as this reason is universal, all individuals coincide. The State is a creation of thought, hence Hegel's rationalist idealism. The State unites universality and individuality: it will seek its particular end by acting through laws and principles that have been thought out and are therefore universal.[79]

The transition from the family, horde, clan, or multitude to the condition of State requires the realization of an ethical idea. A people is still not a State. Without personality and self-consciousness, a people has no laws that are thought-out determinations and, therefore, is not independent or acknowledged by others. Hegel situates pre-State collectives in prehistory, where 'are found uninteresting stupid innocence and the bravery arising out of the formal struggle for recognition and out of revenge'.[80] The stage *State* overcomes all that and achieves the culmination of social life through rational and real harmony between person (individual and family) and society, and with the agreement among volitions that leads to the achievement of general freedom.

Hegel distinguishes three phases in the Idea of State: *internal polity*, *international law*, and *world-history*. Internal polity or constitution is the State in reference to itself. It forms the *legislation* that structures and organizes the State. The State is the reality of concrete freedom, that is to say, that the personal individuality and private interests not only obtain their recognition and the right to develop, but themselves pursue the interest of the universal.[81]

The particular interest shall in truth be neither set aside nor suppressed, but be placed in open concord with the universal. In this concord both particular and universal are enclosed. The individual, who from the point of view of his duties is a subject, finds, in fulfilling his civic duties, protection of person and property, satisfaction of his real self, and the consciousness and self-respect implied in his being a member of this whole. Since the citizen discharges his duty as a performance and business for the state, the state is permanently preserved.[82]

The State is articulated in *institutions*, which are its objective guarantees. The group of these comprises the *constitution* or developed and actualized rationality.[83] These are embodied in different *State organisms*, which carry out the tasks according to which the universal is produced uninterruptedly.[84] Hegel distinguishes three constitutional organisms: *legislative*, *governmental*, and the *function of the prince*. The first determines what is universal[85] and sets the laws that establish what of good comes to individuals to enjoy at the hands of the State and what they must perform for the State.[86] Hegel is not in favour of universal suffrage, but of State representation in which much weight is granted to nobility[87] and the dominant classes in general. The deputies do not represent private individuals but 'essential spheres of society' (to represent is not to be in the place of another, but that interest itself is already present).[88]

The second organism comprises legal and police authorities and also concerns civil servants in general as servants of the State tied by a necessary duty in which capriciousness is intolerable. Both authorities also take charge of the necessary mechanisms to control the civil servants by higher instances, in order to avoid possible misuse of power.[89]

The third power, the authority of the prince, is the subjectivity with which rests the final decision of will.[90] The different powers are united in the prince in correct individual unity. The constitutional monarchy, a creation of the modern world, is for Hegel the highest perfection of the State. It is the culmination of world history in that it liberates its members (citizens recognized as such) and, at the same time, maintains the unity of State rationality. The prince's function contains three elements of the totality: the universality of laws, counsel as reference between the particular and the universal, and the element of the final decision or self-determination.[91] He personifies and guarantees the unity of the State,[92] and is the depository of *sovereignty* in its totality. Hegel does not agree that sovereignty resides in the people, since a 'people' without monarchs and all the articulation mechanisms (sovereignty, government, law courts, and classes) is a formless mass that is neither State nor anything.[93]

Hegel expresses his opposition to the possibility of imagining a constitution that is universally valid, even by following rational principles. The constitution of a people depends on the 'kind and character of its self-consciousness', thus every nation 'has the constitution that suits it and belongs to it'.[94] In this way, he defends historical particularism *avant la lettre* by conceiving the existence of 'people' with *personality*, that is to say, who know that their end is the objective of their will. Therefore, the communion of its members is characterized by a certain form of self-consciousness. Inversely, it was also a curb on Napoleonic *interventionism* and imperialist urges in general, as it is not possible to 'export' revolutionary formulas of socio-political organization by arguing that they reflect the universality of just principles. Each 'people' will have the forms of organization it is *capable of imagining and establishing*.

International law is the second spirit of the expression of the State. It refers to the relationship of an individual State with other States. It is concerned with treaties and international right and is compulsory because of the rights of the nations that transcend it. As the State also exists as individuality (the exclusiveness, the *being-for-itself* of each State), it is also expressed in the relationship with other States, each one of which is independent.[95] Hegel speaks of the 'ethical element in war', as the need to defend the independence of the State at the price of property and life.[96] The State, in so far as it is substantial rationality and direct reality, is the absolute power on earth. Therefore, each State is opposed to others in sovereign independence. Therefore, international law arises from the relationships between independent States, who establish treaties that must be respected. However, it is acknowledged that no universal will exists above these States (a State of States) and therefore Hegel accepts *war* as an 'institution of international law'. Conflicts between States, when the different wills can find no agreement, can only be settled by war.[97]

The third spirit, world history, is not a spirit in itself as, once internal and external policies of the State manifest themselves, the State fulfils reality with justice and culminates the development of individual and community under the common criteria of its sovereignty. However, after it, with it and over it, being it, history has been setting the pace, *actualizing* destiny and gradually *realizing* transformations. Therefore, the final spirit is no more instant than the air freedom breathes in its development; the universal history of the spirit that returns self-consciousness to itself in all its magnitude.

The history of the world is thought of as the world's court of judgement. It is the necessary development of the concepts of freedom, self-consciousness, and reason. It is the exhibition and actualization of universal spirit.[98] World history is the explanation of how spirit works to know what it is in itself. In the development of the idea, as the progress of the conscience to be conscious of freedom, a series of stages are crossed. In each of these there is a dominant nation which is responsible for producing this stage of progress. The other contemporary nations that are not bearers of the present stage of the development of the universal spirit are void of right (their time has passed) and no longer count for world history.[99]

As we have said above, for Hegel, history commences when legal determinations and objective institutions emerge. As the movement of the spirit is to know itself absolutely and to free its consciousness from its natural surroundings, Hegel distinguishes four 'world-historic empires' in the liberation process of this self-consciousness: the Oriental, Greek, Roman, and Germanic periods.[100] In this way, he contributes to building the foundations for the processualist and evolutionist series of the second half of the nineteenth century. For Hegel, 'history is the process that influences itself',[101] it marks the spatial and temporal boundary of free will and expresses the scenario in which the spirit manifests itself.

CONCLUSION: PROBLEMS WITH THE HEGELIAN STATE

The first critique of Hegel's politics arises in relation with what we have just mentioned. To differentiate one nation as 'chosen' or 'protagonist' of an epoch and dismiss other nations as incompetent in the growth of civilization is a symptom of chauvinism and messianism and, at the same time, a justification for their subordination. Hegel repeats this hierarchical way of thinking in other places in his work, and it reaches its most extreme expression when he puts the development of history in the hands of the great men of the different nations. They have shown *the* illustrious synthesis of the way that mankind must follow. With this idea, he also contemplates the historical process once prehistory was abandoned.[102]

This *obedience owed* to the hierarchy is even more striking when he refers, as we have commented above, to the prince as the concrete synthesis of *sovereignty*, the sphere and protagonist of subjectivity in so far as the final decision of will. A person who united in his subjectivity all the objective rationality of the State and embodied the essential link between the individual and the particular became, without doubt, an easy target for Marxian critique.[103]

If we continue heeding Marx, the true contents of the State are very different from the fictional rationality that Hegel believed he could see in it. The State lies beyond the constitutions that are said to express it: its true content is private property.

The supposed *common business* that for Hegel was the decisive content of the State, for Marx only represents the interests of a dominant class, the owners of the means of production. The State, understood as a political entity, comprises only the ceremonial part of social reality.[104] The State appeals to its own abstraction and effectively disassociates itself from private responsibilities, that is to say, from the concrete life of citizens in relation with private property. In fact, the more abstract and ceremonial it becomes, the harder it will be to put an end to inequalities. In addition, individuals are denied their own precise reality when they become true citizens. With the Hegelian State, politics possesses its own entity, independent of all socioeconomic reality. Under the banner of 'we are all now equal before the law', the State sanctions as true what in reality is distance and dissymmetry. By claiming that equality is a *common thing* when it is not, he alienates the citizen from his life and situates his freedom in the only sphere where it can be fitted: thought.

The State, for Hegel the maximum expression of rationality and the determination of human beings, presents the appearance of egalitarian reality, where only division, difference, and private interests exist. By exchanging the dialectics of things for the dialectics of ideas, Hegel shifts the meaning and reference of words to imaginary universes that reassure the conscience of those who fear for the conditions of life they possess, at the same time as he instructs the disadvantaged on their duties, neglecting in a paradise of formalities their right to live and work in conditions of real equality.

It is likely that Hegel's desire to draft a possible Constitution for his country and his time made him formulate assertions that today we might consider inappropriate for his analytical capabilities, as paradoxical and even contradictory. Therefore, we remain in doubt, and we may wonder whether he also weighed up the possibility of developing a more straightforward and less rhetorical and contradictory political theory than the one he proposed, and whether that one would have gone further than this, given the conditions of the social reality in which he lived.

In the formation of the revolutionary ideas of the nineteenth century, the critique of Hegel and the dialectic procedure of his discourse carried equal weight. Without the appeal to the concrete in the Hegelian philosophy and his demand of *realization* for all thought in order to gain self-consciousness, it would have been difficult to *conceive* a formal change of consciences. The ordered outline of a 'back-to-front world' (as his critics called it), whose pieces match reality, however, simply by inverting the process and his subject (being and existence by idea and essence) displays the quality of his philosophical and political contribution.

NOTES

1. About this topic, see J. D'Hondt (2002: 373–80).
2. G. W. F. Hegel (1821) *The Philosophy of Right*. The version we are using here is the translation by S. W. Dyde (1896), available online at <http://libcom.org/files/Philosophy_of_Right.pdf>. The work will henceforth be cited as *Phil. Right* (*Phil. Right*, section 181).
3. *Phil. Right*, section 181.
4. *Phil. Right*, section 270.
5. *Phil. Right*, section 31.
6. *Phil. Right*, Preface.
7. ibid.
8. ibid.
9. ibid.
10. *Phil. Right*, section 32.
11. *Phil. Right*, Preface.
12. ibid.
13. *Phil. Right*, section 31.
14. *Phil. Right*, section 30.
15. *Phil. Right*, section 5.

16. *Phil. Right*, section 21.
17. *Phil. Right*, section 4.
18. *Phil. Right*, section 35.
19. *Phil. Right*, section 35 (Note).
20. *Phil. Right*, section 57.
21. *Phil. Right*, section 40.
22. *Phil. Right*, sections 45 and 46.
23. *Phil. Right*, section 48.
24. *Phil. Right*, section 48 (Note).
25. *Phil. Right*, section 80.
26. *Phil. Right*, section 74.
27. *Phil. Right*, section 79.
28. *Phil. Right*, section 72.
29. *Phil. Right*, section 43. Hegel includes here knowledge, science, and talent which may obtain an external existence.
30. *Phil. Right*, section 200.
31. *Phil. Right*, section 99.
32. *Phil. Right*, section 102.
33. *Phil. Right*, section 104.
34. *Phil. Right*, section 108.
35. *Phil. Right*, section 113.
36. *Phil. Right*, section 121.
37. *Phil. Right*, section 124.
38. *Phil. Right*, section 125.
39. *Phil. Right*, section 126.
40. *Phil. Right*, section 127.
41. *Phil. Right*, section 131.
42. *Phil. Right*, section 134.
43. *Phil. Right*, section 137.
44. *Phil. Right*, section 137 (Note).
45. *Phil. Right*, section 142.
46. *Phil. Right*, section 145.
47. *Phil. Right*, section 146.
48. *Phil. Right*, section 147.
49. *Phil. Right*, section 148.
50. *Phil. Right*, section 149.
51. *Phil. Right*, section 150.
52. *Phil. Right*, section 155.
53. *Phil. Right*, section 157.
54. *Phil. Right*, section 158.
55. *Phil. Right*, section 161.
56. *Phil. Right*, section 162.
57. *Phil. Right*, section 163.

58. *Phil. Right*, section 166.
59. ibid.
60. *Phil. Right*, section 167.
61. *Phil. Right*, section 170.
62. *Phil. Right*, section 171.
63. ibid.
64. *Phil. Right*, section 173.
65. *Phil. Right*, section 175.
66. *Phil. Right*, section 181.
67. *Phil. Right*, section 181 (Note). Nationalist feelings may find their roots in nature in the Fichtean style, if we heed this expression of Hegel's.
68. *Phil. Right*, section 183.
69. *Phil. Right*, section 192.
70. *Phil. Right*, section 196.
71. *Phil. Right*, section 199.
72. *Phil. Right*, section 200. The classes Hegel recognizes are agricultural, industrial, and civil service (*Phil. Right*, sections 203, 204, and 205).
73. *Phil. Right*, section 229.
74. *Phil. Right*, section 230.
75. *Phil. Right*, section 257.
76. *Phil. Right*, section 258.
77. *Phil. Right*, section 258.
78. *Phil. Right*, section 258 (Note).
79. ibid.
80. *Phil. Right*, section 349.
81. *Phil. Right*, section 260.
82. *Phil. Right*, section 261 (Note).
83. *Phil. Right*, section 265.
84. *Phil. Right*, section 269.
85. *Phil. Right*, section 273.
86. *Phil. Right*, section 299.
87. *Phil. Right*, section 300.
88. *Phil. Right*, section 309.
89. *Phil. Right*, section 287 and following.
90. *Phil. Right*, section 273. For this reasoning, Marx criticizes Hegel in his *Critique of the Philosophy of Right* (see below). The randomness of the Hegelian system of right is illustrated by Marx in the need to embody the highest State power in the monarch, and therefore situate the greatest work of reason at the height of the flesh.
91. *Phil. Right*, section 275.
92. *Phil. Right*, section 273.
93. *Phil. Right*, section 279 (Note).
94. *Phil. Right*, section 274.

The Absolute State

95. *Phil. Right*, section 330.
96. *Phil. Right*, section 324.
97. *Phil. Right*, section 334.
98. *Phil. Right*, section 342.
99. *Phil. Right*, section 347.
100. *Phil. Right*, section 354. The Oriental period represents the infancy of mankind, freedom is in the hands of one alone, and is denied to all except the monarch. The Greek and Roman periods represent adolescent mankind. It is the first call of consciousness that, from now on, seeks freedom. In both phases, community prevails over the individual. The Germanic empire represents the maturity of mankind and covers the period between Christianity and Hegel's own time. In this phase, after an unfruitful search in which forms of slavery continued, full conscience of freedom and its historical realization through the State is achieved.
101. G. W. F. Hegel (1807), *Phenomenology of the Spirit*.
102. *Phil. Right*, section 350.
103. Marx's critique was crushing:

> Hegel here defines the monarch as the personality of the state, its certainty of itself. The monarch is personified sovereignty, sovereignty become man, incarnate state—[or political] consciousness, whereby all other persons are thus excluded from this sovereignty, from personality, and from state-[or political] consciousness. At the same time however Hegel can give this '*Souveraineté—Personne*' no more content than 'I will,' the moment of arbitrariness in the will. The state-reason and state-consciousness is a unique empirical person to the exclusion of all others, but this personified Reason has no content except the abstraction, 'I will.' *L'Etat c'est moi*'

> The analogy that he suggests is even coarser: 'Birth would determine the quality of the monarch as it determines the quality of cattle'. K. Marx (1843b) *Critique of Hegel's Philosophy of Right*. (Trans. Joseph O'Malley and available online at <http://www.marxists.org>.) Remarks to sections 279 and 280.

104. 'The constitutional state is the state in which the state-interest is only formally the actual interest of the people... It has become a formality, the *haut gout* of the life of the people—a ceremony. The Estates are the sanctioned, legal lie of constitutional states.' K. Marx (1843b) *Critique of Hegel's Philosophy of Right*. Remark to section 301.

7

The Critique of the State in Marx

Marx's work is a fundamental reference point to understand the panorama of contemporary thought and, in a certain way, a singularly important part of the recent history of mankind. Perhaps, the main reason for his enormous influence lies in his having fomented a dialectically related commitment between, on one hand, the scientific knowledge of social reality and, on the other, ethics and political praxis. Marx drafted the most recent proposal of emancipation that has appeared in the Western world, whose objective consisted, and still consists, of overcoming the conditions imposed by capitalist exploitation and achieving a fairer society.

Marx was the witness of the revolutionary victory of the bourgeoisie and, at the same time, foresaw that only another revolution as violent as the first would put an end to the bourgeois order. In order to succeed in this, he proposed an ethic that demanded an act of solidarity and a collective practice aimed at the revolutionary transformation of the material conditions that supported social reality at a given moment of its history. In this sense, the objective knowledge of this reality became an instrument at the service of its own revolutionary change. With this goal in sight, the task of thought and historical research should focus on discovering the contradictions existing in social reality in order to fight against it and change it, not to encourage reflection as if this was an objective in itself ('engrossed in itself'). Marx aimed to put an end to speculative and contemplative philosophy, and inaugurate the science of History, through a materialist study of society that today we know as historical materialism.

Marx is a materialist because thought and will are products of prior material and real experience; of the production of life in society; of the tension and contradictions arising between the development of the productive forces and the relations of production prevailing at any given moment; between what is produced and the place of social groups within the organization of this production. All thought is objective, but not due to the pure will of a 'subject' or of an autonomous and also metaphysical entity, but as a historical product, influenced by the objective and subjective conditions of social life that shape any will or reflection. Marx is also dialectical because, in turn, any wish or desire can only take effect if it actively favours, in practice, changes in those unfavourable conditions for social life. Contradictions should be resolved in reality; it is not enough for them to be explained in a philosophical discourse.

Thought is a synthesis, a result, and a possible instrument for social change; not a starting point or a self-dependent driving force, as Hegelian philosophy is said to postulate. For Marx, however, Hegel's philosophy was a true starting point, to such an extreme that certain fundamental aspects never left him. In other questions, such as the one that interests us about the philosophy of the State, the divergence took place early and radically, although, as we shall see, the true separation from Hegel took years to be consolidated and occurred in the ontological field rather than in the procedure (dialectics). For Marx, the meaning of 'State'* varied as his ideas about reality underwent their material adjustment. The method to approach its study also went through the same process of adjustment. Method and concept were modified mutually and gradually until the real subject of things replaced in Marx the 'Hegelian essence' of them.

FROM IDEALIST HUMANISM TO HISTORICAL MATERIALISM

The diachronic review of the notion of State in Marx commences when, as editor of the *Rheinische Zeitung*, the newspaper of the bourgeois opposition to Prussian despotism, he wrote one of his editorials[1] about the State and religion. In this text of his youth, Marx seems to support a concept of the State as an association of free men who aspire to obtain freedom: 'philosophy interprets the rights of mankind, demands that the State is the State of human nature'.[2] According to Marx, 'Fichte and Hegel began to regard the state through human eyes and to deduce its natural laws from reason and experience'.[3] Following in the wake of these philosophers, the State was seen as 'the great organism, in which legal, moral, and political freedom must be realized, and in which the individual citizen in obeying the laws of the state only obeys the natural laws of his own reason, of human reason'.[4]

Although at that time, freedom was for Marx the essence of mankind and right was an effect of human reason, there are signs that he began to glimpse a conviction that gradually matured and was extended to politics in general: the State, apparently the consequence of a rational aspiration and, once established, the guiding element of human life, is no more than a simple formalism. Social reality was and is a very different matter, and in an article against the law that punished illegal tree-felling,[5] Marx denounced that with this law, 'all the organs of the state become ears, eyes, arms, legs... of the forest owner'. Even so, until mid-1843, Marx's political position continues to offer different readings, from the cynicism with which he criticized the Prussian State when he called it a dynastic property,[6] to the longing for a State and a new world founded on democratic humanism.

The true critique with which he surmounted the Hegelian 'trap' began to take shape in the *Kreuznach Manuscript*,[7] written in summer 1843. Although he maintains his idealist and humanist opinions, they occasionally give way to an incipient historical materialist analysis. It is generally believed that the *Kreuznach Manuscript* was written under the influence of L. Feuerbach's *Provisional Theses for the Reform of Philosophy*. According to this author, 'Hegel has not thought of objects other than as the predicates of the thought that thinks of itself',[8] when it would be more correct to say that the being is the subject and thought is the predicate and, therefore, thought emerges from being and not the other way round. Nevertheless, the *Manuscript* was more than a simple inversion of Hegel's dialectic, an inversion that substituted the ideal Hegelian subject (the State) with a real subject (civil or bourgeois society).[9] Apart from that, the text is a first call for (scientific) research into the material and historical structure of the societies that in fact support State political forms. Therefore, the work is not limited to a simple change of one logical process for another, but attempts to find the determination of the political institution in the very materiality of society, as well as attacking Hegelian philosophy of Right and the State, which conceived them as the culmination of history and human conscience.

Despite denouncing Hegelian proposals, the Marxian concept of State in the *Kreuznach Manuscript* is not without the idealist components for which he reproached the Jena philosopher for. Thus, Marx considers the State an abstraction but, paradoxically, when he refers to the single concrete aspect found at its roots, he places another abstraction: the 'people'.[10] It is clear that 'people' does not reveal anything more concrete than 'State'. Therefore, Marx shifts the emphasis from one concept to another without modifying Hegel's procedure in practice. For Hegel, notions such as 'State' have their place in the alienation or mediation process in which the Spirit is realized historically.

Another of Marx's debts to idealism at this time is seen in reference to the new subject provided by the Feuerbachian–Marxian inversion: the family and bourgeois society: 'This is to say that the political state cannot exist without the natural basis of the family and the artificial basis of civil society; they are its *condition sine qua non*'.[11] The statement provokes two considerations. The first and most obvious one refers to the quality of the concepts 'family' and 'bourgeois society'. The former reduces the family, an institution which is itself political and polymorphous in its exact manifestations, to a naturalist and ahistorical representation, while the latter is loaded with presentism. The former also owes much to Rousseau,[12] and would only be given an imprecise historical content by Marx many years later.[13] The latter makes us understand that for Marx in 1843, the notion 'State' and the rules of the game that accompanied it, as a concrete reality, could only occur as the culmination of an ideal humanist process, guided by the demands for freedom coming from the bourgeoisie, rather than, as he would have said later, depending on a given level of historical development and the dialectic between productive forces and the social relationships of production.

The crux of the matter is found in the critique of sections 305 and 306 in Hegel's work: 'at its highest point the political constitution is the constitution of private property. The highest political conviction is the conviction of private property'.[14] The political State would be the power belonging to 'private property', its essence brought to existence. What remains to the political State in opposition to this essence? The illusion is that it determines when it is rather determined; indeed, it breaks the will of the family and of society, but merely in order to give existence to the will of private property lacking family and society, and to acknowledge this existence as the highest existence of the political state, as the highest ethical existence'.[15] The conclusion then becomes inevitable: 'private property has become the subject of the will, and the will is merely the predicate of private property'.[16]

This critique is connected implicitly with a new viewpoint on the *true meaning* of the State: 'The constitutional state is the state in which the state-interest is only formally the actual interest of the people... It has become formality... a ceremony. The Estates are the sanctioned, legal lie of constitutional states, the lie that the state is the people's interest or the people the interest of the state'.[17] This formal and ceremonial reality of the modern State was to colour all Marx's considerations about the institution from this point onwards, as he compared its alienating effects with those of religion: 'just as the Christians are equal in heaven yet unequal on earth, so the individual members of a people are equal in the heaven of their political world yet unequal in the earthly existence of society';[18] and a citizen, 'as a state-idealist he is a being who is completely other, distinct, different from and opposed to his own actuality'.[19]

Despite this realist shift that the text begins to take in its final pages, the *Kreuznach Manuscript* still maintains a humanist and democratic aftertaste, which continues to appear in other texts, such as *On the Jewish Question* and the 'Introduction'[20] to the mostly unpublished *Manuscript* itself, until the proletariat began to personify for Marx the possibility of a real and radical social transformation.[21] Meanwhile, bourgeois society remained the real condition of politics[22] and, this aspect, the target of his criticism as a fiction created through the bourgeois representation of 'liberty'. As it guarantees private interests, bourgeois freedom is neither relational nor common, but individual and selfish. Marx argues that the political freedom championed by the bourgeoisie is not real freedom, as it originates and is oriented towards the interests of the uncharitable bourgeois individual, who understands liberty as the emancipation of the collective and uses a supposed natural assumption, individual property,[23] in order to impose his private egoism on social relations as a whole. For Marx, political emancipation, as demanded and articulated around the figures of 'individual' and 'citizen', only aims to sanction a division by means of which the bourgeoisie grant themselves the freedom to appropriate common property and strew the world with laws designed to protect private possessions.[24] This reality of the bourgeois world creates a made to measure political fiction, by apparently making the rights of individuals equal and making them believe that they govern their inequality through the opinion of suffrage.

With crystal-clear reasoning in one of his articles published in the journal *Vorwärts!* (1844),[25] Marx maintains that the political sphere, instituted as the characteristic form of the bourgeois State, will disappear when the bourgeoisie itself dissolves following the revolutionary self-emancipation of the proletariat. Some years later, Marx himself, in the Preface to *A Contribution to the Critique of Political Economy* (1859), took up once more his reflections on the State in this period of his youth:

> My inquiry led me to the conclusion that neither legal relations nor political forms could be comprehended whether by themselves or on the basis of a so-called general development of the human mind, but that on the contrary they originate in the material conditions of life, the totality of which Hegel, following the example of English and French thinkers of the eighteenth century, embraces within the term 'civil society'; that the anatomy of this society, however, has to be sought in political economy.[26]

Political economy became the main objective of Marx's thought with the *Paris Manuscripts*.[27] Private property was no longer considered mechanically the source of all evils, but according to the alienated labour that supports it,[28] as this is the cause and the consequence of wealth and misery. This shift is shown by fewer explicit references to the category 'State'. State and other political concepts lost their central position, as social determination does not lie in the forms of government or political constitutions, but in political economy. In fact, Marx explicitly observes that 'it will be found that the interconnection between political economy and the state, law, ethics, civil life, etc., is touched on in the present work only to the extent to which political economy itself *ex professo* touches on these subjects'.[29] 'Religion, the family, the state, law, morality, science, art, etc., are only particular modes of production and therefore come under its general law. The positive suppression of private property, as the appropriation of human life, is therefore the positive suppression of all estrangement, and the return of man from religion, the family, the state, etc., to his human – *i.e.*, social – existence'.[30]

THE HISTORICAL CONDITIONS OF THE STATE: *THE GERMAN IDEOLOGY*

The subordination of politics to production would not disappear from Marx's later works, whether they were theoretical texts of a general nature or concrete historical analysis. In *The German Ideology*,[31] we find paragraphs that unmistakeably show the firmness of this structural change, as well as a clear materialist orientation towards the process of historical knowledge:

> The fact is, therefore, that definite individuals who are productively active in a definite way enter into these definite social and political relations. Empirical observation must in each separate instance bring out empirically, and without any mystification and speculation, the connection of the social and political structure with production. The social structure and the State are continually evolving out of the life-process of definite individuals, but of individuals, not as they may appear in their own or other people's imagination, but as they really are; i.e. as they operate, produce materially, and hence as they work under definite material limits, presuppositions and conditions independent of their will.[32]

In the analysis of the historical process that led to capitalism, on several occasions Marx drafts a characterization of the 'particular forms of production' that preceded it historically. In *German Ideology*, the thread through the text is the development of the division of labour, which in each stage 'determines also the relations of individuals to one another with reference to the material, instrument, and product of labour'.[33] The division of labour brought with it 'unequal distribution, both quantitative and qualitative, of labour and its products, hence property'.[34] Based on this premise, Marx and Engels sketched out three kinds of property (later, 'forms of production') that characterize pre-capitalist societies: tribal, ancient, and feudal. The State appears as the typical political institution of the final two stages and its different appearances do not depend on idealist driving-forces such as the progress of reason, advances in liberty through the spirit of each period, or individuals' will for happiness and power, but on the forms of property that drive production at different historical times. Those forms that admit private property, either as the sum of individual titles or as the right of a sector of society, indicate that society has been divided into classes and provide the context in which the State acquires its *raison d'être*. The State is thus established as

> the form in which the individuals of a ruling class assert their common interests, and in which the whole civil society of an epoch is epitomized.[35]

Consequently, 'the State mediates in the formation of all common institutions and that the institutions receive a political form'[36] and also a legal form (laws). This *intermediate* role (rather than of mediation) means that the mandate of the law appears to be the result of general will. It is precisely there, in the illusion of the independent character of the State and the free will[37] that supposedly inspired it, where the private interest of the dominant class finds the means to pass itself off as the common will. Therefore, the State is the 'practical-idealistic expression'[38] of the power of a dominant class, as it combines the real social inequality which it serves and its negation, under an illusion of generality.[39]

The break with traditional political philosophy is hence definitive. The abstract individual of Modernity and the Enlightenment loses its importance as the central subject of history, of a history guided by reason and will, the inspirers of political decision. Also is left behind the idealism according to which the State picked up the ethical precepts of a time and set itself up as the governor of social relationships. In its place, the State is the necessary *consequence* of certain previous relationships. The battles that are fought in its interior (between democracy, aristocracy, monarchy, etc.) are not the driving-force of history; but 'are merely the illusory forms in which the real struggles of the different classes are fought out among one another'.[40]

Tribal, ancient, and feudal forms of property are dealt with concisely and, logically, conditioned by the limitations of historiographic and, above all, ethnographic and archaeological knowledge in the first half of the nineteenth century.[41] The earliest form of property was tribal. This, when it did not coexist with any other form in a particular society, is the only one which did not need a State. It was characterized by incipient production based on hunting, fishing, pastoralism, and 'at the most' agriculture, and by a low degree of the division of labour, which existed naturally within the family. At the head of the family was the patriarch (the husband) who dominated women and children in a relationship that contained the germ of slavery. This developed steadily in relation with increases in external exchanges and wars. Social organization was an extension of the family structure: at its top, the council of the patriarchs, below these the members of the tribe and finally the slaves. At first these were only present in small numbers.

The second form of property has Greek and Roman antiquity as its reference point. Here, tribal property has not disappeared but it coexists with private portable property and land-ownership that was increasingly concentrated and determinant because of the growth of slavery. The division of labour has crossed a decisive threshold that involved the separation of industrial work and trade from agriculture. This division had its most significant result in the contrast between town and country. At first, towns and cities were founded by the fusion, through agreements or conquest, of several tribes. At the same time, the State emerged as the instrument through which the association of citizens (that is, the collective of husbands–patriarchs) could 'hold power over their labouring slaves only in their community, and on this account alone, therefore, they are bound to the form of communal ownership. It is the communal private property which compels the active citizens to remain in this spontaneously derived form of association against their slaves'.[42] The appearance of cities initiated a new situation in which conflicts were frequent: between masters and slaves, between urban and rural interests, between one city and another, and between civilian sectors within cities (industry, trade), which opened several new horizons for historical development.

The third form of property, called feudal or by estates, had the country as its starting point. A huge leaderless territory after the fall of the Roman Empire had, following the struggle with the conquerors, a low dispersed population, and agriculture and trade in decline. On this substrate grew feudal property which, for Marx, possessed a hierarchic structure similar to that of the conquering Germanic army. The feudal form was articulated around land-ownership in the hands of nobles. The serfs tied to the land formed, in contrast, the productive and dominated class. While this occurred in the country, in the cities the feudal organization of craftsmen took place through the establishment of guilds. In the guilds, property came from the individual labour of all, and their *raison d'être* lay in the need to face up to the 'greed' of the nobles, at a time when the craftsman and the trader were usually one and the same person.

The peasants in conditions of serfdom were the direct producers who came to take the place of slaves in the country. Their miserable conditions of life caused them to find shelter in the cities, where they were added to an increasing mass of labourers. They stood on the bottom rung of a class ladder also formed by master craftsmen, skilled workers, and apprentices, whereas in the country the social structure clearly separated peasants, clergy, and nobles. At the peak of feudalism, the division of labour had a very limited reach: agriculture was still at a very rudimentary level, and in the crafts industry the division of labour within each trade, and even between trades, was small. Later, the development of the division of labour between production (craftsmen) and exchange (merchants), the subsequent geographical division of labour between cities, and the appearance of manufacturing, were the historical conditions for the formation of the bourgeois class and the establishment of capitalism.

THE HISTORICAL CONDITIONS OF THE STATE: *THE FORMEN*

Just as occurred with *German Ideology*, the second time that Marx examined the past of mankind in certain detail remained as an unpublished manuscript until long after his death. We are referring to the text known as *The Formen* (forms that precede capitalist production), included within an extensive preparatory study for the composition of the *Critique of Political Economy* and *Capital*. This study, *Grundrisse der Kritik der Politischen Ökonomie*, was written between 1857 and 1858 but did not appear until 1939/41 in Moscow and some years later, in 1953, in Berlin, the edition that made the work known in Western Europe.[43]

One of Marx's main objectives when he included past stages of human development in his analysis was to demonstrate that 'free' paid work, a characteristic of capitalism, was a historical product and not an inherent condition of the human species. Thus, Marx's historical excursion should be understood as an attempt to show the precise trajectory that led to the institution of paid employment and, at the same time, to remember that human history has followed numerous courses which cannot be apprehended by alluding to supposed unchanging essential ideas or by reducing them to prearranged stages in the development of the Idea. In other words, what comes from a historical change, can in turn be changed. Paid work arose in the confluence of a series of factors, which were the dissociation of workers from the land and the means of labour, and the possibility that labour can be used as a use-value that could be exchanged for money in order to raise the value of money itself. Such premises could only have been proposed in modern Europe after the dissolution of the previous forms of property which, in turn, was the consequence of the historical transformation of even older forms.

As in *German Ideology*, the category 'property' holds the central position. It is defined in a wide sense of the word as the 'the relation of the working (producing or self-reproducing) subject to the conditions of his production or reproduction as his own',[44] relationships that vary historically. Marx starts by fixing his attention on a series of forms of production based on the 'property of the community' of the land, understood as the 'great workshop, the arsenal which furnishes both means and material of labour, as well as the seat, the *base* of the community'.[45] These forms share a decisive characteristic, which is that the belonging of an individual to the community is the presupposition for the appropriation of the land through labour.[46] Individuals are, above all, members of a community who, in addition, work, and who, as the result of this work, reproduce the community. In their different variants, individuals are related with one another as owners or possessors of the land, which is a condition that must be fulfilled as a prior requirement to be a member of the community.

Marx tiptoes around the first form of community property,[47] whose premise would lie in a 'natural community' based on the family, the family widened to a clan, or the combination between families and clans. The 'natural community', or its synonym 'clan community', is characterized by being nomadic, as it is initially based on pastoralism or hunting. With the passage of time, when this community settles in one place, it undergoes greater or lesser changes, depending on several factors. As we have just pointed out, belonging to the community is the main supposition for the 'appropriation of the objective conditions', all contained in the land, as the instrument and material for labour and the physical basis of the community, and also for the objectification of the activities that maintain life (hunting, animal-husbandry, and agriculture).

The form of community property can be achieved in other ways, although always respecting the communal appropriation of the land as its main characteristic. Marx comments first on the case of Asiatic forms.[48] In these, the society is articulated in local communities that combine agriculture and manufacturing, so that they are practically self-sufficient. By belonging to a community, an individual has access to the *possession* of a plot of land temporarily or hereditarily, but is never the owner of it. On other occasions, the work on the land is simply carried out communally. In the Asiatic forms, ownership lies with the local community which, in turn, has received it from an overall unit which is seen as the ultimate owner. This unit, personalized as 'the despot, the father of many communities' and represented locally by a tribal chief or a council of heads of family, is able to appropriate the surpluses produced by the communities. A part of this surplus may be used for various common objectives (from war to worship) and another part is given as a tax. In this context, the city, which makes its first appearance, is the place where the despot and his court centralize taxation and spend or exchange it. However, the basis is always the countryside, the city being a more excrescence of this, 'the camp of the prince'.[49]

When he illustrates the variety in the Asiatic forms, Marx briefly mentions examples that are as remote in time and space as the early Celts, 'a few clans of India', and pre-Hispanic Mexico and Peru. Although he does not tackle the question directly, the existence of the State is given as taken in all of them. In this respect, Marx refers to the despot as 'the head of the state' on one occasion,[50] and in other places it seems to be understood that communities live in a situation of generalized slavery, which enables the inference of a class division coherent with the *raison d'être* of the State, explained so clearly in *German Ideology*.

The role of the State is treated more explicitly in the ancient form of property, in which membership of a community is still a precondition for appropriation. Here, in fact, two forms of property occur. The first is communal and is articulated around the basis of the association of families in a city, united against an outside threat and represented in a State. The city, as a public entity, is the owner of a common territory. However, each citizen, as a member of this community, may also be a land-owner individually. Both forms of property require the existence of a community: only by being a member of it can an individual have access to public land, and only through common enterprises, mainly war, can the individual property existing next to the former be guaranteed.[51]

The clearest examples of the ancient form of property are found in Greece and Rome. The ideal is a society where, unlike the Asiatic forms, the city predominates over the country and where the social basis is made up by the sum of free and equal proprietors of land, who may hold, strictly speaking, the title of citizens.

Unlike the above situations, the basis of the Germanic form[52] is established in the individual ownership of land by country families who avoid city-life and live separated one from the other, producing for themselves independently and practically autonomously. The community is only formed in occasional or periodical meetings of the families for common goals such as, for example, war, religious worship, and the administration of justice. It is true that some common land exists, apart from the individual property of each family, but its role is reduced to a mere complement of the latter and only acquires importance when it is defended against enemy tribes.

The Germanic community is supported by ties of language and blood (descendants) rather than political bonds. The State does not develop from the Germanic forms, as it is not necessary to guarantee individual-family land-ownership, which is the basis of economic and social life. Marx notes that in the Germanic forms: 'The commune therefore does not in fact exist as a state or political body, as in classical antiquity, because it does not exist as a city'. Out of all the forms of property mentioned so far, the Germanic one is the form which grants least importance to the existence of the community as a prerequisite for the appropriation of the land. In fact, he seems to propose quite the opposite, by defining the community in terms that might be described as almost virtual However, the need for this can be glimpsed in the consideration that language and blood ties inevitably refer back to a common past (without which the dispersed but continuous occupation of a land would not have been possible) and also to present relationships, without which the fore-mentioned blood ties could not be renewed (families are not autonomous communities as regards their biological reproduction).[53]

FORMS OF PROPERTY AND STATE

Marx used the categories 'forms of property' and, later, 'modes of production' in order to represent the historical expression of social production in certain places and at certain times; categories to which a political organization of the state type may or may not correspond. In *German Ideology* and *The Formen*, the forms of property were not sealed categories; they are not self-explanatory nor do they follow one another in a pre-arranged order, although all these characteristics have been attributed to them in certain evolutionary readings of Marx's texts.[54] Instead, they should be thought of as 'situation diagnostics' expressed within a dynamic reality whose true situation should be studied in each moment of its development. Marx made clear that the forms of property were only fulfilled materially in production.[55] This production was in practice a 'development of productive forces' that, sooner or later, would cause a crisis in the previous conditions that guided it, their dissolution and the formation of new ones according to rules that cannot be established by a strictly rational and deductive intellectual exercise. For this reason, there is no substitute for historical research, as it is the way to discover how a specific reality formed within the general framework of production that characterizes the whole of human societies. In this respect, Marx's historical method is totally different from the previous idealism and later evolutionism (see below). Marx provides the tools to be used to discover the specificity of certain orders of human societies and their diachronic variation. The key lies in insisting on finding out what produces each society and how they are organized to achieve this. This objective proposes a general interest for research which helps to guide it, but without prejudging it or anticipating the result of the inquiry. The forms of property mentioned in *German Ideology* and *The Formen* are *points reached* by empirical research. Idealism and evolutionism, however, work in a very different way. They begin by considering the many realities that can be observed at a given time, they dissect them with a universal analytical tool (separating the observable reality into categories such as 'technology', 'kinship', 'beliefs', etc.), and then draw up synthetic sociological categories ('Savagery', 'Barbarism', 'Civilization', etc.) which are supposed to cover the full range of human variability, even though they do not illustrate exactly any one society in particular. Assuming that the limits of these abstract generalizations include all human diversity, the task of research then consists of *identifying* one or other of these 'frozen moments of social time' in the human realities that new empirical research brings to light. By doing this, the categories of idealist–evolutionist synthesis are no longer the points reached by actualist research, and from this time on become the *starting point* of an activity that is more re-view and classification than true discovery.

Through their very origin, the synthetic idealist–evolutionist categories postulate a universal applicability, whereas the Marxian forms of property do not. The former comprise a necessarily limited set; the latter one as large as research is able to devise. With the exception of the lightly dealt with original 'tribal property', the other forms of property commented on in *German Ideology* and *The Formen* were taken from the analysis of mainly European historical realities, chosen precisely because of their proximity to and influence on the formation of capitalism. Their value lies in that, and not in the provision of a hypothetic periodization for the history of mankind, which needs to be investigated, and not imposed, in places and times different from the recent past of Western Europe. In this respect, the fact that some of the structural characteristics occasionally seen in certain scenarios in the Old World coincide with developments observed in other times and geographical scenarios, should not condition the research into these other realities. The aim is not to classify the new discoveries in one or other of the pre-established set of synthetic categories but, quite the contrary, to be able to describe the category (the corresponding 'form of property') after discovering the new aspects in a reality which had previously been unknown.

After making these general comments, we should now focus our attention specifically on the topic of the State. The first, and perhaps the most important point is that, after holding a significant place in Marx's earlier works, the 'State' is not a major category in his later thought. From the above explanations, it can be seen that after the mid-1840s Marx stressed the question of production, although the term 'forms of property' displays clear legal connotations. The State- its form, evolution and its internal conflicts- does not guide the historical process. On the contrary, it is a political institution characteristic of societies divided into classes, which implies it is absent in other kinds. In two of the three forms of property considered in *German Ideology*, the ancient and the feudal, the State plays a clear role in defending, respectively, the community of citizen-owners against the outside and the slaves themselves, or the nobles' land-ownership against the serfs of the glebe. It is not so in the form of tribal property, where the limited development of the division of labour would not have favoured the creation of antagonistic classes and where, therefore, the State remained unknown.

However, from our point of view, there are several reasons for not ruling out the development of state institutions in societies where the only form of property was tribal. In the first place, because Marx and Engels themselves pointed out, in a passage that was not taken any further, that the first form of property is contained within the family, 'where wife and children are the slaves of the husband', although they then admit that this form of slavery was 'still very crude'.[56] Therefore, may we not classify as a state the governing bodies of a community where a group of patriarchs use the labour of other members of the group as they see fit?[57] Perhaps a conception of the family restricted to biological union, in which the leading role is taken by the male (in the line of *ius naturale* tradition), made them see everything relating to it in the 'animal world' rather than in the human sphere. Marx and Engels are over-naturalistic in some passages when they consider the family, or the clan comprising the group of families, as pre-political, when in fact the family is possibly the first and most persistent form of political relationship. Thus, if the family is not 'natural' but, like any other political form, displays enormous historical diversity, it should not be assumed that the division of labour within it arises 'naturally', beyond the activities connected with gestation and suckling. Therefore, a wide field of social variability lies open, for research to elucidate.

The second reason is closely related with the first and emerges from the methodological considerations described above. We should recall that Marxian 'forms of property' are not tools to classify and explain other societies, but products of research into historical realities that no category formulated a priori can replace. In the case being studied here, even if we admit that in a given society the only land-ownership is communal (and therefore it can be called 'communitarian' or 'tribal'), we should still use suitable methodologies to examine whether the level of the division of labour and its distribution within the group is accompanied by mechanisms of materially differential appropriation and possession. In this case, it would be possible to identify the existence of a political organization of the state kind.

Finally, in *German Ideology*, neither Marx nor Engels possessed the interest or the empirical means to tackle detailed research into tribal forms of property, among other reasons because of the embryonic stage of archaeological and ethnological studies in the middle of the nineteenth century. Thus, 'the earliest form of property of the earth' was covered briefly and non-specifically, and in its characterization, supposed tribal vestiges in later forms had greater weight than firsthand data about one or other society. In short, it is unlikely that Marx believed that the tribal forms of property of which he might have known could have developed into the State, but at least they never explicitly ruled out that possibility, because neither their method nor the available data allowed them to do that. In fact, it is significant that a decade after writing *German Ideology*, with a larger collection of empirical knowledge, Marx was able to establish differences in societies based on communal land-ownership and he identified the state component in each of them, grouped under the label of Asiatic forms.

THE FUTURE OF THE STATE

We have already noted that the increasingly important role of production in Marx's thought followed a trajectory inversely proportional to the importance of the notion of 'State'. From the second half of the 1840s onwards, this question rarely came to his attention, except briefly and occasionally, nearly always in connection with a report and comments on contemporary historical events (for instance, in *The Eighteenth Brumaire of Louis Napoleon* and *The Civil War in France*) or otherwise in contexts related directly with his political activism. A text of this kind, titled 'Critique of the Gotha Programme'[58] will serve as our example to illustrate the clarity with which Marx conceived politics in relation with the State and in which terms he predicted the historical future of the institution.

The text was aimed at questioning the foundational programme of the United Workers' Party of Germany, arisen from the unification of the Social-Democratic Workers' Party and the General Union of German Workers. Marx criticized the orientation of the new party vigorously, as he believed its ideological and political programme was innocuous for the bourgeoisie. One of the aspects which best shows the programme's conformity with capitalist legality can be seen precisely in its position with regards to the State. According to the aspirations expressed in the Gotha programme, the State of the future society had to be a 'free State', whose missions included encouraging the formation of production cooperatives, overseeing 'popular education', and putting into practice a series of demands of the party in Germany, such as universal suffrage, direct legislation, popular right, and a people's militia. In addition, the party restricted its field of activity to within the German borders.

Marx's criticism of these ideas was made from the defence of a revolutionary objective that excluded all forms of control and even complicity with the bourgeois State and which, in fact, augured in the short or middle term the disappearance of the state institution itself within the framework of a classless communist society. From this viewpoint, Marx argued that the points in the programme of the future United Workers' Party of Germany, instead of conceiving a revolutionary scenario of that kind, aspired to *reform* the German State of the time[59] into a democratic republic. This form of government was already in place in some capitalist countries, like the United States of America and Switzerland. Thus the programmed reforms in no way subverted the bourgeois order and merely modernized it according to the most progressive forms of a bourgeois state (it may be added that these reforms were also demanded by the more liberal sectors of the bourgeoisie itself). This was in complete contrast with the ideas of Marx, who foresaw that 'it is precisely in this last form of state of bourgeois society that the class struggle has to be fought out to a conclusion'.[60] Marx thought it was intolerable that the party should ignore the reality of the confrontation between classes and consider the State as an autonomous body, unconnected with this confrontation when, in fact, it acted in favour of one of the parties: the bourgeois class. The only possible reading was that the leaders of the new party were working in an opportunist way, to obtain small improvements in the economic and political situation of the German proletariat in exchange for leaving the pillars of bourgeois society untouched.

In contrast, for Marx, the priority consisted of subverting, through revolution and violence, the material conditions of capitalist production, of which the State is only the instrument that guarantees property and the bourgeois monopoly of the means of labour. The final goal was the establishment of a communist society, organized around the collective ownership of the material conditions of production; a collective ownership that must impose new rules for the distribution of consumption goods and new political forms. However, it could not be expected that this goal would be achieved overnight, but only after 'prolonged birth pangs': 'Between capitalist and communist society there lies the period of the revolutionary transformation of the one into the other. Corresponding to this is also a political transition period in which the state can be nothing but *the revolutionary dictatorship of the proletariat*'.[61] Although the State continued to exist during this transition period towards a full communist society, it now served to defend by force a social order very different from the bourgeois one. In the dictatorship of the proletariat, the ownership of the means of labour has been taken away from capitalists and landowners, and in this way capitalist exploitation (the appropriation of paid work) has been eliminated. State violence, now led by the proletariat, is directed against the final resistance of the previous system. Certainly, the changes are radical, but nonetheless, within the society arisen from the revolution still lie the remains of bourgeois right, according to which each worker will receive from the social deposits the equivalent to what has been produced by his labour, after deducting the part going towards the collective fund (reserves or insurance against unforeseen expenses, maintenance of the disabled, schools, health service, administration, replacement of consumed means of production and their enlargement). Under these conditions, inequality will not be made to disappear automatically by the elimination of capitalist exploitation, as individual differences in the amount and intensity of the work that can be performed will also produce differential reception and accumulation of products.

The 'higher phase of the communist society' will be reached when the bourgeois right that survived during the dictatorship of the proletariat is left behind, and the communities organize production according to the principle: 'From each according to his ability, to each according to his needs!'[62] In this time, the disappearance of class differences will lead to the extinction of the State, as the basic reason behind it will also have disappeared. For Marx, the State was neither a vehicle of human essence nor the start of a journey of no return within the social future. Its validity and its disappearance, like any other institution, are tied to the economic and social conditions arising in history. If the *raison d'être* of the modern State resides in maintaining capitalist exploitation and the consequent class divisions, just as other earlier states guaranteed the exploitation of slaves or serfs, in a classless communist society the State will simply become extinct, as the motives that once gave it meaning cease to be.

MARXIST TRADITION AND THE STATE

Marx's critique of the State, together with the new position of this institution within social life, has had considerable weight in social and humanistic thought and, as could not fail to be, in political action. A review, however brief, of the meaning and reach of these influences would go far beyond the aims of the present book, as it would have to consider both the proposals rooted in Marxian thought, in its many forms, as the non-Marxist ideas, inspired or conditioned to a greater or lesser degree by the previous existence of Marx's work. Here we must be content with noting that historiography, anthropology, and prehistoric archaeology are the disciplines that have worked the hardest to reveal the origins and development of state institutions. Although the incidence of Marxist positions in these fields of research is and has been very different, both in rigour and in extension, several elements remain:

- The State is a historical product. It is a specificity in the field of political organization, occurring in the places and times in which social production has caused the division of society in antagonistic classes and when their relationship has reached a certain level of conflict.
- The State, as the prime exponent and decisive factor in the political life of class societies, is not, however, the driving force behind the process of their development. This role almost always belongs to the social production of material conditions.
- According to the previous point, political life and its ups-and-downs have overtones of being ceremonial with no autonomy. In this respect, we should not confuse *types of State* with *forms of government* ('monarchy', 'aristocracy', 'democracy', 'republic', etc.). The former are defined by the priority social relationship dictating the production of the means of living, so we should speak in each case of slavery States, capitalist States, etc. The latter, in contrast, describe the exact state institutions in each kind of State. The same type of State may have different forms of

government. Therefore, the changes and substitutions that occur between these do not produce in themselves any decisive breaks in the progress of societies. They comprise, in the strictest sense, an appearance of change and, therefore as an appearance, are ceremonial.

- For the proletariat, the revolutionary class in our times, the objective should not lie in replacing the present forms of government with 'fairer', 'freer', or 'more progressive' ones, but in ending with the property relationships that determine the existence of a capitalist type of State. Over and above that, the revolution aspires to a classless communist society, in which the State no longer has any reason to exist.

The contributions made after Marx, and therefore rightly called Marxist, began with Engels himself, and his famous work *The Origin of the Family, Private Property and the State*[63] in which he reiterated the role of the State as an instrument of the exploiting classes to maintain within an 'order' (obviously the order that interests them) the irreconcilable class antagonisms by which production divides up society.[64] In addition, it was Engels who noted several aspects which add greater depth to the definition of State, independently of the types and forms it might take throughout history.

1. The first is the territorial dimension of the State. Unlike previous kinship organizations, the State groups together individuals on a territorial basis.[65] In other words, rather than possessing certain relatives or ancestors, what is really important is to have been born within the borders of one State or another.
2. The State institutionalizes a public armed force, which is not identical to the people's own organization of an armed power.[66] This force is formed by detachments of armed men and also by prisons and other forms of coercive institutions, which are unknown in societies organized strictly according to ties of kinship.
3. A bureaucracy capable of gathering taxes for the upkeep of the repressive public forces and, consequently, itself as an institution.[67]

Bureaucracy and standing army, as the basic institutions of any State, were characteristics that Engels and, some years later, Lenin[68] underlined most emphatically. As we shall see below, the empirical definition of both is currently at the heart of the archaeological debate on the origins of the State. However, there seem to be no doubts about the relevance of these institutions in fully consolidated states. At the present time, when neo-liberal states are said to be in retreat and are not afraid to rid themselves of many traditional attributions, by privatizing them, sub-contracting them, or simply ignoring them, the bureaucracy of the tax system and 'specialized and permanent detachments of armed personnel' (no longer only of 'men') are still the banners of the State and receive special care.

NOTES

* Marx did not develop a theory of the State systematically. However, as we shall see, he made clear his position on the topic in several of his works.
1. The text entitled 'Leading Article in Number 179 in the Cologne Gazette (*Kölnische Zeitung*)' was published in the *Rheinische Zeitung* (Rhineland Gazette) on 10, 12, and 14 July 1842.
2. *Rheinische Zeitung*, 14 July 1842.
3. ibid.
4. ibid.
5. Published in *the Rhineland Gazette* on 25, 27, and 30 October, and 1 and 3 November 1842.
6. Letter from Marx to Ruge (Cologne, March 1843).
7. This text is known in English as *Critique of Hegel's Philosophy of Right*. We have used the translation by Joseph O'Malley, available online at <www.marxists.org>. It is cited below as *CHPR*.
8. Cited by Ripalda in note 18 in his translation of *CHPR* (1978, Crítica, Barcelona), according to L. Feuerbach, *Aportes para la Crítica de Hegel*, translated by Alfredo Llanos, La Pléyade, Buenos Aires, 1974, pp. 80–1.
9. Thus states Engels in his text: *Biography of Karl Marx* (1869):

    Proceeding from the Hegelian philosophy of law, Marx came to the conclusion that it was not the state, which Hegel had described as the 'top of the edifice,' but 'civil society,' which Hegel had regarded with disdain, that was the sphere in which a key to the understanding of the process of the historical development of mankind should be looked for.

10. *CHPR*, Remark to section 279.
11. *CHPR*, Remark to section 262. The modern State, or true political State, could not emerge outside bourgeois society, a society which in this text is only characterized philosophically as the producer of alienating and empty realities only travelled by reason: 'Property, contract, marriage, civil society appear here ... as particular modes of existence alongside

the political state; that is, they appear as the content to which the political state relates as organising form' (*CHPR*, Remark to section 279).

12. In the words of the Genevan philosopher, 'The most ancient of all societies, and the only one that is natural, is the family' (*Social Contract*, book I, chapter 2); 'The family then may be called the first model of political societies: the ruler corresponds to the father, and the people to the children' (*Social Contract*, book I, chapter 2). Locke also touched on the topic when he pointed out that 'The first society was between man and wife, which gave beginning to that between parents and children; to which, in time, that between master and servant came to be added' (*Second Treatise*, chapter VII, section 77).

13. The historicity and polymorphous nature of the family was at least known to Marx later, as can be gathered from the summaries and comments made to the works of anthropologists like H. Morgan. See *Los apuntes etnológicos de Karl Marx* (transcribed, with notes and an introduction by Lawrence Krader, Pablo Iglesias/Siglo XXI, Madrid, 1988), especially pp. 77–101.

14. *CHPR*, Remark to section 306.
15. ibid.
16. ibid.
17. *CHPR*, Remark to section 301.
18. *CHPR*, Remark to section 307.
19. ibid.
20. Here, we have used Joseph O'Malley's translation of *Introduction to A Contribution to the Critique of Hegel's Philosphy of Right*, and the version of *On the Jewish Question* (cited as *OJQ*), equally available online at <www.marxists.org>.
21. For the revolution of a nation, and the emancipation of a particular class of civil society to coincide, for one estate to be acknowledged as the estate of the whole society, all the defects of society must conversely be concentrated in another class, a particular estate must be the estate of the general stumbling-block... a particular social sphere must be recognized as the notorious crime of the whole of society, so that liberation from that sphere appears as general self-liberation... which can invoke no historical, but only human, title... a sphere, finally, which cannot emancipate itself without emancipating itself from all other spheres of society and thereby emancipating all other spheres of society, which, in a word, is the complete loss of man and hence can win itself only through the complete re-winning of man. This dissolution of society as a particular estate is the proletariat' (*Introduction to A Contribution to the Critique of Hegel's Philosophy of Right*).

22. 'Practical need, egoism, is the principle of civil society, and as such appears in pure form as soon as civil society has fully given birth to the political state' (OJQ, part II).
23. With what the bourgeoisie call political freedom, man 'was not freed from property, he received freedom to own property' (OJQ, part I).
24. Security is the highest social concept of civil society, the concept of police, expressing the fact that the whole of society exists only in order to guarantee to each of its members the preservation of his person, his rights, and his property... The concept of security does not raise civil society above its egoism. On the contrary, security is the *insurance* of egoism. (OJQ, part I).
25. The article is entitled 'Critical Notes to the Article: "The King of Prussia and Social Reform." By a Prussian'.
26. K. Marx. *Preface to A Contribution to the Critique of Political Economy* (trans. S. W. Ryazanskaya, online at <www.marxists.org>.
27. The Paris Manuscripts were not published in Marx's lifetime, and the first edition only appeared in 1932. We have used the English translation, titled *The Economic and Philosophic Manuscripts*, by Gregor Benton, available online at <www.marxists.org>. This work will be cited as *EPM*.
28. 'It is clear from an analysis of this concept that, although private property appears as the basis and cause of alienated labour, it is in fact its consequence.' (*EPM*, First Manuscript.)
29. *EPM*, Preface.
30. *EPM*, Third Manuscript.
31. *The German Ideology* is a manuscript written jointly by Marx and Engels between 1845 and 1846, but which remained unpublished until 1932. Here, we have used the English translation made available online at <www.marxists.org> (cited as *Ideology*).
32. *Ideology*, part 1A.
33. ibid.
34. ibid.
35. *Ideology*, part 1C.
36. ibid.
37. ibid.
38. *Ideology*, part 1D.
39. If power is taken as the basis of right, as Hobbes, etc., do, then right, law, etc., are merely the symptom, the expression of *other* relations upon which state power rests. The material life of individuals, which by no means depends merely on their 'will,' their mode of production and form of intercourse, which mutually determined each other—this

is the real basis of the state and remained so at all the stages at which division of labor and private property are still necessary, quite independently of the *will* of individuals. These actual relations are in no way created by the state power; on the contrary they are the power creating it. The individuals who rule in these conditions—leaving aside the fact that their power must assume the form of the *state*—have to give their will, which is determined by these definite conditions, a universal expression as the will of the state, as law, an expression whose content is always determined by the relations of this class, as the civil and criminal law demonstrates in the clearest possible way... The state does not exist owing to the dominant will, but the state, which arises from the material mode of life of individuals, has also the form of a dominant will. (*Ideology*, part 3).

40. *Ideology*, part 1A.
41. In the mid-1840s, such basic questions as the 'Antiquity of Man' were still a mystery. Charles Darwin was contemplating the evolution of the species after publishing his notes on the voyage of the Beagle and obviously, L. H. Morgan had not applied the theory of evolution from an anthropological viewpoint. Information about the human past at Marx and Engels' reach at that time came above all from classical sources and the European historiographic tradition.
42. *Ideology*, part 1A.
43. The translation used here (cited as *Forms*) is included in the version of the *Grundrisse* available at <www.marxists.org>.
44. *Forms*, part II. A few lines earlier, Marx had expressed this idea more extensively: 'Property thus originally means no more than a human being's relation to his natural conditions of production as belonging to him, as his, as presupposed along with his own being; relations to them as natural presuppositions of his self, which only form, so to speak, his extended body' (*Forms*, part II).
45. *Forms*, part I.
46. The relationship of the individual with the land 'is instantly mediated by the naturally arisen, spontaneous, more or less historically developed and modified presence of the individual as member of a commune—his naturally arisen presence as member of a tribe etc.' (*Forms*, part II).
47. *Forms*, part I.
48. ibid.
49. ibid.
50. ibid.
51. 'Membership in the commune remains the presupposition for the appropriation of land and soil, but, as a member of the commune, the individual is a private proprietor' (*Forms*, part I).

The property in one's own labour is mediated by property in the condition of labour—the hide of land, guaranteed in its turn by the existence of the commune, and that in turn by surplus labour in the form of military service etc. by the commune members. It is not cooperation in wealth-producing labour by means of which the commune member reproduces himself, but rather cooperation in labour for the communal interests (imaginary and real), for the upholding of the association inwardly and outwardly. (*Forms*, part I).

52. *Forms*, part I.
53. Let us pause in our explanations here. Marx mentions an additional form of property, called 'Slav', which he barely describes and which is said to be a modification of the Asian form (*Forms*, part II). He later focuses his attention on the origins and immediate historical preconditions of capital, which he places in the context of European feudal society.
54. Engels himself contributed to these readings to a large extent in his work *The Origin of the Family, Private Property and the State*, which was greatly influenced by the uni-linear evolutionism of L. H. Morgan. The way to this simplification followed other routes in the twentieth century, including the linking of the different modes of production defined by historical research (socio-economic translation of 'forms of property') and in uni- or multi-linear sequences of supposed universal necessity.
55. *Forms*, part II.
56. *Ideology*, part 1A.
57. In this respect, it is necessary to make a careful distinction between 'use' and 'exploit', especially examining whether differential material accumulations benefit the patriarchs. In short, whether the surplus obtained is of private use or not.
58. The main text was written as 'critical marginal notes on the Unity Programme of the German Social-Democratic Worker's Party' and sent by Marx to W. Bracke on 5 May 1875, for him to read and communicate to the other party leaders. The manuscript was not published until 1891, on Engel's initiative, in the journal *Neue Zeit*. The translation used here (cited as *Gotha*) is available at <www.marxists.org>.
59. Described by Marx as 'a state which is nothing but a police-guarded military despotism, embellished with parliamentary forms, alloyed with a feudal admixture, already influenced by the bourgeoisie' (*Gotha*, part IV).
60. *Gotha*, part IV.
61. *Gotha*, part IV. This expression first appeared in *The Communist Manifesto* (1848). Events such as the Paris Commune contributed to

separating it from the realm of utopias and filling it with real contents. See K. Marx, *The Civil War in France* (1871); F. Engels, *Letter to Bebel* (18–28 March 1875) and V. I. Lenin, *The State and Revolution* (1917).
62. *Gotha*, part I.
63. The work was published in 1884, a year after Marx's death. The translation used here is available at <www.marxists.org> (abbreviated as *The Origin*).
64. *The Origin*, chapter IX.
65. ibid.
66. ibid.
67. ibid.
68. V. I. Lenin, *The State and Revolution* (1917). See chapter 1.

8

Evolutionism and State

The idea that human societies, or even mankind as a whole, have followed a trajectory through different successive stages can be traced back at least as far as classic antiquity; it is found in Christianity and appears more often in the philosophy of the Modern Age and in Enlightenment thought. The stories that string together the different trajectories obviously contain terminological variations and can be classified according to the kind of moral connotations that guide their storyline. Thus, for some, the journey has followed an ascending, positive, and progressive course, in which each stage has involved an improvement in the material and intellectual conditions of human life. Beginning in the darkness of the caves, subservient to nature, violence, and precariousness, the human race has advanced along a route that has made it a master of its own fate and that of its environment. In contrast, other proposals have suggested a completely opposite opinion. Far from reaching higher and higher standards of well-being, happiness, or freedom, mankind has slowly degraded in the course of history, more in the moral sense than in the strictly material or technical fields. Nowadays hardly anything is left of that original situation in which humans lived happily and innocently, before calamities of one or another kind eroded the situation away or removed it at a stroke. According to this view, 'any past time was better'.[1]

Until relatively recent times, many of these stories, in form and content, played the role of a mythical genealogy for the human groups who accepted them as part of their historical world view or their religious and moral creed. As we shall see below, by this we do not mean that contemporary proposals are exempt from this ideological component; only that references to original and former social realities, those out of reach of written records or memory, were mainly nourished by legends, oral tradition, or simply imagination, while the arguments that judged that distant past time were inspired by direct projections of one or another scale of moral values.

In the nineteenth century, evolutionism, in its application to the study of human societies, approached the question from different viewpoints. It developed in an intellectual context rooted in the Enlightenment, which postulated knowledge based on empirical observation and a causalist method applied to any reality, either organic or inorganic. The project of a unitary objective science achieved basic success in Geology (Lyell) and Biology (Darwin). With this background, studies were undertaken into social evolution by such scholars as Tylor, McLennan, Spencer, Lubbock, and Morgan. This 'Anthropology', understood in its widest sense, combined ethnographic observations, historical tales and records, philological data and archaeological discoveries. The information obtained through this empirical research, which became increasingly rigorous, was articulated by a comparative procedure justified by resorting to the principle of the psychic unity of our race or, in other words, the unitary character of 'human nature'. The reasoning began with the discovery, in societies belonging to very different times and places, of the similar appearance or development in or between some of the fields in which human experience was divided, such as technology, kinship rules, forms of justice and government, language, art, and religion or beliefs. If these similarities were shown to exist with sufficient frequency and consistency, they might be understood as regularities. On this basis, always under the basic premise of the psychic unity of mankind, the regularities can be explained by the effect of similar causes. The final objective is to formulate generalizations, that is to say, statements in the form of laws aimed at explaining human behaviour, in the same way that the laws of natural evolution explain the behaviour of other living species.

Anthropological research attempted to understand scientifically those societies different from Western society that, to use a simile still near to those times, were still in the 'state of nature' or halfway between that and civilization personified in bourgeois society. Although we shall return to this important topic below, here we should propose that the two premises at the foundations of this research were:

1. The supposition that the societies 'living' at the time of the observation were evidence of different levels of development within the same reference scale.
2. The data obtained from the observation of these 'living' societies provided the keys to the reconstruction and explanation of the remote past of all societies.

The data used as the basis for this research came from the observations made by army officers, chroniclers, travellers, bureaucrats, traders, and religious missionaries in the colonies of European powers and, later during the main imperialist expansion of capitalism, by professional ethnographers. Thanks to the information obtained by all of these, in the nineteenth and twentieth centuries, evolutionist anthropology drafted sequential and hierarchical proposals for the classification of human diversity. At the same time, they noted factors aimed at explaining the social change that would culminate in the appearance of civilization or the State. This will be the topic of the present chapter, which will approach its objective through the study of the works of several anthropologists.

The first scholar to be the focus of our attention will be L. H. Morgan, who earned his place here as one of the 'founding fathers' both of evolutionist thought and of the subject of anthropology in general. His work went beyond the frontiers of the theoretical details of his discipline to leave its influence, for example, in Marxist tradition through the intermediary of Engels. The other two researchers we shall include here, M. Fried and E. Service, contributed decisively to shaping the sociological interpretation large sectors of modern archaeology give to the sequences of material finds in many regions of the world; a sequence that is usually understood in terms of a steady increase in social 'complexity' which finally culminated in the rise of civilization and the State. A fuller examination of this wholly archaeological aspect will be the theme of the second part of the book.

LEWIS HENRY MORGAN (1818–81)

As well as other outstanding works in the field of his anthropological studies, we are especially interested here in his most important book, titled *Ancient Society or Researches in the Lines of Human Progress from Savagery through Barbarism to Civilisation* (1877). Morgan's objective was expressed concisely at the start of the book.

> It will be my object to present some evidence of human progress along these several lines [subsistence, government, language, religion, house life and architecture, the family and property], and through successive ethnic periods, as it is revealed by inventions and discoveries, and by the growth of the ideas of government, of the family, and of property.[2]

The 'ethnic periods' Morgan refers to are: 'Savagery', 'Barbarism', and 'Civilization',[3] where the first two are subdivided into three levels ('Lower', 'Middle', and 'Upper'). The criteria for their definition come from the sphere of 'inventions and discoveries', that is to say, from technology and, to be more exact, from the 'arts of subsistence' which covered the ways of obtaining food and crafts.[4] Morgan granted great importance to technological aspects of human progress, and for this reason these form the backbone of his periodization. Hence the transition from one stage to another is marked by significant technical innovations, in the form of landmarks that enabled a qualitative leap forward. However, *Ancient Society* did not propose reducing human evolution to stages in technical progress, as can be seen immediately in the contents of the book. Here it is clear that the explanation of the ethnic periods only takes up the first part, titled 'Growth of Intelligence through Inventions and Discoveries', while the main part of the work is concerned with the developments occurring to the *concepts* of government, family, and property. In the first of these he outlines the evolution of social organization, from the one based on sex, through gens, phratry, tribe, confederacy, and, finally, the State. The evolution of the family follows a path marked by primitive forms, and the consanguine, the Punuluan, Syndyasmian and patriarchal, and, lastly, monogamian families. Finally, the historical development and the concept of property begin with initial communitarian kinds and culminates with private, individual, and alienable property.

In fact, technology and the 'concepts' whose development results in successive institutions of government, family, and property, make up two parallel, but inter-connected lines of research:

> As we re-ascend along the several lines of progress toward the primitive ages of mankind, and eliminate one after the other, in the order in which they appeared, inventions and discoveries on the one hand, and institutions on the other, we are enabled to perceive that the former

stand to each other in progressive, and the latter in unfolding relations. While the former class have had a connection, more or less direct, the latter have been developed from a few primary germs of thought.... Two independent lines of investigations thus invite our attention. The one leads through inventions and discoveries, and the other through primary institutions. With the knowledge gained therefrom, we may hope to indicate the principal stages of human development.[5]

It is important to stress that Morgan did not propose univocal or direct relationships of causality between technology and social institutions. He highlights the differences in the dynamics of change between both spheres and simply suggests the existence of links owing to the observation of certain regularities. Therefore, without denying the leadership of technological factors, he gives the impression that ideas such as government or property possess certain independence from their most common technological correlations. In fact, on occasions it seems that the driving force behind social development is one of the conceptual lines, as occurs with property.

> It is impossible to overestimate the influence of property in the civilization of mankind. It was the power that brought the Aryan and Semitic nations out of barbarism into civilization. The growth of the idea of property in the human mind commenced in feebleness and ended in becoming its master passion. Governments and laws are instituted with primary reference to *its* creation, protection and enjoyment. It introduced human slavery as an instrument in its production; and, after the experience of several thousand years, it caused the abolition of slavery upon the discovery that a freeman was a better property-making machine.[6]

As a hypothesis, he points out that the explanation for the regularities seen between 'inventions' and 'institutions' must lie in societies finding similar solutions in the face of similar conditions and needs, as mental capabilities are the same everywhere (the principle of the psychic unity of mankind).

> It may be remarked finally that the experience of mankind has run in nearly uniform channels; that human necessities in similar conditions have been substantially the same; and that the operations of the mental principle have been uniform in virtue of the specific identity of the brain of all the races of mankind.[7]

Before continuing with the comments on the importance and implications of Morgan's proposal, we must make a short description of the ethnic periods.[8]

Savagery

Lower

This period coincided with the 'infancy of the human race', that is to say, it is the first and oldest period after leaving the mere animal condition. Its characterization was made through a simply deductive exercise, as Morgan could not find any surviving human group to illustrate this period. Food, basically fruit and nuts, was obtained by gathering. Life took place partially in trees, within a forest environment, and also in caves. Articulate speech existed, but there was still no art. The family was of the consanguine type – that is, articulated around the marriage between brothers and sisters in a group. Property did not go beyond a personal level, while government existed through a pact between men.

Middle

The use of fire and fish subsistence indicate the transition to this new period. However, despite this innovation in subsistence strategies, contingencies in food supplies often led to cannibalism. In the middle status of savagery, we now find chipped stone implements and the first weapons (clubs and spears). The typical form of family was the Punaluan, which excluded marriage between uterine siblings and cousins. The government and property laws now correspond to the *gens*, understood as a kinship group similar to lineage, whose members are forbidden to marry amongst each other. On the basis of gentile organization would later appear the phratries, tribes, and confederacies of tribes. At the time when Morgan carried out his research this status was exemplified by the Australian aborigines and different Polynesian groups.

Upper

The main technological innovation which made it possible to reach this status was the invention of the bow and arrow, which in turn enabled hunting to acquire greater importance in subsistence. This change was further favoured by the consumption of farinaceous roots. At the same time, the first attempts were made at a sedentary life and progress in manufacturing. The Punaluan family and the gens government continued to dominate. Several coastal tribes in North and South America illustrated the typical upper period of savagery.

Barbarism

Lower

The manufacture of pottery vessels is the technical innovation that best marks the transition to barbarism, although Morgan also refers to other important inventions, such as hand-weaving on a loom, which made it possible to make clothes that would provide better protection against inclement weather. The previous ways of obtaining food still prevailed, although sedentism was consolidated with the construction of larger houses and villages defended by a palisade. The Punuluan family would continue, but it now coexisted with the Syndyasmian family, characterized by the fact that a man would live with one or several women. However, they did not occupy an exclusive residence, but lived in a common home which they shared with other family units. Social organizations such as the phratry and the confederacy appeared, and government was exercised through a council of chiefs, although in times of war a single chief would be in command. Different European and Asian tribes who practised the art of pottery, and tribes living to the east of the Missouri, typified this lower status of barbarism in the nineteenth century.

Middle

The technological key indicating the commencement of this stage is the domestication of animals and plants, a phenomenon which was expressed differently in terms of its time span and consequences in the Old and New Worlds. The use of adobe brick and stone in architecture was also stressed together with bronze-smelting in the Old World. The Syndyasmian family, which had appeared in the lower status of barbarism, is now the dominant modality. The government was in the hands of a council of chiefs, while the figure of a military commander acquired greater importance. This time, the tribes who exemplified this status were located in different regions of America, and also included the ancient Britons.

Upper

As well as being an indication of the final stage of barbarism, for Morgan, iron-smelting was an invention of the first order.[9] The reason lies in the fact that iron allowed a wide range of tools to be produced, and their application in different economic sectors, from agriculture to the crafts, formed the basis for the later development of civilization. In the field of family organization, the Syndyasmian and patriarchal forms became more widespread, implying the marriage of a man with one, or more usually, several wives. The group that was formed lived in a house exclusively. Slavery existed. Government was divided between a general assembly, a council of chiefs and the figure of the leader or military commander. Although portable goods were individual property, land was still generally owned collectively. The examples of the upper status of barbarism were found, among others, in the Greek tribes as described by Homer, the Italian tribes before the rise of Rome, or the German tribes contemporary with Julius Caesar.

Civilization

Finally, writing based on a phonetic alphabet was the invention that marked the arrival of civilization.[10] This ethnic period is sub-divided into ancient and modern (the capitalist society in which Morgan lived), although Morgan did not go into the distinction in depth. Civilization is characterized by the spectacular development of manufacturing and the arts. The monogamous family predominates now, and individual alienable property, handed down from father to son by hereditary arrangements, is transmitted within it. Individual property is guaranteed by the State and also coexists with direct State ownership. In civilization, the traditional gentile organization is replaced by a truly political organization based on the territorial ascription of people: the State. For Morgan, the appearance of the State marks a before and an after in the development of the institutions of government:

The experience of mankind, as elsewhere remarked, has developed but two plans of government, using the word *plan* in its scientific sense. Both were definite and systematic organizations of society. The first and most ancient was a *social organization*, founded upon gentes, phratries, and tribes. The second and latest in time was a *political organization*, founded upon territory and upon property. Under the first, a gentile society was created, in which the government dealt with persons through their relations to a gens and tribe. These relations were purely personal. Under the second a political society was instituted, in which the government dealt with persons through their relations to territory, e.g. the township, the county, and the State. These relations were purely territorial. The two plans were fundamentally different. One belongs to ancient society, and the other to modern.[11]

The reasons explaining the substitution of a social organization by a political one are sketched out by Morgan in the final part of *Ancient Society*, where he discusses the development of the concept of property.[12] The transition is situated in the closing stages of the upper status of barbarism, at the time of an increase in individual property, and the origin of slavery and the patriarchal family. The abundance of food produced by a booming agriculture favoured population growth. The tribes, rooted in fixed areas and under the pressure of the rising population, intensified their struggle for the control of the most fertile lands. The result was that 'it tended to advance the art of war, and to increase the rewards of individual prowess'.[13] The development of these factors in antiquity led to certain societies entering the status of civilization.

The meanings of evolutionary periodization

Morgan proposed the ethnic periods as classifying categories, in a sequential and hierarchical order, with the aim of including all knowledge about human diversity. He presented his evolutionary plan in the first part of *Ancient Society*, but did not explain how it had been developed nor, in any systematic way, the consequences involved in adopting it as a tool to study mankind. Apart from this criticism, we can point out a double meaning in Morgan's theory, as we shall describe below.

Unidirectionality and hierarchy

The evolutionary plan follows a stepped line in a series of successive stages through which all human societies have passed or should pass. It is evident that clear differences can be seen among the studied societies in their technical means, organizational forms, customs, and beliefs. However, evolutionism understands this diversity in terms of hierarchic differences in a vertical scale. The societies that have reached the highest stages possess a level of *complexity* that is greater than in the lower stages, which for that reason are described as *simple*. Humans thus keep the general law applied to all species, according to which the development tends to go from the most simple to the most complex. However, unlike other living creatures, the driving force behind progress is the accumulation of knowledge, which results periodically in technical advances. For Morgan, the condition *sine qua non* for overcoming one stage and reaching the next is the acquisition of certain technological innovations in the field of the production of food and manufacturing. When a society reaches a new status, it maintains contacts and relationships with others that remain in stages that it has overcome. In this way, the inventions spread and favour progressive advances in the same direction.

> The most advanced portion of the human race were halted, so to express it, at certain stages of progress, until some great invention or discovery, such as the domestication of animals or the smelting of iron ore, gave a new and powerful impulse forward. While thus restrained, the ruder tribes, continually advancing, approached in different degrees of nearness to the same status; for *wherever a continental connection existed, all the tribes must have shared in some measure in each other's progress*. All great inventions and discoveries propagate themselves; but the inferior tribes must have appreciated their value before they could appropriate them.[14]

Morgan's evolutionism possesses an undeniable materialistic component in its explanation of the reasons for social change, as it grants most importance to the technological aspect directly linked to subsistence. However, he accepts the influence of other causal factors that twentieth-century evolutionism was to abandon, such as the abovementioned role of diffusion in social change and also certain particularism related to it. In this respect, it could be said that while the technological vector was in the vanguard of human evolution, the decisive innovations only arise within one or a few groups with the right intelligence or 'genius'. This is the case of iron-smelting, whose technical complexity makes Morgan suggest that it was unlikely that it could have been invented more than once. Thus, despite assuming the principle that under similar conditions and needs, human groups produce similar responses, in practice Morgan accepts differences in the supposed human psychic unity. This results in the existence of 'families' (not in the meaning of kinship), to be exact, the Semitic and Aryan families, capable of leading the progress of mankind in recent times.[15]

The acceptance of a hierarchic structure implies expressing opinions in terms of superiority and inferiority, and advances forwards or steps backwards. Morgan connoted civilization positively,[16] placing it at the top of the human evolutionary pyramid. To be more exact, Western civilization, with Aryan roots, of which Morgan was a member, was considered the most successful achievement of the human race and therefore, according to the unidirectional reasoning we have just explained, was set up as the model to which all other societies should aspire. Contemporary technical progress and the bourgeois institutions associated with it should be the goal, or if you prefer, the necessary end that awaited all others. From this viewpoint, Morgan's theory contains ideological prejudices that draw it near to the traditional mythical genealogies we referred to at the start of this chapter. Morgan has been criticized for the ethnocentrism that made him raise the society to which he belonged to the summit of human development. In addition, he supplied a 'scientific' justification for 'Western superiority' and, in consequence, for the colonial and imperialist actions of Western capitalist powers.

> In strictness but two families, the Semitic and the Aryan, accomplished the work [reaching civilization] through unassisted self-development. The Aryan family represents the central stream of human progress, because it produced the highest type of mankind, and because it has proved its intrinsic superiority by gradually assuming the control of the earth.[17]

The present preserves the past

In his research, Morgan used ethnographic information corresponding to roughly contemporary societies, as well as historiographic references to Greco-Latin antiquity. Therefore, the chronological range he took into account might be considered recent, in comparison with the huge time span of human existence. Despite this, Morgan's evolutionary theory aims to represent *all* the historical and prehistoric development of mankind. Such an aspiration is based on the premise that the present time contains sufficient evidence of the past to be able to make a reconstruction of it. This premise is, in turn, based on another three:

- Mankind progresses through the accumulation of knowledge, so that the most recent stages preserve, totally or partially, material elements (technology) and concepts (institutions) without which it would not have been possible to reach the present stage.
- Nineteenth-century Western civilization personifies the highest level of progress ever reached by mankind. Other societies have stopped in different stages that Western society has already gone through. Consequently, it can be said that '*their* present illustrates *our* past'.[18]
- The simplest ways of life that have been described ethnographically inform us of mankind's oldest ways of life and, at the same time, the most widespread.

These premises clearly show the deductive character of evolutionist procedure. Morgan even came to surmise that human presence on the Earth went back a hundred thousand years, of which savagery would have occupied the first three-fifths, i.e. sixty thousand years.[19] However, it is clear that deductions like this do not become per se true pronouncements about the reality of the past, because they have been made by a combination of formal theoretical premises and not through empirical observations. All statements about the past need a *real* past to be validated or not; that is to say, proofs belonging to the past in which forms that today we can only infer or imagine are fully in force. This is exactly where archaeology comes into play.

If Darwinian biology favoured the development of palaeontology, anthropology encouraged the growth of archaeology,[20] although it is true that the science had been born some time before and had begun to fit the premises of scientific method to the specificity of its materials with the 'three age system'. Morgan was aware of this fundamental achievement of Nordic archaeology. In fact, he weighed up the possibility of structuring his ethnic periods according to the

Ages of Stone, Bronze, and Iron, although he finally discarded that idea.[21] In general terms, although Morgan considered some teachings of archaeology when he gave contents to some of the ethnic periods,[22] the contribution of the science to his evolutionary theory is not significant. In the 1870s the scientific study of the past through its material remains was in its infancy. Archaeology won prestige through a number of great discoveries, which encouraged the passion of antiquarians and students of ancient art, while slow progress was made in the task of developing a chronological order for the series of finds that steadily increased in number.

When Morgan wrote *Ancient Society*, archaeology was still not able to offer him a solid background about the depth and time rhythms of human evolution, nor about how this had taken place on the five continents. On the contrary, the work of the evolutionary anthropologist was an encouragement to widen the scope of archaeological research, as it implied a large number of premises and claims about the human past that only archaeology was able to prove or disprove. To confirm or deny the sequence of ethnic periods itself was one of the crucial aspects, if not the most important. Archaeology had already begun by developing its own method to obtain relative chronologies (the typological–contextual method contained within the three age system), and in this task it found the assistance of the stratigraphic laws formulated by Geology. The question was not only to check the correctness of an empirical sequence, but also the validity of the premises on which the method was based. Naturally, there was also great curiosity to solve other more specific problems. Morgan expressed one of these when he referred to the origins of iron-smelting, which he believed to be the greatest discovery of mankind: 'It would be a singular satisfaction could it be known to what tribe and family we are indebted for this knowledge, and with it for civilization'.[23]

In short, evolutionism was an incentive for the science of archaeology which was still in an incipient form in the mid-nineteenth century. Although it was at that time that they consolidated their separate academic lines, it is also true that anthropology and archaeology laid the foundations for a relationship that has continued until the present time; one of their most interesting topics has been research into the formation of civilization and the State.

NEO-EVOLUTIONISM

After contributing decisively to the consolidation of anthropology as a discipline, evolutionism began to be questioned and lost its position of hegemony as a guide to research. Historical particularism then took its place. In the warmth of German idealist philosophy, the study of the diversity of human beings abandoned the aim of discovering regularities, of formulating generalities and much less of drawing unilinear evolutionary trajectories of universal validity. In contrast, the multiple forms of human life began to be understood as a mosaic of *cultures*. Culture is defined as an entity of significant and ideal nature which belongs to the realm of thought and is, therefore, resistant to any causality of the technological and, in general, materialist kind. Each culture displays its own distinctive essence, shaped by a particular concatenation of historical events, which lead to different configurations of customs, beliefs, and material objects. Therefore, if each culture is unique, we would seek in vain, as pointed out above, any causes applicable to a generality of them. If they were to be detected, the similarities between cultures are due to phenomena of diffusion, loan, or influence, whose reach and intensity are thought to depend on the idiosyncrasy of the parts involved and the historical situation in which they occurred. It would also be a mistake to propose hierarchical orders among human groups following universal criteria, whether they be technological or any other kind. Conviction in the singularity of cultural phenomena leads to relativist postures that oppose attributions in terms of superiority–inferiority or developed–underdeveloped with which evolutionism connoted the comparison between the societies being studied. Even so, bourgeois ethno-centrism is too deeply rooted for many supporters of cultural historicism to stop acknowledging differences between 'high' and 'low' cultures. Evidently, civilizations are prominent among the former...

Archaeology provided arguments that contributed to discrediting nineteenth-century evolutionism. On one hand, it proved there were errors in Morgan's evolutionary sequence, such as, for example, that the first civilizations arose *before* the development of iron metallurgy and not as a more or less direct consequence of it; or, in fact, the practice of metallurgy has not even been a requirement fulfilled by all civilizations.[24] On the other hand, the excavation of multi-phase sites,

Evolutionism and State

the definition of prolonged stratigraphic sequences, and the establishment of the first regional periodizations made it clear that the development of human groups was far from uniform and that periods in which great technological, institutional, and even artistic progress was made were followed by others with clear backward steps in all these fields. In short, archaeology contributed in its small way to the critique of uni-linear evolution, the causality of technological factors and the universality of the idea of progress, while at the same time it united with those who considered that diversity (material, in the case of archaeology) was a sign of cultural idiosyncrasy.

However, as usually happens when 'that part of truth' which sometimes makes a theoretical proposal hegemonic is not extinguished completely, in the second half of the twentieth century, evolutionary theories were reformulated and revived. In anthropology, the works of J. Steward and L. White are usually indicated as fundamental landmarks in the resurgence of a tradition which lived its best years in the 1960s and 1970s, mainly within the scenario of certain American universities. This neo-evolutionism put new stress on old ideas, while also supplying new arguments. The anthropological evolutionism of the nineteenth century owed more to the philosophical tradition of the Enlightenment, especially to the idea of progress, than to the direct influence of Darwinist biology. In contrast, in neo-evolutionary postulates, this influence was felt much more clearly. Human societies are expressions of the *human* species which, like all other living species, must go through the process of natural selection in order to survive. Hence the importance given to ecological variables, which characterize the habitat in which social life is carried out, and to the category 'adaptation'. This measures the success with which human groups confront survival only that, unlike other animals and plants, the role of genetic mutation is minimal compared with technology, socio-political organization and, culture in general, defined by White as the 'extrasomatic means of adaptation'. In explaining change in human behaviour, again we witness the primacy of material variables of the techno-economic and demographic kind. Humans are a species that uses technology to take from the environment all the resources enabling it to survive and reproduce successfully. Cultural rules and meanings, from institutions to language and religion, exist according to these absolute necessities, and for this reason neo-evolutionism establishes determinist links between the realm of material subsistence (hunting, gathering, horticulture, irrigated agriculture...), the true driving force of existence, and the other instances in which social reality is analysed.

However, this emphasis on techno-economic variables is combined with the great importance of forms of political organization, to such an extent that many studies published under a neo-evolutionist heading have become part of the domain of political anthropology. In fact, both the method used to draw up new evolutionary schemes and the terminology employed to designate their studies, reflect the influence of a liberal-bourgeois political philosophy based on individualist ontology that gives precedence to the criterion of the centrality of leadership in the understanding of human groups. Therefore, neo-evolutionism favours the correlations between degree of political centrality and subsistence technology in the definition of the set of social types. Each one of these would exemplify advantageous solutions, either from the strictly adaptive point of view (survival) or material in the widest sense of the word (higher level of general benefits or well-being). In turn, these types are used to synthesize all human diversity, a project coinciding with one of Morgan's primordial goals: explain in simple terms all the apparent human diversity at any time or place.

Neither is it chance that the increase in inequalities, measured in terms of 'complexity', as well as the origin of the State as the culmination of this process, has again been a key topic in the neo-evolutionary programme. Above all, these are developments that have occurred with greater or lesser intensity all over the world and, in a certain number of cases, within societies with no contacts among each other, so the diffusionist explanations so beloved of cultural historicism can be ruled out. In this way, one of the main premises of classical evolutionism can be vindicated, which is the basic unity of humankind as the cause of regularities in social behaviour: similar responses to similar conditions and needs, even though they may sometimes differ in their formal appearance.

Instead, unlike nineteenth-century evolutionism, neo-evolutionism does not insist on the uniformity or universality of the evolutionary process. Basically, it maintains that the general trajectory runs from simple organizational forms to complex ones, distinguished as civilizations and States. However, it does not rule that the intermediate steps have to be fulfilled obligatorily and, above all, admits the reality of reactionary phenomena, which would have their own field of study linked to the causes of crises and collapses.

Evolutionism and State

The most distinguished representatives of anthropological neo-evolutionism include M. Sahlins (in his earlier works), E. Service, and M. Fried. As noted above, we will focus on the contributions of the two latter authors because of their special repercussion on archaeological research into the formation of the State and civilization.

ELMAN R. SERVICE (1915-96)

Two of E. Service's works are to be discussed here. In the first, titled *Primitive Social Organisation: An Evolutionary Perspective*,[25] the author gave an initial version of a scheme of the evolution of societies which was an indubitable success, both in its contents and on the terminological level. This scheme was subdivided into four stages, whose characterization is summarized below:

Bands

This is the simplest and oldest form of social structure, some testimonies of which have survived until today such as the Athapascans, the Andaman islanders, or the *!Kung* Bushmen. The bands consist of between thirty and a hundred individuals, linked in nuclear or extensive families created by the practice of exogamy. The maximum population density is stipulated at only one inhabitant per square mile, although this figure varies according to the availability of food, obtained mainly by hunting and gathering. The division of labour is inexistent on the supra-family level.

Tribes

As happens in the bands, tribal societies have no political hierarchies. The only forms of leadership are situational in character and are based on personal qualities. There is an increase, however, in the number of positions of recognized status. The size of the aggregations of people and the number of residential groups also increases. The tribal organization contains associations of kinship, such as lineages and clans, and also accepts the formation of secret societies. Finally, disputes and violent relationships occur between the tribes, ending in assaults and sudden attacks.

Chiefdoms

Chiefdoms involve the formation of denser aggregations of population and larger groups of residence. This development runs parallel to an increase in productivity in the subsistence sector (well-developed agriculture) and also to higher levels of complexity and internal organization. Political leadership implies centralized direction in the hands of chiefs. This position has a description assigned to it and the performance of its duties is bound to rules about the succession and the enjoyment of luxury goods. One of the functions accepted by chiefs is managing re-distributive exchange between groups of producers with some regional specialization because of ecological particularities.

Primitive States and archaic civilizations[26]

Finally, States are characterized as possessing bureaucratic governments that monopolize the legitimate use of force. They may expand until they form empires, including different cultures and ethnic groups within the framework of civil order. Primitive States and ancient civilizations are not qualitatively different entities, rather variations within a same stage of development. Archaic civilizations represent successful attempts at stable integration which leads to the formation of a new type of culture, different from that of its initial components. In this way, archaic civilizations would represent the culmination of the integrating potential of primitive pre-industrial States.

The second of Service's works, *Origins of the State and Civilisation. The Process of Cultural Evolution* (1975),[27] is a longer, documented book about the characteristics and functioning of types of sociopolitical organization, In fact, for Service, the evolutionary vector corresponds to politics and, more precisely, to the institutionalization of leadership. In contraposition to the Marxist thesis, championed by V. G. Childe, among others:

Evolutionism and State 153

The alternative thesis to be presented here locates the origins of government in the institutionalization of centralised leadership. That leadership, in developing its administrative functions for the maintenance of the society, grew into a hereditary aristocracy. The nascent bureaucracy's economic and religious functions developed as the extent of its services, its autonomy, and its size increased. Thus the earliest government worked to protect, not another class or stratum of the society, but itself. It legitimized itself in its role of maintaining the whole society.

Political power organized the economy, not vice versa. The system was redistributive, allocative, not acquisitive: Personal wealth was not required to gain personal political power. And these first governments seem clearly to have reinforced their structure by doing their economic and religious jobs well—by providing benefits—rather than by using physical force.[28]

In fact, Service reserves the term 'State' to refer to political forms characterized here by the use of physical force as an instrument to achieve repressive control. Some of these organizations have been documented ethnographically (for example, the Zulu and Ankole States) and he dedicates part of the book to them, designating them as 'Primitive States'. However, Service insists that they are relatively recent phenomena, whose origins are generally due to the repercussions of European colonial expansion on theocratic chiefdom societies. In contrast, he uses the expression 'archaic civilizations' to refer to the first hierarchical and institutionalized political structures that appeared in Mesopotamian, Egypt, China, the Indus Valley, Mesoamerica, and Peru, several thousand years ago. Service then focuses his attention on how these civilizations 'developed out of the matrix of egalitarian primitive society',[29] initially structured in egalitarian segmental societies and later in chiefdoms. Let us pause here to show the characterization of these evolutionary types.

Egalitarian or segmental societies

Most egalitarian societies obtain their food by hunting and gathering. They consist of small groups where political leadership is based on personal qualities (skill, intelligence, physical conditions) conferring advantages in certain contexts in life and which in exchange receive social recognition in the form of status. The character of this leadership is ephemeral, as the leader lacks sufficient means to dominate other persons permanently. In the absence of coercive force, collective decisions or the solution of interpersonal conflicts depend on the verdicts given by people holding moral authority (for example, the elders) or on the arbitration of distant relations or the inclination of public opinion. Conflicts occasionally end in violent actions, although these are limited to expiatory combats or small-scale battles. When this type of society suffers an external aggression, the affected groups may flee or disperse, or instead form large confederations to face up to the attack. The chiefs at the head of these may hold a much larger authority than do leaders in times of peace.

Equally, the solution to internal conflicts may take the form of segmentation, the process by which a part of the local group breaks away and settles in another location, reproducing an analogous social unit to the original one. This process of segmenting is precisely the source of the second term that Service uses to designate these societies.

Finally, bartering and marriage are the most common forms of exchange, both guided by the principle of reciprocity. The exchange of goods and persons does not represent an activity aimed at obtaining an economic profit in capitalist terms, but a means of consolidating alliances and reducing the risk of conflicts.

Chiefdom societies

Chiefdoms form a socio-political type acting as a bridge between egalitarian societies and civilizations. They are a firm step towards the institutionalization of leadership and the consolidation of a structure of hierarchically organized status. In these societies, the leadership is the responsibility of a chief, who occupies a post transmitted hereditarily by primogeniture. Among the reasons for the development of this type of organization, Service emphasizes the managing role of the chief within a redistributive system of exchanges. Sedentary chiefdom societies normally inhabit areas with a range of natural resources. This favours local and regional symbiosis resulting in the development of the distribution of products between settlements, as they become increasingly specialized in the exploitation of the ecological niches where they are located. When this practice is combined with rudimentary forms of leadership, such as, for example, the so-called 'big men', the formation of an institutionalized system of power is stimulated, centralized around the chief and the group of his kin.

The management of redistributive exchanges, necessary in a society formed by increasingly specialized collectives, sees the addition of other functions, such as justice, warfare, religion, or the organization of foreign trade, which are taken over by a hierarchy of posts headed by the chief. This is the origin of bureaucracy, whose development is explained by Service in terms of the benefits involved in its management role and which the population perceives positively. This unanimity, reinforced ideologically by religion and the frequent investiture of the chief with supernatural attributes, is the basis of the ability of chiefdoms to mobilize large labour-forces for the construction of public works or collective enterprises, such as building irrigation systems, temples, and tombs. The production of craftsmen increases noticeably. In this respect, we may mention the manufacture of symbols to be used by the persons wielding authority. These are occasionally made from allochthonous raw materials, obtained through the establishment of long-distance exchange networks.

Despite Service's insistence on stressing that the conscious support of the population is a decisive factor in the explanation for the consolidation of chiefdom systems, the author also suggests the practice of coercive behaviour. Thus, any action against the chief is interpreted as an attack on the society and is deserving of punishment. In a similar way, Service indicates that the tendency of chiefdoms to grow, with the subsequent expansion of the bureaucracy and conspicuous consumption associated with high-ranking persons, may lead to the rebellion of the governed part of the population. If this is successful, the system undergoes a crisis and reduces its scope. However, if the system survives the rebellion, it may be in the position of crossing the threshold separating chiefdom from civilization.

Archaic civilization and State

As we noted above, for Service, it is preferable to talk of civilizations in the ancient world, rather than States. Civilizations are systems of government characterized by centralized leadership with the aim of management, without resorting to physical coercion. They are led by persons, invested with authority with a theocratic tinge, whose leadership is accepted and enjoyed by the whole society. In its management duties it is assisted by a bureaucratic class with responsibilities in very varied functions, from the construction of infrastructures to the organization of religious worship. However, its original and most important function is the administration of a redistributive exchange system, which guarantees the general supply system in a situation of increasing productive specialization.

The immediate precedents of archaic civilizations were hereditary chiefdoms, where the efficient management of an incipient bureaucracy provided benefits to society as a whole. Measures of self-preservation instigated by the bureaucracy itself, combined with the support of the rest of the population, contributed to an increase and expansion of governmental functions until, in some cases, the extent of the changes led to the evolution of some chiefdoms to the rank of a civilization. Therefore, the differences between one and the other are a question of degree, within the same scale, rather than qualitative differences.

> Civilizations of the classical type were not created *de novo*; their basic characteristics were all foreshadowed in earlier stages of society. The term civilization is thus a relative concept and should not be defined in terms of the appearance of some single attribute... From an evolutionary standpoint, the relativity is achieved by thinking not in terms of arbitrary demarking points but of a continuum of directional change... Then the key becomes concerned with 'more' or 'less' advancement along the directional line. The most commonplace, because most obvious, notion of the direction cultural evolution has taken is from simple to complex cultures, or the corollary, small to large societies.[30]

In the context of the first archaic civilizations, violence, if it existed, was restricted to episodes of power struggles among different governmental factions or, exceptionally, to conflicts between political units for the access to certain resources. Service stresses that internal social control was based on the consent of the majority of the population due to the perception of the benefits of the redistributive economy, a consent strengthened additionally by a religious ideology which attributed the supreme governor an halo of sacredness and even divinity. From this point of view, the 'state as a repressive institution based on secular force'[31] was a later development, foreign to the archaic civilizations.

MORTON H. FRIED (1923-86)

In *The Evolution of Political Society. An Essay in Political Anthropology*,[32] Fried explained the detailed characterization of a four-part evolutionary scheme, whose main lines will be summarized as follows.

The egalitarian society

The account opens with a warning that sounds paradoxical: 'Equality is a social impossibility',[33] as individuals themselves display multiple marked differences among each other (age, sex, endurance, speed, auditory, or visual acuity, etc.). Therefore, Fried adds that the heading should read as '*relatively* egalitarian society' and that the societies being alluded to have in common the lack of hierarchic or stratified structure, but that does not mean they achieve total equality.

Having made this proviso, Fried focuses the definition of an egalitarian society from the consideration of the concepts of 'status', 'role', and 'prestige'. 'Status' is equivalent to social standing, 'role' is defined as the active counterpart of status, while 'prestige' is viewed as the ideological component of status and is associated with the concept of 'authority', understood as 'the ability to channel the behaviour of others in the absence of the threat or use of sanctions'.[34] Using this approach, Fried defines egalitarian society in the following terms:

> An egalitarian society is one in which there are as many positions of prestige in any given age-sex grade as there are persons capable of filling them. Putting that another way, an egalitarian society is characterized by the adjustment of the number of valued statuses to the number of persons with the abilities to fill them.[35]

As it is based on authority, not on coercion, leadership is transient in character and is limited to occasional situations in which this authority is recognized. Social organization is based on families and small mobile exogamous bands, occupying a territory with a low population density. Subsistence comes from hunting, fishing, and gathering, activities providing food which is not usually stored in large amounts. Access to essential or 'critical' resources for subsistence, such as food and raw materials, is egalitarian.

The division of labour is based on sex and age, where the family is the minimum production unit, although certain activities may occasionally require cooperation at a larger scale. The technological level is low. Reciprocity, occurring immediately or in time, is the dominant way of putting products in circulation and takes place in the course of visits or celebrations. Finally, war is a brief, occasional event of low intensity, whose causes lie in the competition for resources. Confrontation does not produce or presuppose any professional warriors, and the weapons used are normally the same as the ones used for hunting.

!*Kung* Bushmen and Eskimos provide the closest examples of this type of society.

Hierarchized or rank societies

A rank society is defined as one in which 'positions of valued status are somehow limited so that not all those of sufficient talent to occupy such statuses actually achieve them'.[36] This is because social mechanisms act to restrict the positions of status or authority, which are typified in the figure of the chief or 'big man'. The appearance of rank societies coincides with the introduction of agriculture and pastoralism, the commencement of sedentary life in villages, where the houses are gathered together and collective activities are carried out. Demographic density increases in comparison with egalitarian societies. Almost all the food requirements are produced locally, which gives the groups a high level of self-sufficiency. In fact, only certain raw materials are obtained through exchange.

The new farming strategies, with their implications in the production, accumulation, and management of large amounts of food, sedentism, and the growing importance of redistribution as the dominant form of the internal exchange of goods are the reasons that help to explain the transition from egalitarian to rank societies. Fried agrees with Service that the importance acquired by redistribution explains the appearance of the figure of a charismatic chief as an economic administrator with no power to exploit: the chief gathers, he does not expropriate; he distributes, he does not consume.[37] In this respect, another important characteristic in the definition of rank societies is that equal access to basic subsistence resources, such as land and water, is maintained. Therefore, the political hierarchy does not lead to clear or permanent inequality.

As in egalitarian societies, the division of labour is mainly organized according to criteria of age and sex. However, a certain degree of part-time specialization in tasks, based on different criteria, can now be observed. Thus, for example, the procurement of raw materials or the manufacture of goods may tend to be taken on by a certain group who, in compensation for the time spent on these tasks, receive the food they were unable to produce from the rest of the community.

Finally, the social organization rests upon kin networks, in the form of lineage or clan. Interpersonal and economic relationships depend on the individual belonging to a family group of this kind.

Some of the best-known examples of rank societies have been documented in Polynesia and Melanesia.

Stratified societies

Stratified societies comprise a transition stage between rank societies and the State. Their rise is connected to demographic increase and the problems derived from the pressure on subsistence resources that this causes, and which social organization based on kinships has difficulty in solving. Stratified society is inherently unstable, and may drift towards State forms or go back to more egalitarian kinds of society. In fact, Fried admits that it is almost impossible to document stratified societies which have not become States, as the main characteristic defining them is shared by States:

> A stratified society is one in which members of the same sex and equivalent age status do not have equal access to the basic resources that sustain life.[38]

In practice, this means that certain individuals or groups control the resources and that, for this reason, others suffer from scarcity. In order to have access to such basic resources, they must provide products or labour to those who hold control and direct access. This situation is accompanied by complex arrangements about the hereditary transmission of rights and obligations among groups of closed kinship that are stratified amongst themselves.

Food resources are obtained by intensive technologies, which might include the use of the plough, irrigation systems or the custom of specialized husbandry. New methods also affect the sphere of the division of labour. Full-time craft specialists now appear, some of whom manufacture luxury goods, which means that a sector of the population is remote from the direct production of food. The complexity of manufacturing also increases, so that in general, the necessary technology cannot be made by a single individual, such as occurs in metallurgy.

War increases in frequency and intensity, as it enables the accumulation of resources (booty, the annexation of land, slave labour) in the hands of the victors. In parallel with the greater importance of war, specialists in coercive actions appear (the army) and military commanders find the ideal scenario where to increase their social influence.

The State

Most of the characteristics of the stratified society are also valid for State societies. The definition of the State is: 'The complex of institutions by means of which the power of the society is organised on a basis superior to kinship'.[39] In this way, a bureaucracy arises whose members are not united by kinship and whose main objective is to maintain and strengthen unequal access to the basic resources that sustain life; that is, the order of stratification. In order to fulfil this aim, the State possesses instruments of coercive power, in the shape of armed forces. In the same way, the borders are defined, within which are to be found the resources and the individuals who are under the control of the institutional complex. At the same time, a tax system is created which mobilizes resources for the State institution. Finally, punishable behaviour is established in the form of explicit laws in written records.[40]

Fried consolidated the distinction between pristine and secondary States, formulated by V. G. Childe and also accepted by J. Steward some years before. The first term refers to those States which arise as the culmination of processes with no record of the influence of other States. The history of mankind has provided six cases of pristine or independently arisen States: Mesopotamia, Egypt, Indus Valley, North China, Mesoamerica, and the coast of Peru. In contrast, secondary States will be all the others, that is, those in which other already-consolidated States intervened directly or indirectly in their formation.

NEO-EVOLUTIONISM: DISCUSSION AND ASSESSMENT

The studies of Service, Fried, and other neo-evolutionist researchers have generated a huge bibliography which includes all kinds of publications, from the addition of clarifications to the initial proposals, to critiques in greater or lesser detail. Instead of attempting to be exhaustive in the inventory of all these reactions, here we shall simply highlight the fundamental aspects of the evolutionary theories and outline a critical comment on them, some of whose arguments we put forward in the previous chapter.

We shall begin by examining aspects of the method for the construction of the sequences of evolutionary social types. The definition of each one of these types is based on the consideration that political relationships form the basic dimension of social life. This dimension, abstract at first, becomes a category in a list in order to be operative in empirical analysis, by establishing:

1. the essential aspect of political relationships becomes apparent above all in the institutionalization of political centrality, understood in terms of leadership; and
2. this institutionalization can be graded, in this case from ephemeral, flexible, simple, and barely formalized types of leadership, to other permanent, centralized, complex, and highly regulated kinds. As we have seen in the above description, the graded scale usually provides for three or four levels.

According to these premises, neo-evolutionist research undertook the organization of a large amount of data on numerous social groups, documented ethnographically all over the world. Taking political relationships as a guide, each particular case was assigned to one or other of the levels that express the degree of institutionalization of the leadership. Then, they observed which characteristics of aspects, such as technology, exchange, division of labour, demography, settlement patterns, kinship system, laws, warfare, and organization of the religious cult, occurred most frequently among the societies ascribed to each level. Based on this, the recurrent elements set the guidelines for the general characterization of the level. As a result of this process, the levels of political centrality became condensed into abstract social types, the synthesis of a generality of real, different and distant, human groups. None of these groups matched the definition of one or other type exactly, but neither did any of them fall outside the boundaries marked by the typological sequence.

In what way did this aspect of the methodology condition the understanding of social life in all its diversity? To answer this question, it is worth pausing to consider the effects caused by taking as given that politics is the fundamental dimension of social relationships. Some neo-evolutionist researchers grant it greater autonomy than others in comparison with the technological, demographic, and environmental factors which play their part in the ever-crucial everyday challenge of adapting to survive. However, despite these differences, they agree that the fundamental element distinguishing some societies from others is rooted in their political organization. Nonetheless, 'politics' has a potentially large semantic field. To progress, it is necessary to be more precise or, in other words, to opt in favour of one out of several possible definitions. Where does neo-evolutionism come from to make its choice? From a conception of political relationships that stresses the ideas of *consensus* and *need*.

Chiefdoms or hierarchized societies first, and civilizations and States afterwards, would indicate that the cited success had come to strengthen male leadership. In the successive forms in which it has appeared, from the first Big Men to the theocrats and kings, it is always assumed that the action of government received collective consent. Service, for example, even claims that popular support for the leader and bureaucracy becomes the main driving force behind the increase in political complexity. The core of the reasoning justifying social consensus is as follows: if the political organization contributes decisively to the survival of the group and, on occasions, even to its abundance and growth, it would be absurd to question it, as that would mean going against basic human instinct.[41] Need and conformity thus become inseparable. Consequently, human populations generate leaders and they institutionalize them and extol them if it is *necessary*. The measure of that *need* is given by the material conditions that could put physical subsistence, and therefore survival, at risk: in short, the provision of food and shelter. As it affects everyone equally, politics becomes the means to achieve the general interest.

From this point of view, neo-evolutionism connects with the political philosophical tradition which, since Plato, understands government, or leadership, as a service to society as a whole. The difference in comparison with other approaches lies in the materialist arguments which accompany it. Thus, instead of pursuing the realization of an ethical idea, in neo-evolutionism, political organization forms an adaptive mechanism oriented at achieving the survival of the group in certain material conditions. General political evolution, summarized in a sequence of types, thus illustrates a continuum of successful solutions that have enabled the proliferation and expansion of our species.

Let's take the argument a step further. We have stressed that contemporary evolutionism proposes a scenario where political relationships comprise the essence of social life. However, for neo-evolutionism, 'politics' is above all an inter-person relationship, between people, between individuals, as in all living species natural selection always takes place at that level; it is the flexible groups of *individuals* who *authorize* a Big Man at a given moment and who deprive him of authority later; it is all the *individuals* of a society who approve the establishment of permanent posts of leadership and who give their consent so that bureaucracy governs them more, and supposedly better, each day. To sum up, neo-evolutionism links the political dimension, which takes priority in their proposal, with individual decisions guided by instinct or the will for survival. In this way, it takes us along very familiar paths for modern thought, which were followed particularly by natural law philosophers. The agreement with this tradition is again shown when it is stated that successful individual decisions are those that consent and favour individual leadership, generally male.

If neo-evolutionism was to stop there, it would not go far enough, as its only merit would consist in varnishing old ideas with new words. The old ideas recall the belief in *ius naturale*, a juridical postulate embraced by philosophies that use it to propose individualist and integrating ethics and morals. However, evolutionism is not content with offering just another philosophical point of view, but aspires to construct a *science* of human behaviour; and a science cannot base its method (only) on a conviction or philosophical opinion. Neo-evolutionism understood this, and for that reason resorts to Darwinist biology. However, it should insist on applying the adopted methodology rigorously and it should explore all the paths that are opened when doing so. We should bear in mind that, according to the theory of evolution, it is essential to take into account how intra-species variations occur (mutation) and how inter-species natural selection works (competition). Yet, the human species shows some significant differences. First of all, the place reserved for intra-species mutation, of a stochastic nature, would in our case be occupied by political decision, of a rational nature. Secondly, competition, which is inter-species in the general theory, among human beings also acquires an intra-species dimension when it is shown that this competition takes place between political units, which is the anthropological translation of *population* as understood in biological terminology (certainly a controversial translation, may it be said).

The two differences that we have just mentioned do not exist in the rest of nature. Therefore, we must ask whether despite this, the Darwinian theory of evolution can be a suitable tool for understanding human affairs, or as useful as it has proved to be for animal and plant species. However, even if we sidestep this doubt or grant a vote of confidence with an affirmative answer, it must be admitted next that *variation is the norm* and in consequence, that human societies have generated and generate multiple forms of political relationships, both in the internal aspect and among different social groups. Therefore, to assume that *all* political relationships are based on conformity and consensus towards leadership and/or *only* these have proved to be 'adaptive', as neo-evolutionism claims, is a *pre-judgement* that the basic theory does not support.

This critique can be expressed in a series of questions. If we admit that variation is one of the pillars of the evolution of the species and that, in humans, conformity towards the leader could be an organizational criterion but not necessarily the only one, how do we know which criterion or criteria have prevailed? How can we determine which criteria have shaped civilization and the State, eventually established as the hegemonic forms of political organization? Is the State the most appropriate solution for the species or is it the best one for only part of it?

Neo-evolutionist methodology in anthropology finds difficulties in giving satisfactory answers. One reason for this comes from the bias in certain ethnographic observations. In these cases, the autochthonous leader was promoted to a higher status by the colonial administration, which needed interlocutors and delegates, instead of by a process of local internal generation. In connection with this, the consensus noted around the figure of the leader was above all the result of the *pax* imposed by colonial garrisons and, to a more uncertain extent, of the prestige, charisma, and occasional services in favour of the community. At other times, the result was simply predetermined, by assuming from the start the criterion of male political centrality and the idea of social consensus around the authority or power of the leader. It may happen that a society is classified as egalitarian because the political relationships *between men* appear to take that form, even though the female collective is totally subjugated to them. In this case, the initial pre-judgement has simply hidden over half the population and the relationships maintained with the rest. The paradox arising here would lead to a patriarchal society that exploits and oppresses most of its members being classified as egalitarian.

The above objections take modern ethnographic reality as their scenario. However, the main source of difficulties appears when the allusions are related to the human past, prior to ethnographic recording. As we pointed out in the description and comments on *Ancient Society*, the construction of social evolution typologies was produced from data referring to human groups which were still functioning at the time of ethnographic observation or historiographic narration, which is to say, in the last two or three centuries. Even so, despite the present or sub-present chronology of the empirical sample, the typologies are supposed to cover the entirety of human diversity. In addition, the authors are confident they can follow its diachronic development since its origins, assuming that the simple or slightly institutionalized forms observed at the present time are illustrative of the stages which more complex and stratified societies have already gone through.

The assumption that neo-evolutionist socio-political types configure a summary of human behaviour and, therefore, are able to illustrate mankind's remote past, rests on the conviction that the ethnographic present covers the totality of social variability and the material conditions that determine it. However, anthropology is unable to prove this, as it lacks access to the evidence about the material, natural, and social conditions of past times. This deficiency cannot be made good by appealing to the uniformitarian principle of human psychic unity and by supposing on this basis that modern behaviour is a valid sample for any other time. It is clear that the common biological characteristics of our species propitiate behavioural regularities in and between human groups, but the genetic, physiological, psychic, or cognitive dimensions cannot by themselves explain the space-time polymorphism of social organizations and their mechanisms of change. The reason for this insufficiency lies in the impossibility for common and general aspects to provide a full explanation of specific features. All these dimensions are constant elements of our species, and therefore provide a substrate of abilities found in each individual; they establish the conditions of possibility for any human situation, but they do not determine the exact direction of what might happen. Imagine that if the dynamics of human societies depended directly and wholly on biological constants, then a sub-speciality of Ethology would suffice to approach their study. In that case, it would surely be difficult to discern anything that could be called political evolution. If, instead, we place the emphasis on the material conditions surrounding the existence of human groups, such as climate, relief, or biological abundance and diversity, neither can we complete the argument. We still do not know what the environment was like in the past. And finally, if we grant more importance to subsistence and craft technologies, it has to be admitted that these are means that must have *been produced*. Production is a collective act that cannot be explained simply by combining biological, psychic, or environmental factors, some of which can be identified today, but by referring to *historically* variable social conditions: accumulated work, and forms of the division of labour and cooperation. It is this historical variability of which we cannot be sure whether it is contained within the ethnographic sample, as all of this belongs to a single period: the present.

As we first mentioned in the comments on Morgan's work: the transfer of the situations sketched out by neo-evolutionist typologies to the pre-capitalist past, as occurred with the American anthropologist's succession of 'ethnic periods', creates hypotheses, not clear certainties. The socio-political types are abstractions which remain on the fringes of History. The process of devising them eliminates this, as it places all the empirical cases being studied in a present 'zero' time; once they have been defined, the types do not need time to take on meaning. Hence, to give them a historical dimension is an intellectual operation a posteriori which, strictly speaking, is to propose a possibility, not to establish a truth. However, submitting this possibility to scrutiny lies beyond the boundaries of anthropology since, as we said above, it has no access to the past material conditions it is aiming to reconstruct. The understanding of societies' past should begin with a different field of knowledge and also be devised following a different method other than the comparative one. With it, evolutionism can only invite us to *recognize* past worlds as they have been constructed from snippets of present-day worlds, but it is unable to guarantee the *knowledge* of a real past.

The recent trajectory that has linked the inability of the method and the object of neo-evolutionist anthropology on the one hand and the development of processual archaeology on the other, will occupy our attention in the next chapter. For the moment, we shall dedicate the final lines of the present chapter to certain points that will also be taken up in the next.

Each one of the evolutionary sequences of social types provides a reference scale in order to *classify* societies. This enables us to compare them, as an essential step in the detection of associative recurrences and, in this way, establish generalizations with a causal value. As the forms of political organization are understood as social responses to certain material conditions, the aim is to elucidate whether any factor or set of factors can be identified as appearing repeatedly in one or another stage and which might be assigned an explicatory value. Service and Fried went to greater efforts to produce classificatory sequences than to propose possible causal relationships that might explain the transition from one social type to another. Both agreed on the importance of the implementation of a redistributive economy when outlining the path from egalitarianism towards hierarchical forms and institutionalized leadership. However, their opinions are less unanimous as concerns the rise of civilization and the State. Hence, Service stresses the conscious and open support of the population for the work of the leader and the bureaucracy as the main factor in understanding the transformation of some chiefdoms into ancient civilizations. In contrast, Fried is more ambiguous, and makes allusions to the effects of population growth and the need to apply certain subsistence technologies.

The explanation of the transition to the State from an evolutionist point of view has provoked numerous publications. Since the mid-twentieth century, a large number of models have been proposed, and only to enumerate them and describe them here would fill many pages. Most of them have been drafted by anthropologists or by archaeologists trained in anthropology, and have been applied through regional archaeological research into the formation of the State in different parts of the world. For this reason, we prefer to wait until the next chapter to assess them. Even so, we can note here that they differ in whether the weight of its causes tends to fall on one factor (monocausal models) or if it is spread across a network of interactions that involves several factors of a similar order of importance (multivariate models). Other differences are related to the exact nature of the factors. Some of them highlight demographic growth and its consequences in the form of pressure on resources; others, the effects of technology for the management of water, especially oriented towards agriculture; others, the management of exchanges and the reach and importance of these; others, finally, the importance of inter-community conflicts and war, above all. Despite these distinctions and differences, one principle inherent in nineteenth-century evolutionism and contemporary neo-evolutionism tends to remain invariable: the first leaders, rulers, and elites arose because they were able to offer crucial services to the community. Their function resided in *solving problems* that had put the survival of the population as a whole in danger and therefore, their work was always advantageous, even when the process of their rise is understood as the lesser of two evils. In other words: what happened, happened because it was necessary; the need affected everyone equally: this general need takes as understood a unanimous consensus in the solution that was finally agreed upon.

CONCLUSION

The above critique has attempted to show the theoretical and methodological deficiencies of evolutionism as a way to explain the social evolution that resulted in the formation of the State. However, this does not mean that the research inspired by this approach has been in vain or fruitless.

One of the successes of evolutionism has been managing to find causal relationships that can be put in objective terms through material variables, mainly those included within the field of technology. The search for cause–effect relationships forms part of the cognitive mechanisms of human beings. When we approach the study of human groups it is difficult to attribute most observed aspects of social life to chance. Therefore, the scientific community is divided between those who aim to find the causes ruling social functioning and change, and those who do not deny that causes might exist but are sceptical about the possibilities of ever finding them. The evolutionist approach aligned with the first group at a very important time for the development of social and human sciences. Thanks to this, the evolutionist project of transforming the study of societies into a scientific activity favoured the development of disciplines like anthropology and archaeology.

It is hardy surprising that revealing the causes that led to civilization and the State has captured the attention of evolutionist research for over a century. The experience of having lived within State societies provides the certainty which leaves little room for chance. If we add the fact that State political organization developed in different parts of the world independently from each other, the intuition that universal mechanisms were at work becomes particularly intense. Evolutionism criticized the cultural particularism that sees all human aspects as a rosary of unique configurations, and set off in search of the regularity lying beneath diversity, the trend among the chain of singularities; in brief, it observed similar effects and tried to discover the causes that had given rise to them. From our viewpoint, we must acknowledge the merits of this project. In the above pages, however, we have shown that the search for general causal principles cannot neglect the specificity in the (pre)history of each case, also full of material causes and conditions. To ignore this reality in favour of sweeping generalizations only allows the formulation of extremely lax principles with little cognitive value. Thus, to observe that no State has developed in societies based on hunting and gathering within an extreme ecological niche (such as the desert or arctic conditions) has limited utility. In the same way, to claim that civilizations and the State, described as complex societies, arose from previous uncivilized or pre-State societies, considered simpler, is true, but merely expresses a trend that can be observed at a human scale and is almost a platitude.

Despite all this, evolutionist schemes have exercised an undeniable appeal on other theoretical and methodological approaches. The Marxist tradition is a good example of this. Engels incorporated Morgan's periodization into his work *The Origin of the Family, Private Property and the State*. In the twentieth century, V. G. Childe applied these parameters in his account of the prehistory of the Old World. Later, we find canonical expressions of historical unilinearism in the form of a rigid succession of means of production (Stalin) as well as more open debates on questions of historical periodization in the light of Marxist structuralism in the 1960s and 1970s. This, as we saw in the previous chapter, is all very different from the historical materialism as it was applied by Marx himself.

We cannot conclude the discussion on the proposals of neo-evolutionist anthropology yet. One of the critiques we have made stresses its theoretical and methodological deficiencies when attempting to validate hypotheses about the remote past. In the next chapter we shall deal with the way in which archaeology has modified this state of the question.

NOTES

1. Translator's note. In the Spanish original text 'cualquier tiempo pasado fue mejor', a quotation from the Spanish poet Jorge Manrique, 1440?-79.
2. *Ancient Society*, chapter 1.
3. Such a tripartite sequence, identical in its terminology, had been proposed by several Enlightenment thinkers in the eighteenth century. For a review of the theoretical stages of modern Western thought, see R. Meek (1981).
4. Morgan did not propose his ethnic periods out of nothing, at a conceptual level or even in the terminology. Modern Enlightenment thought in the seventeenth century and above all in the eighteenth century had developed the idea of periods of mankind according to a succession of stages characterized by the strategies employed to obtain food (see C. Lisón, 1975).
5. *Ancient Society*, part I, chapter 1.
6. *Ancient Society*, part III, chapter VI. In this respect, Morgan does not abandon the leading role attributed to property in the process of social development, as the *ius naturale* tradition had maintained since the seventeenth century (for example, see the section about Locke in this volume).
7. *Ancient Society*, part I, chapter I.
8. See *Ancient Society*, part I, chapter III. A presentation and summary of the ethnic periods is given in chapter I.
9. 'The production of iron was the event of events in human experience' (*Ancient Society*, part I, chapter III).
10. 'The use of writing, or its equivalent in hieroglyphics upon stone, affords a fair test of the commencement of civilization. Without literary records neither history nor civilization can properly be said to exist' (*Ancient Society*, part I, chapter III).
11. *Ancient Society*, part II, chapter II.

12. *Ancient Society*, part IV.
13. *Ancient Society*, part IV, chapter II.
14. *Ancient Society*, part I, chapter III (our italics).
15. 'From the Middle Period of barbarism, however, the Aryan and Semitic families seem fairly to represent the central threads of this progress, which in the period of civilization has been gradually assumed by the Aryan family alone' (*Ancient Society*, part I, chapter III).
16. 'It must be regarded as a marvellous fact that a portion of mankind five thousand years ago, less or more, attained to civilization' (*Ancient Society*, part IV, chapter II).
17. *Ancient Society*, part IV, chapter II.
18. 'In studying the condition of tribes and nations in these several ethnic periods we are dealing substantially, with the ancient history and condition of our own remote ancestors' (*Ancient Society*, part I, chapter I).
19. *Ancient Society*, part I, chapter III.
20. In this respect, see V. G. Childe (1951).
21. *Ancient Society*, part I, chapter I.
22. For example, when he points out that 'Flint and stone implements are older than pottery, remains of the former having been found in ancient repositories in numerous instances unaccompanied by the latter' (*Ancient Society*, part I, chapter I).
23. *Ancient Society*, part I, chapter III.
24. See the illustrative reappraisal of this topic in Childe (1951: chapter 2).
25. Published in 1962 by Random House, New York.
26. In this book, Service paid little attention to the definition of the stages situated between the level of chiefdom and modern industrial states (see Service, 1965: 174–7).
27. Published by W. W. Norton & Company, and cited here as *Origins*.
28. *Origins*, 8.
29. ibid.
30. *Origins*, 305–6.
31. *Origins*, 307.
32. Published by Random House, New York (1967), and cited here as *Evolution*.
33. *Evolution*, 27.
34. *Evolution*, 13.
35. *Evolution*, 33.
36. *Evolution*, 109.
37. Fried, 'On the evolution of social stratification and the state'. In *Culture in History: Essays in Honor of Paul Radin*, edited by S. Diamond. Columbia University Press, New York, 1960.
38. *Evolution*, 186.

39. *Evolution*, 229.
40. For a more detailed description of the basic characteristics of the State, see *Evolution*, 235–40.
41. Individuals who would rather die than live are the exception, and the suicide of whole societies is even rarer.

Part II

Archaeology of the State

9

Archaeology and Research on the State

Archaeology has devoted a great deal of time and effort to discovering how and why the first states formed. Although a high degree of consensus has been reached about certain theoretical and methodological aspects, some problems still hinder progress in research or cause it to take controversial courses. Our main aim in writing these lines is to make clear the roots and forms these obstacles take through a critical diagnosis of the dominant research structure at the present time, as well as to suggest certain ways in which they might be overcome.

In the preceding chapter, we have been able to see that reflections on the political phenomenon that is now known as the 'State' have formed part of the history of Western thought since antiquity, and therefore, are far older than the institutionalization of archaeology. For a long time, propitiated by the works of classical philosophers and Christian doctrine, arguments about the essence and functions of the 'Republic', the *'Polis'*, the *'Civitas'*, the 'Government' or the 'Kingdom' have been indissolubly connected to more general reflections on the nature and goals of human societies. Later, beginning with the Enlightenment and above all with the emergence of social sciences in the nineteenth century, the 'State', as a clearly differentiated political institution, and the stage of social and cultural development to which it corresponded, 'civilization' came to be understood as particular manifestations of human diversity, relatively recent in their appearance and still undergoing expansion. The historical nature of the State, that is, its consideration as the result of a series of previous conditions and not consubstantial to human nature, contributed to its study leaving the realm of philosophical speculation. This cleared the way for empirical disciplines to take it as a research subject and in doing so, in turn found an incentive for their own development and consolidation.

The conviction of what we might call the 'historicity of the State', and through this, the need to inquire into the exact circumstances in which this historicity was expressed, provided an invitation for archaeology to take an interest in the recently established intellectual perspectives. In the previous chapter, we showed how the evolutionary schemes proposed by authors like Morgan took a kind of chronological transposition for granted, according to which some modern societies illustrated stages that others had gone through in the past. This premise was the final point in equally deductive reasoning based on another two premises:

1. The evolutionary course always runs from the most simple to the most complex.
2. Technology provides a suitable reference scale to measure the distance between the above extremes and to establish the appropriate intermediate grades.

However, as the product of deductive reasoning, the evolutionary conclusions about the course of human development could not go beyond the field of hypotheses. To verify or reject the succession of stages proposed by anthropology (in Morgan's case, 'Savagery' and 'Barbarism' with their internal sub-divisions and 'Civilization') required a direct empirical inquiry into the societies living on the planet in more remote times. It was precisely there that archaeology entered into play. Only this discipline was capable of diving so deep into the human past as to reach ages out of the range of memory, beyond even that we have been bequeathed in writing.

During over a century of research, archaeology has tried out different strategies to approach the problem of long-term social evolution, until it has outlined a way that is followed by a large part of the profession. In the next few pages we shall explain and comment on its main aspects.

DEFINITION OF THE OBJECT OF STUDY

Which were the first states in mankind, and where were they located? Several accounts in the Bible and in texts of classical antiquity mention the existence in remote times of kingdoms, republics, and empires in Sumer, Egypt, Babylon, Assyria, Israel, Persia, the Aegean shores, and Rome. They refer to political units generally headed by a supreme ruler who became famous for having extended lasting dominion over wide territories and numerous populations. This type of political system was always familiar to medieval and modern Europe. This meant that the old sources stood as compulsory references when philosophical essays and doctrines were being drafted about the nature and origins of government, and also for reflections on the causes of human inequality in the distribution of wealth and power.

Throughout the nineteenth century and in the early twentieth century, the contribution of archaeology grew in importance. In the first place, it took charge of illustrating, with objects and images, the written texts on great civilizations, mainly Rome, Greece, and Egypt, with which bourgeoisie society wished to be associated. This task was given additional touches of adventure and excitement when it discovered the existence of cities and kingdoms, mentioned in the texts but unknown in their details or even their precise geographical locations. The romantic halo and initial prestige of archaeology owes much to occasions such as the discovery of Troy and the palatial centres of Homeric Greece and Minoan Crete, the excavation of Chaldean Ur, the exploration of biblical sites in the Holy Land, or the search for mythical kingdoms such as Tartessos.

Whether it was through these exceptional occasions or archaeological expeditions with better known objectives, the finds that were made went to increase the private collections of patrons belonging to the aristocracy and the bourgeoisie, who used them as elements to show off their aesthetic refinement, financial success, or simply, social distinction. Another important destiny was the collections of the large national museums of colonial and imperialist powers, where they were exhibited and celebrated as signs of national ostentation.

At this time, archaeology still played a subsidiary role with respect to history based on texts. The excavations rediscovered the cities mentioned in ancient written sources, found the luxurious burials of kings, princes, priests, and aristocrats, and revealed the magnificence of the state centres. Yet they also achieved something else of great importance: numerous finds of texts written on clay tablets, papyri, or blocks of stone, written by real people living in the past, and most of which could be deciphered thanks to the work and ingenuity of distinguished philologists. Many of these records were found to be for accountancy and administrative purposes; but some of them listed the genealogies of the rulers of a land, reaching further back in time than the memory of the chroniclers. This acquired great significance for research, as it sketched out a scenario which has remained fully valid until the present time. *Archaeologists, historians, and anthropologists began to assume, tacitly or explicitly, that the first states or civilizations appeared at the precise time and place that certain rulers and their scribes had taken care to record; that is, coinciding with the specified start of the dynastic genealogies or with the appearance of the writing systems in which they were recorded.* Since then, and until today, the cities in southern Mesopotamia and the Egypt of the Pharaohs have held the title of the earliest states in the history of mankind. The appearance of writing on the clay tablets in Level IV of the stratigraphy at Uruk, and the reign of the first Pharaoh in the first Dynasty of unified Egypt, Menes-Narmer, respectively marked the turning points. In chronological terms, these are situated at the end of the 4th millennium BC; that is, a little over 5,000 years ago.

It is therefore no accident that writing has become the basic element to diagnose the existence of a state. On one hand, it is the way in which this was 'confessed'. On the other, it is the empirical element attributed with the transcendence capable of marking a before and an after, an intellectual achievement of the first order, a means for the lasting expression of thought, the beginning of History. This is so much so, that the identification of a codified system of signs, whether or not it can be deciphered nowadays, is enough to qualify the society that used it as a state. In contrast, the few societies without writing that have been admitted into the exclusive club of textual-states have had to prove the presence of the most frequent requirements in these, basically the emblems of ostentation and power associated with the figure of a supreme centralized government.

This analogical and inductive course of action that we have just outlined has shaped a model of state-ness, whose final and basic reference points are, strictly speaking, *only certain states*, but which in practice has come to cover the full semantic field. The wide acceptance of categories like 'pristine states', 'primary states', 'archaic states', 'first civilizations', and 'earliest civilizations' among others, even with the small nuances of meaning of each one, has contributed to internalize these reference points further, so that a yardstick that distinguishes which societies deserve to be classified as states or civilized has been fixed in the depths of the conscience of research. Sumer[1] and Egypt,[2] with their systems of writing and their greater age, are the earliest and provide most of the classification criteria. Based on these, other societies were added to the group: the civilizations of the Indus Valley,[3] Yellow River,[4] Central America,[5] and the Central Andes.[6] All societies either previous or contemporary to the ones mentioned above are automatically placed one step below the State, while the diagnosis of later societies depends on whether they fit the standard derived from the characteristics the members of the founder group hold in common.

We could reach a first conclusion about what has been said so far. Archaeological research has not decided what the threshold of the state was and where to place it through a conceptual process and its own methodology, but has adopted the boundaries of this condition just as it was pronounced by the same ancient states, conveniently translated by philology and glossed since then by historiography. It might be said that research accepted that the object of its interest was established by the 'voice' of the object itself. In this way, archaeology has taken as the first states those which in fact correspond strictly to *the states-who-named-their-rulers-in-writing-on-durable-surfaces*. Indirectly, this reality expresses the situation of under-development, or if you prefer, of dependence that archaeology has suffered and continues to suffer with respect to other social and humanistic sciences. Accordingly, there appears to be no problem in identifying a society as a state if this was set down in writing by the centralized government that ruled it, or if qualified observers, such as historians and ethnographers have certified it. That is to say, everything is clear if anthropology and historiography testify in favour. However, many doubts are posed when this classification is proposed based exclusively on arguments arising from the archaeological record, and reasoning linked with this. It is time that the reasons for this apparent inability were examined in greater depth, paying attention to how archaeology has approached this question, once the standard of the first state has been accepted. We are especially concerned with the mechanism of research and how this obliges us, if we equip ourselves with it.

THE IMPACT OF V. G. CHILDE (1892-1957)

As we pointed out in the previous chapter, at the end of the nineteenth century, evolutionism began to lose credit in favour of historical particularism. Archaeology, which owed so much to the impulse of evolutionism, contributed to its deceleration when it began to provide more and more evidence contradicting the linearity and unidirectionality of human development. The study of cultures, unique mental configurations shaped in the course of particular historical trajectories, began to substitute the search for common material factors underlying human diversity. This statement describes a general trend in academic development, but if we take it on its simplest terms we are in danger of forgetting that in the world of knowledge, complete substitutions and radical theoretical breaks are unusual. New theories never leave behind the whole baggage of previous ideas and the most brilliant approaches have known how to choose prior elements in successful and fertile combinations. Perhaps with this phrase we have summed up what Childe's works have meant for archaeology. Few have known how to harmonize apparently contradictory concepts and methods like he did, and succeed in influencing how his colleagues worked and also, how many generations of readers understood the past.

The theoretical orientation of his work stressed different aspects throughout his life. In general, he was decisively influenced by Marxism, especially by Engel's *The Origin of the Family, Private Property and the State*, although he also accepted contributions from evolutionism and functionalism. He took the category of 'culture' from the idealism of G. Kossinna and German geographical tradition, and applied it to the arranging of the archaeological record. He understood 'archaeological culture' as the material expression of a certain population united by common social traditions, divesting it of the definition of racial connotations that Kossinna attributed to cultures. In addition, this material expression was not the physical product of a given mental make-up, in the style of historical particularism, and instead its *raison d'être* lay in the field of technology (productive force) and, with greater emphasis in his later works, in social relationships of production.

Childe denied the possibility of formulating universal laws for human behaviour, the goal pursued by evolutionism. Instead, he sought the determination of social evolution (whose Morganian terms 'Savagery', 'Barbarism', and 'Civilization' he used repeatedly for classification purposes) in the exact processes in which this always appears, granting priority to economic variables above political forms and beliefs. He explained in one of his best known works how economic revolutions respond to man's position to nature and promote the development of institutions, science, and literature, that is, of civilization in the widest sense of the word.[7]

Like Morgan, but unlike the main current of evolutionism occurring later, Childe accepted diffusion as the means for social transformation. This could take place through the migration of people, conquest, or as an effect of the development of trade and exchange networks. Migration and trade produce profits, signifying progress, mixing, and the multiplication of variables for behaviour. However, in any of these eventualities, the adoption of innovations was not an automatic or natural occurrence, but depended on previous social and economic conditions among the local communities.[8] This also distanced him from historical particularism, even though this research strategy also considered diffusion as the basic agent of cultural change. However, the historicist approach rarely adduced the causal framework which led to the adoption of one or another trait by certain groups at a particular time. Nonetheless, generally speaking, this silence did not come from ignorance or lack of interest in the need to give explanations about cultural change. Simply, the explanation was taken for granted and this was possible by an idealistic kind of evaluative scale: 'high' cultures exported innovations and the remaining cultures adopted them, In other words, some cultures are more ingenious and superior to others and, for this reason, they are 'melting pots' irradiating influence. In contrast, for Childe, the core of historical explanation does not lie in the arbitrariness inherent in a value judgement. He does not doubt that material determination takes primacy over ideas and that it is based on the economy, largely understood as technological development.

We should now concentrate on his contributions to the problem of the formation of the State. Childe was the author of some of the most brilliant summaries of the prehistory of the Old World, in which he combined an encyclopaedic knowledge of archaeological discoveries with a materialist interpretation of the studied trajectories. He maintained a progressive conception of History, according to which human societies accumulate and transmit experiences from one generation to another, which enables technological improvements to be adopted to satisfy the basic needs of food and shelter. This has resulted, through time, in a growing ability of adaptation and mastery over nature.

However, this progressive and accumulative development is marked out by qualitative changes of great transcendence, which are worthy of the name of 'revolutions'. Childe coined the famous expression 'urban revolution' to allude to the rise of the State and civilization. Two aspects were stressed with it. On one hand, the word 'revolution' underlined the reach and transcendence of the organizational changes that came with the appearance of the first states. On the other, the phrase made clear the importance of living in cities for this process, a landmark of extraordinary significance, taking into account its role in human life until the present time.

The Urban Revolution had actors with names and surnames. Childe's merit consisted in going beyond the boundaries of the individual cultures that populate the archaeological landscape and divest it of evolutionary straightjackets, and provide a historical explanation of the phenomenon in the regions where it took place and the exact societies who participated in it, as well as noting the repercussions on other human groups whose trajectory was for ever marked by this event. The topic was first dealt with, fully and systematically, in *The Most Ancient East* (1928), where he analysed the appearance of the Urban Revolution in Egypt, Mesopotamia, and the Indus Valley. However, it was in *Man Makes Himself* (1936) and in *What Happened in History* (1942)[9] where Childe expounded most clearly and completely on his view of the origins of civilization in the Old World. Let us recall its most significant aspects.

The Urban Revolution could not have happened without the background provided by the other great revolution, called the 'Neolithic Revolution', which took place when human beings ceased being mere 'parasites' on nature and began producing their food artificially with agriculture and animal husbandry. The earliest Neolithic manifestations appeared in the Near East, first in Palestine and soon afterwards in the whole arch going from lower Egypt to northwest Iran, the region known as the 'Fertile Crescent'. The Neolithic, which Childe considered equivalent to the evolutionist stage of 'Barbarism', led to sedentary societies living in villages and towns, where the inhabitants maintained a high level of self-sufficiency.

However, despite the progress that had been made, this form of life had to tackle two serious restrictions. The first was caused by the limitations of the available resources to feed a growing population. As long as there were lands to be cultivated and unoccupied areas for grazing, the population could spread without problems. But when these started to become scarcer, the tensions between the local groups could easily end in territorial conflicts. The second limitation came from one of the main traits of Neolithic communities: their ability to be self-sufficient. This meant that quite small food reserves were stockpiled, so that any setback in the farming harvests could be the cause of severe penury and even death by starvation. Thus, it might be said that the strength of these communities, their self-sufficiency, was also the source of their fragility.

Both limitations began to be overcome by the Copper Age populations in the Near East. One of the keys was the invention and use of metal implements, which were better than those made from stone or bones as they allowed an increase in productivity in the economic sectors where they were used. Their advantages were evident, but the complexity of the process of metallurgical production made compulsory the creation of the figure of specialists who worked full-time in this activity, and therefore took no direct part in food production. In this way, if the community wanted to use metal tools, it had to take charge of the subsistence needs of the people specialized in metallurgy. They must, in Childe's words, produce a food *surplus* which, distributed by bartering or trade, could be used to maintain the metallurgical specialists. In doing this, they took the first, decisive step in destroying and overcoming Neolithic self-sufficiency.

New inventions, like the plough, contributed to an increase in agricultural productivity, which further helped the production of food surpluses. Other innovations, like the wheel, favoured the spread of exchanges, which encouraged the creation of new specialists manufacturing an ever-increasingly diverse range of goods.

Not far from the Fertile Crescent, on the flood plains of lower Mesopotamia, the optimal conditions soon arose with which to exceed the Neolithic framework and develop forms of social organization that were qualitatively different. In reality, the surrounding aridity and the lack or scarcity of basic raw materials, like stone, wood, and metals, imposed very severe restrictions. Yet, the potential of irrigated farming land for obtaining surpluses was enormous. The communities worked together in order to tackle the large investment in labour needed to build and maintain the hydraulic infrastructures. From that moment, dykes, channels, and irrigation ditches enabled the huge but irregular flow of the Tigris and the Euphrates to convert an inhospitable desert into a garden. The decisive step forward had been taken to leave behind local self-sufficiency and inaugurate a new era characterized by a centralized economic organization. Thanks to the planning in food production and distribution, and the excellent conditions for communications and transport, the food surpluses made it possible to obtain the required raw materials through long-distance exchange, and also to maintain a growing number of craftsmen specialized in manufacturing goods with them.

The social authorities who planned the economy and administered the surplus were a class of priests associated with the institution of the temple. The place which gathered together the temple itself and the priests ascribed to its service, the workshops of the specialist craftsmen, and also a variable mass of people working in other professions, from agriculture to trade, was a completely new kind of settlement: the city had been born. Its earliest examples have reached us in the form of sites like Eridu and Uruk where, as well as the characteristic architectural remains of the new urban reality, the oldest evidence of written records has been found. With them, the temple administrators controlled the accountancy of numerous economic transactions.

Until that time, the surpluses had been the fruit of a huge collective effort which was also to the collective benefit by means of the temple management. However, in Childe's opinion, before 2500 BC, the priests and leading civil servants began to appropriate the surplus through extortion, concentrating it in only a few hands and using it for their own benefit. At this time, the society was already divided into conflicting classes.[10] Quoting Engel's phrases, but without referring to him explicitly as the sources, Childe states that in order to 'restrain' both the class struggle and the invasions of 'starving' barbarian tribes, a new institution was needed: the State. The germ of the State would be found in the so-called 'urban ruler' or 'king'. The oldest examples can be identified in the Uruk and Jemdet Nasr phases, although at that time the hegemony of the temple still relegated the figure of king to second place. They later fully assumed the ruling function in which the State was 'a power, apparently standing above society, but necessary to moderate the conflict of classes and keep it within the bounds of order'.[11]

Despite accepting the Marxist definition of the State, Childe had no doubts about assessing general aspects of the state positively in an attitude that seems more in agreement with evolutionist progressism. The quotation given above comes from a paragraph in which he relates how Urukagina, ruler of the Sumerian city of Lagash, intervenes in a decree to check the exaction of the rich. Thus, on occasions like these Childe tends to consider the State as a mediatory institution playing its role from a position of neutrality, a claim that is totally foreign to the ideas of Marx and Engels. In other cases, his opinion even becomes more favourable: 'State organization, based on residence instead of kinship, abolished blood-feuds between clans, mitigated the violence of other internal conflicts, and probably reduced the frequency of wars'.[12] In short, his treatment of the State is a somewhat eclectic synthesis between functionalism, evolutionism, and Marxism.

Towards the end of his life, Childe published a brief informative article summarizing the most significant traits for the definition of the Urban Revolution.[13] These traits were based on the archaeological evidence found in Egypt, Mesopotamia, the Indus Valley, and the Mayan area. The question was not focused from a different viewpoint to that in earlier works, but the precise and synthesized nature of this publication resulted in it holding considerable influence on research into the origins of the State. It is therefore worth pausing to present the ten diagnostic traits of the Urban Revolution:

1. Urbanism. The first cities were larger settlements (figures of between 7,000 and 20,000 inhabitants have been suggested) with larger population densities than any previous town.

2. The composition and function of the population living in the first cities was also quite new. To be exact, we find groups working on different tasks within a wide division of labour, which could be maintained thanks to the food surplus. The collectives not linked with food production did *not* obtain their food through the direct exchange of their products with the peasant population living in the city and/or dependent villages.

3. The food surplus was concentrated under the form of a tax or tithe given to an imaginary deity or a deified king. Without this concentration, the rural economy would have been unable to

obtain the 'effective capital' needed to take on greater economic challenges.

4. Construction of monumental public buildings, like temples, palaces, and tombs. The warehouses where the social surplus was stored are often found near these large buildings.
5. Formation of a ruling class made up of priests, civil and military leaders, and civil servants. This class was totally separate from manual labour and kept a substantial part of the accumulated surplus. According to Childe, the ruling class brought substantial benefits through aspects like planning and organization.
6. Invention of recording systems (writing, numerical notation), necessary to carry out the duties of centralized administration.
7. One of the corollaries of the invention of registry systems and notation was the development of exact and predictive sciences (arithmetic, geometry, and astronomy). Among the most outstanding achievements is the design of a calendar with which to plan the work in the agricultural cycle.
8. Art as an activity carried out by specialists also maintained thanks to the social surplus. Sculptors, painters, and engravers depicted people and objects in sophisticated and distinctive styles.
9. Regular long-distance trade, aimed at obtaining the raw materials needed for industry and worship. Part of the previously stockpiled social surplus was used to pay for these imports. Some of the materials acquired through exchange, like metal and obsidian, were vital for the first cities to a greater extent than they had ever been before.
10. The State: an organization based on residential adscription rather than to family relationships. The State provided the specialized craftsmen security, as well as the raw materials with which they worked. However, both craftsmen and peasants were relegated to the lower classes. In part, Childe points out that the whole citizenship, from the rulers to the peasants, carried out mutually complementary functions. This interdependence is a form of 'organic solidarity' according to Émile Durkheim's classic distinction. However, the concentration of the surplus provoked an economic conflict between a minority dominant class which controlled this surplus and the majority of

the population whose lives were reduced to the level of mere subsistence, on the sidelines of the 'spiritual benefits of civilization'. In the face of this conflict, ideological mechanisms supported by the force of the State were required to maintain social solidarity.

This list of ten points[14] includes characteristics of different kinds. Some possess a direct empirical reference point, such as monumental buildings (point 4) or writing (point 6). However, others involve a combination of kinds of evidence, such as job specialization (point 2), the ruling class (point 5) or 'state organization' (point 10). Later researchers, like R. Adams[15] and C. Redman,[16] noticed this and re-ordered the list by distinguishing between five 'primary characteristics', related with organizational aspects, and another five 'secondary characteristics', alluding to certain material elements that prove the existence of some of the primary characteristics. We shall examine the consequences of this sub-division below, in the context of the research carried out within processual archaeology. However, for our immediate purposes it will suffice to recall that Childe did not draw up a list with ten criteria of equal importance and weight. He was working with a necessarily small sample, consisting of the four earliest and only civilizations considered by mid-twentieth-century archaeology to have arisen independently, and of which sufficient information was available. His main intention was to detect common traits linked structurally in the four empirical cases being studied. However, far from presenting a list of discrete equivalent characteristics, the structure articulating them is hierarchical and is built on two fundamental ideas:

1. Centralized concentration and management of surpluses produced socially. The collective labour of peasant communities is the foundation of all.

2. Division of labour, including full-time specialization, between those who produce and those who manage the accumulated social surplus.

This is the conceptual core defining the Urban Revolution. In itself, the city is no more than the spatial and material expression of this economic and social situation, while literacy, monumental public works, the calendar, long-distance trade, etc. are elements functionally related with the core ideas that we have just listed and which are *expressly and precisely linked* with the four civilizations Childe was bearing in mind. Childe himself admitted that even these similarities could only be established at a markedly abstract level[17] and although they provided the 'cultural and material capital' on which later urban revolutions were constructed, these were not mere replicas of those first civilizations.

To summarize, we suggest that Childe's intention was not to offer a closed list of traits that all urban revolutions must fulfil canonically in order to be recognized as such. Although the format of his presentation in the *Town Planning Review* article might lead one to believe that such an intention existed, a more careful examination shows that instead he drew up a structural definition of the Urban Revolution by combining components of Marxist and evolutionist tradition, to which he added certain empirical elements which could be seen in close relationship with the phenomenon *in the four cases being studied*. Childe stressed the decisive importance of the socio-economic base, centred on the concentration of agricultural surpluses and on their centralized management within the framework of a profound and determinant division of labour. The social classes had their origin in this division, and the State was the organization backing the new social situation. This scheme fits within the realm of historical materialism although, just as in the rest of his work, Childe shows certain ambiguity here. Thus, whereas in some parts he describes a scenario characterized by class struggle, at other times he seems to advocate a contractualist or functionalist view of society, in which the dominant class would provide 'organizational benefits' to life in community and would even take on duties that many people would find harder than any physical labour.[18]

Childe combined Marxism, functionalism, and evolutionism in a synthesis which succeeded in making the archaeological view of prehistory enter within the narration of the universal history of mankind. From evolutionism he took the notion of technological progress and also an appropriate terminology for marking its periodization ('Savagery', 'Barbarism', 'Civilization'). However, he avoided using the characteristic evolutionist comparative method, as this led to any explanation being situated outside the history precisely testified to by the remains under study. The comparisons Childe makes are always among results obtained by a procedure that is not comparative. We have seen an example of this in the definition of 'Urban Revolution': Only after completing archaeological research on a series of certain trajectories separately was he in a position to make comparisons in order to summarize common factors.

Childe recognized the power of archaeological remains, in their exact and particular expression, to denote a reality that had to be considered in itself, and avoided subsuming this immediately in a standardizing abstraction of the 'ethnic period' type. For this reason he emphasized the definition of archaeological cultures, as they indicated real and unrepeatable historical trajectories. However, he was not content with listing the material evidence of the cultures, in the style of the archive logic of sceptical empiricism. Instead, the archaeological materials provided information about something else apart from themselves: social relationships. From functionalism he took the vision of society as an interrelated and balanced whole; a balance that could only be broken by an external factor. From Marxism, thus producing the ambiguities or contradictions that we have noted, he took the idea that this balance is always elusive and the unceasing dialectic between the development of productive forces and the state of the relationships of production is the driving force of History/Histories.

PROCESSUAL ARCHAEOLOGY AND RESEARCH ON THE FORMATION OF THE STATE

After Childe's death, the archaeology practised in capitalist countries set up his figure as a compulsory reference point for understanding the prehistory of the Near East and Europe. Explanatory proposals for certain phenomena such as the Neolithic and Urban Revolutions, or perspectives for understanding the overall prehistory of extensive regions (such as those currently known as 'world-systems') are among his ideas most widely accepted and followed. However, in general, the Marxist components in Childe's works tend to be obviated and instead, greater emphasis is placed on evolutionist materialism and the importance given to the notion of 'archaeological culture' as a methodological tool for organizing finds.

During the second half of the twentieth century, research on the origins of civilization and the State underwent acceleration which, over the years, has shown no signs of slowing down. It is still a classic nowadays, a topic which always arouses interest. There are several reasons to explain this. In the 'First World', the so-called 'First Civilizations' are usually considered lost worlds, but by no means foreign ones. That is to say, the first cities became buried millennia ago, but a part of them, whether in the realms of technology, law, religion, or art, lives on in the so-called Western civilization. In agreement with the progressive view of universal history, according to which we progress thanks to the knowledge accumulated by past generations, we preserve the legacy of the earliest Urban Revolutions and, in fact, our present existence would have been impossible without it. The most significant aspects of this inheritance are called 'landmarks' and 'achievements' of mankind; they are given a positive connotation and are praised, with what is often a blatant and alarming lack of self-criticism. The appeal of this feeling of 'so far way, and yet so near' is fostered by the tourist, cinematographic, and even fashion industries, who find a fruitful source of publicity and inspiration in the aesthetics of ancient civilizations.

With the complicity of the general public, archaeology has gone to greater depths in the study of civilizations. Historical–cultural archaeologies have included them within a specific class of cultures, the 'largest and wealthiest'.[19] However, this does not mean they lose their specificity, as each civilization is considered to be unique in that it was inspired by a singular and unrepeatable coming together of ideas, a structure whose core existed prior to the rise of the civilization because it formed part of the 'spirit' or 'genius' of the founding population. Where similarities between civilizations exist, they are usually explained by resorting to diffusion phenomena (sometimes with synonyms like 'influence' and 'cultural loan') which, however, does not lessen the original nature of each one. Going beyond the economic aspects which contributed to their definitions and, of course, leaving behind any materialist determinant to explain their appearance, civilizations above all express a new mental order, a qualitative leap forward in the human conception of living in community. S. Piggott described how the term civilization is used to refer to a society that has come up with a solution to the problem of living in a permanent and relatively large community, on a higher level of technological and social development than that of bands of hunters, families of farmers, independent villages, or tribes of pastoralists. Civilization is artificial, made by mankind; it is the result of manufacturing more and more complex instruments *in response to the increasingly wide concepts of life in community that developed in human minds.*[20]

Historical–cultural archaeologies recognize the convenience of making interpretations about the past, but usually neglect the task of defining precise criteria in order to do this, and distrust the ways proposed by other theoretical and methodological positions as they are 'speculative'. The only hope of linking the present and the past interpretatively is based on humanist arguments, according to which human beings are 'deep down' the same, basically, in how their minds work, which allows us to understand the experiences of other people. In the case of civilizations, this task is more feasible as we share certain significant components of a common history. Aesthetic aspects, through the artistic depictions in which they are expressed, represent one of the best ways in which spiritual sensibilities of the past and present can find understanding. Hence the proximity between classical archaeology (precisely the field responsible for the study of ancient civilizations) and Art History, so clearly shown in the structure of university courses still taught in many countries today. Historical–cultural archaeology of civilizations has led to an aesthetic humanism, vindicating values of tolerance from a liberal point of view: understand, admire, and preserve the diversity of human achievements at all times and in all places. Its best known and most widely accepted expression is currently the discourse of UNESCO and the International Cultural Forums, which celebrate and watch over so-called world 'heritage' as the result of the spirit of the people who were able to produce it.

In the 1960s processual archaeology, also known as 'New Archaeology', reacted against this way of approaching studies. It rejected empathetic humanism as a perspective and method to understand past objects and, instead, it attempted to re-found archaeology as a scientific project which was deeply rooted in the philosophy of enlightened modernity. Thus, it established that:

1. Ontology: societies are not human groups formed by the chance of historical trajectories or by the obstinate will of its members. They are integrated and self-regulating systems, whose ways of working display inter-cultural regularities. Beyond the multiple forms in which they manifest themselves, human societies respond to material determinants, above all of technological, environmental, and demographic kinds.

2. Epistemology: the objective knowledge of societies through their material remains is possible. It is the responsibility of the scientist to formulate the appropriate hypotheses and the empirical inquiries that will support them or will justify their rejection. Archaeology should aspire to the status of a scientific discipline and, therefore, abandon the field of humanist empathy.

3. Politics: the knowledge of social functioning and process is useful to understand our own present and to guide our future. From this viewpoint, it is not surprising that the formation of the first civilizations has been one of the favourite topics for processual archaeology, since, in this way, it attempts to research our own origins, how our society works, and what its future might be.

An understanding of variation and change in human societies is closely linked with the concept of social ontology that we have just mentioned. In this respect, the most decisive influences come from evolutionism and functionalism. According to these, the ultimate goal of human behaviour is to achieve the adaptation of the group to a given environment, or in less ecological and more functional terms, the balance or homeostasis between the sub-systems making up the social system. In this way, the establishment of relationships of social and political inequality should be understood as a response aimed at achieving the survival of the individuals, and consequently, of the whole social group. The terms of the alternative that society must choose between are clear: either crisis and extinction, or the emergence of rank and stratified systems. Society, faced inescapably with the requirement to satisfy its basic needs for subsistence,[21] is assumed to create a series of directive or managing posts (leaders) for the common good, to grant them a special status and to mark it with distinctive material attributes, the so-called 'prestigious objects'. In short, the elites owe their *raison d'être* to their provision of organizational services and benefits that redound to the satisfaction of social needs.

When it is said that 'society' generates these posts, it is implied that society as a whole approves their creation. However, who makes up that whole? Who is able to decide and give their consent? In the final analysis, it is acknowledged that the individual or the household are the rational authorities of decision, are free and sovereign in their acts (the first of which, in fact, consisted of agreeing to the regulations that govern society).[22] In clear continuity with liberal sociology and its philosophical precedents (Hobbes and Locke), it is said that all individuals are autonomous organisms who pursue the fulfilment of their needs and wishes. In order to achieve this, they use the faculties, skills, and resources at their reach, in competition with other individuals, in order to maximize their goals, whether they are economic (*Homo oeconomicus*), political (*Homo politicus*), or any other which is supposed to be typical of our species. In this way, processualism identifies the satisfaction of individual or private wishes and interests with the common good, taking as granted that the goal is correct (the survival of the society through satisfactory adaptation) and that the means to achieve it can be no other than what they are (individuals in competition seeking their own particular objectives).

The first leaders who occupied the position of management and decision satisfied a series of requirements: they were males and, according to what is generally said, they were the most gifted in terms of their intelligence, skill, or physical strength. This conferred them with social and political prestige, which was expressed in the corresponding material ways. Taking ideas directly from anthropological neo-evolutionism, it is claimed that in the simplest societies the Big Man personified all these characteristics and was the dynamic element transforming the original egalitarianism and enabling an incipient hierarchical order. In contrast, in other more evolved social forms, where personal positions of rank are handed down hereditarily, no competition is produced among all the members of the society. The concepts of 'representation' and 'legitimacy', according to which an individual assumes the collective aspirations delegated in his person, then come into play. He becomes the revitalizing element of his group and those that come into contact with it thanks to the same mechanism that existed in the original inequality; the dynamics of 'competition–interaction', now acting among elites either through mechanisms of emulation (known as *peer policy interaction* and the economies of 'prestigious goods') and/or through conflict, war, and possible conquest. The malleability of 'sociology of competition' allows it to be applied both in an explanatory ecological-adaptationist framework and the less functionalist one involving the maximization of individual or group wishes and needs as the natural tendency of mankind.

In relation to the arguments that we shall put forward below, we should bear in mind that the sociological–anthropological perspective adopted by processual archaeology believes that individual merits and benefits are conditions for the common good and that this is the crux of the origins of social inequality. Thus, certain outstanding individuals perform useful roles and functions in connection with social survival. In consequence, they may come to hold hierarchical posts of *rank*, which are institutionalized to a greater or lesser extent. These involve collective approval (*prestige*) and are symbolized through the display of certain items of restricted use (*prestigious goods*).

Complexity

Let us examine in greater depth how processual research established the precise mechanisms through which social inequality became thoroughly accepted as natural. In other words, let us see how the exact causes that favoured the appearance and development of this inequality, and the socio-political forms in which it was expressed, were defined. As we shall now verify, neo-evolutionist anthropology played a decisive role in all of this.

It is clear that societies change and that their diversity is apparently enormous. However, are these multiple forms due to chance in social events, to the random diffusion of traits, or to unyielding cultural idiosyncrasy? We have already explained that the answer is now negative. Defenders of scientific archaeology share the belief that societies function and change in response to causal imperatives that archaeology is capable of understanding and formulating in general principles or, at least, of representing in the form of models that can be compared with the empirical evidence. In any case, from this viewpoint, it is assumed that the evolution of mankind has been governed by determining factors and has occurred in an ordered fashion, following a gradual scale of increasing political hierarchy and economic intensification.

The study of *graded process* was tackled from the notion of *social complexity*. This has a double meaning, as it designates both a development trajectory in formal terms and, at the same time, the most advanced stages of the trajectory. In this way, it may be said that one society is more complex than another and, equally, a given society may be classified as 'complex' if it displays a stratified or state organization. Thus, complexity *describes*, either in relative terms (comparison between amounts: society 'x' *is more complex* than society 'y') or in absolute, qualitative terms (society 'x' *is* a complex society). 'Complexity' is a frequently used notion in evolutionist thought. In recent times, K. Flannery[23] is the person who has surely defined the word most rigorously. In addition, based on the premises of systems theory, he attempted to show how it could be made operative in archaeology.

For Flannery, complexity can be measured according to two processes. The first has been named *segregation*, and refers to the degree of interior differentiation and specialization in the sub-systems making any society. In this respect, the appearance of new institutions or new levels in the hierarchy of political control would correspond to an increase in segregation. The second process is *centralization*, that is, the degree of bonding between the different sub-systems and the higher-order political controls within a society. In this case, the reinforcement of these controls would reflect an increase in the degree of centralization.[24] The development of segregation and centralization beyond a certain threshold would be equivalent to the development leading to the formation of states.

The main mechanisms favouring this development are *promotion* and *linearization*.[25] The former contributes to the process of segregation, as it generates new higher-order institutions. An example of this could be the emergence of the stable post of 'chief' out of a situation in which the leadership was held in a more informal or unstable way. In contrast, linearization is very common in the process of centralization, when powers and functions that until then had been the responsibility of lower-level authorities are taken over. Linearization acts when, for example, according to Flannery, a state agency begins to govern irrigation mechanisms which had previously been managed by organizations in the local communities.

Flannery's proposal was an attempt to define and formalize the notion of complexity with greater precision. His study focuses on explaining how it works and how it is displayed, and therefore we must acknowledge his merit in having reduced potential sources of ambiguities and misunderstandings. However, it is not enough to draw up the movement of what is complex, but also the use of 'complex' as an adjective should be defined; that is, which elements a society should possess in order to be described as 'complex' and, above all, how these can be identified archaeologically. The first problem is related tothe establishment of category thresholds (what it is and what it is not) and, in this way, we come into full contact with the typologies of socio-political evolution.

The designation of 'complex society' is reserved for those societies that can be classified in the stages of chiefdom, stratified, and civilization or State. Below that line we find 'simple' societies, separated from the complex ones by what are supposed to be conclusive differences. The most outstanding of these refer to the institutional dimension of social life, as both the emergence of the institutions themselves and their proliferation are the clearest indicators of the development of complexity: the society is divided into parts, which are increasingly more numerous, more consolidated, and better related amongst each other both horizontally and, above all, vertically or hierarchically. Chiefdoms and states are characterized by the institutionalization of political leadership, but also by an increasingly wide range of specialized activities. LaMotta and Schiffer have proposed one of the fullest definitions of this basic institutional dimension in order to define the threshold of complexity. For them, any complex society is the product of sectors and institutions that have succeeded in developing in a differential way. An institution is a wide behavioural component with a bureaucratic, or hierarchical, structure. To be more exact, an institution is a field of related activities, organized at a supra-domestic level, in any part of society, such as the government, churches, the army, universities, trade unions, and professional sports. Institutions, which can be assimilated to specialized behavioural systems, devote places and structures to their activities, and regulate the flow of people, objects, energy, and information inside these places and between different places. The functioning of an institution depends on the connections that the system establishes, through factors linking them with other external activities and institutions.[26]

The importance of the institutionalization of social relationships is connected with the loss of influence of kinship relationships as the backbone of social life. For this reason, complex societies are defined, as well as by their level of institutionalization and internal functional relationship between institutions, by how they stand on a territorial, residential, and truly political base.[27]

Evolution, typologies, and surveys

Up to this point, processual archaeology had prioritized an aspect of social life (politics), had defined the order of its variability (complexity understood as a degree of institutionalization), and had modelled its formal development (segregation and centralization). However, to take as its subject the *emergence of civilization* required the adoption of an overall vision of the human societies in which this emergence was the result of a diachronic process governed by objectifiable causes. To explain this process in its full extent, archaeology resorted to neo-evolutionist anthropology. Authors like Service, Fried, and Sahlins proposed new evolutionary schemes following in the wake of Morgan's 'ethnic periods' (see the previous chapter) and the much more recent approach of Steward's 'levels of socio-cultural complexity'. The new processual archaeology has made wide use of these typologies of social evolution. In this way, the sequence formed by bands, tribes, chiefdoms, and states (proposed by Service in 1962) or egalitarian, rank, stratified, and state societies (according to the scheme developed by Fried in 1967) formed the basic reference points with which they worked. It is worth recalling briefly the procedure that was followed to produce these typological sequences.

First of all, the reference criterion was fixed: in human societies the level of institutionalization of leadership, measured in terms of the stability and centrality of political relationships, is a top priority. In addition, it is to be expected that this level of institutionalization will vary significantly. With these guidelines at hand, the next step was to organize the empirical material provided by a large number of groups studied historically or ethnographically all over the world. As, in fact, institutional variability is high, the result of the ordering took the form of a grading of classifications. This starts with ephemeral and situational posts of command where institutionalization is minimal. It continues with societies where political responsibilities appear timidly at first and gain in strength until they become hereditary. Finally, the grading reaches the centralized and rigidly institutionalized forms corresponding to civilized societies. Once the initial intercultural sample had been classified, the definition of each of the stages was supplemented by the economic, demographic, kinship, and ideological aspects associated *most frequently* with the classified societies according to the political reference criteria. Thus it may be said, for example, that egalitarian societies *usually* obtain their subsistence from hunting and gathering or at the most from simple forms of agriculture; or that civilized societies *normally* use systems of writing or build public buildings on a monumental scale. Consequently, the procedure followed in the definition of each stage converts them into ideal types, the synthesis of common factors observed in certain human activities and, at the same time, in geographically and temporally distant groups. All together, the sequence of stages provided a scale with which social and cultural complexity could be measured, from its simplest forms to the most complex.

The contributions of processual archaeology to the redefinition of the evolutionary schemes were not significant initially, even though the American scholars who promoted them had received solid anthropological training. Only a few authors, such as Flannery himself[28] and, some years later, Johnson and Earle[29], introduced variations that did not question in depth the initial neo-evolutionist proposals or the premises on which these were based. In any case, the main point of debate and controversy has consisted in determining how to make these schemes operative. Archaeology does not dig up institutions or political units, whether you call them chiefdoms or states. To affirm the existence in the past of any of these organizations requires the application of a research method that necessarily takes material remains into consideration. Processual archaeology has based its research on the identification in the empirical record of those diagnostic elements that belong to each stage in social evolution. In order to fulfil the requirements of correspondence, recent archaeology favoured a wide field of research based on specific examples or aspects of the empirical record, such as funerary deposits, population organization, forms of food production, or the distribution of objects as a reflection of institutionalized modes of the exchange of goods. In turn, this has resulted in an increasing use of auxiliary techniques in archaeology, from geology to different branches of chemistry. All these initiatives explain in part the proliferation of specialities into which the professional and intellectual field of our science has been divided (archaeology of death, spatial archaeology, economic, or environmental archaeology, etc.).

In a few words, we might state that processual research is based on a procedure of *observation and testing* in order to develop classifications. Thus, a certain group of material remains, analogous or comparable with those of societies that the archaeological-philological-historiographical-anthropological tradition has considered civilizations or states (see the exposition at the start of this chapter) would endorse the identification of a new civilization or State. It would then be attributed a socio-political functioning analogous to the standard that anthropology and historiography had previously defined. This second step is usually called 'explanation' although, to be strict, it is a metaphorical interpretation: if the reference civilizations are expressed in a series of characteristic traits which denote a certain level of organizational complexity, any new similar combination of traits will be a symptom of a comparable complexity.

In its insistence on observation and testing in reference to complex societies, processual archaeology went back to Childe's article in *Town Planning Review*, interpreting the list given there as a series of traits that any archaeological record aspiring to denote a civilization ought to demonstrate. As we have already emphasized, the basic list taken from Childe is an important reference point, which was completed for the stages before civilization with elements derived from anthropological evolutionary schemes (Service, Fried, and Sahlins) and later adapted and enlarged thanks to archaeological research.[30]

However, the procedure of observation and testing soon encountered difficulties in its application to specific archaeological cases. The internal problems of this method arose in the classification of societies when the archaeological remains do not fully match the stipulated criteria for one or other level of evolutionary complexity, to be precise between chiefdoms and civilizations or states. One series of difficulties concerned the archaeological method itself. Thus, for example, controversies have arisen over such questions as: Based on which elements and in what amounts can we start to talk about centralized storage? How can we assess the level of development of craftsman specialization? Which elements denote unmistakeably the urban status of a settlement? Which indicators should support the proposal of a settlement pattern structured on more than three levels and which can be classed as 'hierarchic'?

Other difficulties, equally as or even more decisive than those above, come from formal considerations or about the criteria. Is it necessary to prove the existence of *all*, or is it enough with *nearly all* the diagnostic traits set down for each socio-political type? How many and which would be necessary and sufficient, taking into account that they are not all equally important?[31] Where can we situate the societies with some traits corresponding to chiefdoms and others to civilizations? And between chiefdoms and other 'simple' forms? In other words, where and how can we draw the threshold between simple and complex societies, and among the latter, between chiefdoms and civilizations? As may be guessed, research on chiefdoms has been the cause of many of the controversies. Perhaps their condition as a 'bridge' category between egalitarian societies and stratified societies and states has been a major cause for the wide use made of them in prehistoric studies in the Old and New Worlds. To distinguish only between egalitarian and state societies would be an excessively simplistic polarization which would over-reduce the variability of the political organizations documented ethnographically and archaeologically. This is the large area occupied by chiefdoms. Nevertheless, their extended use has threatened to make them a kind of catch-all item, including all those societies that are not worthy of entering in the select group of the first states, but which display hierarchical traits that would inhibit them being considered egalitarian. In conclusion, as the category has been used to cover societies of noticeably heterogeneous compositions, alarm bells have been sounded about its effectiveness.

The crisis of the chiefdom category exemplifies the problems of research excessively focused on classifications. The initial starting point consisted of proposing sub-divisions of the initial category,[32] but it was soon seen that this was no more than a kind of 'leap in the dark', despite the attempts at claiming its usefulness.[33] The solution usually consists of situating the main delimiting criteria rather in the line separating simple and complex societies than inside the latter group. As a result, chiefdom and civilization often appear together within the general level of complex societies. The differences between both would be of degree rather than of nature: the latter would have a larger population, cover a larger territory, a higher level of internal institutionalization and, perhaps, of centralization.

In the early 1990s Renfrew and Bahn[34] compiled the traits applied most often in the archaeological identification of chiefdoms and primitive states. These authors ordered the techniques of archaeological identification according to several research lines, each of which included diverse empirical indicators. It is worth presenting them here in summary form, as they demonstrate a state of the question which in a certain way is still valid today and which has been maintained thanks to its dissemination at university level in successful handbooks, such as the one published by the two British researchers.

1. *Primary centres (capitals), revealing a centralized administration.*
   - Artefacts indicating a centralized organization, above all of economic activity (archives, seals, writing).
   - Buildings associated with central functions of high order (palaces, large ritual buildings).
   - Other indicators, such as fortifications or a mint.
2. *Evidence of a centralized administration outside the primary centre.*
   - Artefacts of administration (characteristic seals of a redistributive system, emblems of a central authority and power).
   - Standardization of weights and measures (indication of centrally administered economic systems).
   - Good road system.
   - Indications of military power (fortifications, garrisons).
3. *Social ranking, reflected in disparities in ownership, access to resources, facilities, and status.*
   - Elite residences ('palaces').
   - Unusual concentration of great wealth (for instance, treasures).
   - Depictions of the elite and other symbolic emblems of authority.
   - Burial monuments produced by unusually high labour input, magnificent grave goods and sometimes accompanied by human sacrifices.
4. *Economic specialization and indication of a centralized structure, bringing increased efficiency of production.*
   - Intensified farming, generally linked to 'labour-intensive techniques' (ploughing) and public works (irrigation canals).
   - Taxation, storage, and redistribution. Existence of permanent storage facilities for food and goods.
   - Full-time craft specialists, identified by the particular technology of each craft.

5. *Relationships between centralized societies.*
- Organized warfare.
- Ritual competition and emulation, in this case reflected in the spread of certain customs and artefacts.

Renfrew and Bahn's summary was put forward at a time when processual research into the origin of civilizations was showing signs of fatigue. However, the need to classify in socio-political terms has remained of fundamental importance at the epistemological level. Proof of this is that, in 1998, some of the most outstanding researchers in the American processual tradition published a list of criteria which, in their opinion, made it possible to distinguish between chiefdoms and ancient states.[35]

1. Change in the hierarchy of the settlements, from three levels (chiefdom) to four (State).
2. Change in the hierarchy of decision-taking, from two levels (chiefdom) to a minimum of three (State).
3. Fundamental change in the ideology of the stratification, according to which the ruler is given a supernatural sacred origin (divine right to rule).
4. Emergence of two endogamous strata, the result of breaking the kinship ties that had previously linked the leaders with their followers.
5. The palace is fixed as the official residence of the ruler.
6. Change from a single centralized leader (a chief) to a government that uses force in a legalized way, at the same time as it denies citizens the use of individual force.
7. Establishment of laws for government and the capability to enforce them.

Processual archaeology, or archaeology rooted in the processual approach, has persistently pursued the demarcation of category boundaries, because this epistemological operation is fundamental to define *what* needs to be explained; that is to say, classification is the means of establishing the object of research. Once it has been defined, research can approach the object in its static and dynamic dimensions; both in the internal function of the first state organizations and in the process leading to their emergence out of simpler organizations. Let us examine more closely how both objectives have been approached.

Empirical regularity and explanation

When it drew up evolutionary typologies, neo-evolutionist anthropology compared societies according to a reference criterion: the level of institutionalization of political relationships. When these had been decided on, the evolutionary stages acted as a guide for the classification, in our case, of archaeological cultures. The next step consisted of explaining the functioning of complex societies as a whole or of any subset which this general category has been divided into ('complex chiefdoms', 'archaic states', 'first civilizations', etc.). This objective requires the identification of inter-cultural *regularities* among the empirical cases included in each of these subsets. The method applied to achieve this made use of *comparison* as its basic tool.

The term *regularity* is used in its most general sense to refer to the recurrence of a certain association of elements documented empirically. *Regularity* is a fundamental category, since being able to prove it actively refutes the role of chance, of unique occurrences and idiosyncrasy in human behaviour, precisely the basic supports of historical–cultural approaches. As it excludes its opposite, singularity, regularity demands an explanation applicable to a generality of cases. With explanation it enters the realm of science, of the possibility of formulating explanatory laws for human behaviour and its evolution, and it abandons the historical–cultural ways that were content with sceptical empiricism or that led to the empathetic celebration of particular cases.

Where there is no agreement is in how to fix the value of the different empirical regularities that are observed; that is to say, to establish a causal hierarchy for the explanation of the functioning of societies and their change. Steward and Adams, to cite two of the best known figures, indicated the importance of the interrelated group of institutions making up the 'core' of any social system, from a classical functionalist position. Adams pointed out that it is much more likely that the changes in these institutions lead to further cultural changes in technology, subsistence, and religion than vice versa.[36] This involves giving priority to aspects connected with social organization, and relegates other cultural manifestations, especially those linked to beliefs and symbolism, to the role of 'random noise'.

In contrast, other researchers, like M. Harris, locate the basis of determination in techno-environmental variables (technology, population, environment). These form the 'infrastructure' on which domestic economy and politics depend (the 'structure'), and finally, the expressions of the ideological 'superstructure'. On this occasion, it is stressed that infrastructural changes possess a much greater likelihood of generating changes in the system than those occurring to the structure, and certainly, than to the superstructure. Nonetheless, the superstructural elements should not be explained away by supposed random or idiosyncratic behaviour but, however inexplicable it might seem, they gain meaning in reference to the techno-economic determinants that govern the behaviour of individuals and groups in all socio-cultural systems. Harris devoted a very successful publication to casting light precisely on several of these 'enigmas', such as the Hindu taboo on sacrificing cows or the Jewish and Muslim prohibition on eating pork.[37]

As far as the research methodology focused on the first states and civilizations is concerned, this has produced various comparative studies which have marked the course of the state of the question. Steward included five examples;[38] Childe, four;[39] Adams, only two;[40] Service, as many as six.[41] In the most ambitious attempt of recent years, Trigger included the largest and most varied list geographically, with seven cases.[42] In general, these initiatives all follow the same script:

1. Selection of a sample of cases.
2. Comparative study undertaken within the fields marked out by different thematic areas like, 'Demography', 'Kinship', 'Administration', 'Food production', Land-ownership', 'Religious cults', etc.
3. Identification of similarities forming the basis for the establishment of regularities and, in parallel, a review of the differences seen.
4. The drafting of conclusions that highlight the significance of the different regularities, and which open the door to the formulation of causal generalizations about certain facets of human behaviour, going beyond the apparent diversity of the phenomena being analysed.

Unanimity has not been reached as regards the results obtained in point 4, although it has been widely recognized that certain regularities observed among societies very distant in time and space cannot have been produced by chance, nor can they be explained by contact and diffusion. Thus, for instance, Steward[43] noted that the foundation of the developments leading to the civilizations included within his study was the practice of irrigated agriculture in arid or semi-arid environments. The American anthropologist suggested this combination of factors prompted the setting up of political controls that led to the formation of a ruling class with a theocratic tinge. Trigger, in contrast, recently argued that the key variables in the first civilizations were not population density or ecological situation, but the growing need to protect agricultural land and other forms of constructions in which large amounts of labour had been invested. Under the threat of rival political units, nomadic pastoralists or outcasts from their own societies, the peasant land-owners opted to accept an authority which, constituted as their government, would protect them.[44]

The reach of the generalizations that have been obtained has been quite unequal and not without its criticism.[45] The dissatisfaction with the results is partly to do with the small number of cases included in the studies, as this circumstance endangers the reliability of any generalization proposal. However, rather than in the quantitative validity of the sample, in our opinion the problem is rooted in its qualitative make-up. The comparison between civilizations in search of regularities involves first of all selecting the set of cases that are going to be subject to comparison. And, precisely, this selection rests on a previous classification that already took into account the presence of a series of common factors when including one society or another within the very category of civilization. Therefore, it is hardly surprising that the structural and organizational similarities are greater than the differences and singularities, because *the proximity between the units being compared was already settled from the start.* The basis of the entire procedure lies in an initial selection that conditions the result to a great extent. To decide that a certain society belongs to the category of civilization (and thus place it in line to be chosen for a comparative study) presupposes that it has satisfactorily passed the empirical test that measures its proximity to the standard model. This reasoning is somewhat circular. Under these selection conditions, it would be paradoxical if the differences were greater than the similarities. Perhaps our argument is understood better in the light of the metaphor F. Nietzsche proposed to illustrate the search for truth within the limits of dominant scientific reason: When someone hides something behind a bush and looks for it again in the same place and finds it there as well, there is not much to praise in such seeking and finding.[46] In short, it is again necessary to recognize the primordial influence of the original designation of the object of study in the planning and development of research. It could be an irony that those old *states-that-put-down-the-names of-their-rulers-in-writing-on-durable-surfaces* in some way continue ruling thousands of years after their collapse.

The second part of the problem is seen when the research increases the number of aspects subject to comparison and also the details this task goes into. In general, this has made it possible to appreciate increasing numbers of differences among the societies, even accepting the general similarities guaranteed by their belonging to this category of 'Civilization' or 'State'. In practice, as this diversity has come to the surface, it has served to postpone the frequent searches for generalizations and, instead, it has favoured the proposal of new sub-divisions in the classifications. In the late 1990s Marcus and Feinman[47] enumerated a long list of kinds of states as a result of this new interest in typology: bureaucratic, despotic, expansionist, inchoate, mature, mercantile, and militarist.[48] This range of new categories is the consequence of the use of highly detailed and minute empirical analysis. In this sense, we might say that the 'magnifying glass' with which societies are being inspected has increased its magnification. However, this keener eyesight appears to be used above all so that the analytical 'scissors' can dissect the initial political category and produce more and more sub-types. In short, research remains profoundly committed to the task of classification, which seems to take the form of a spiral with no easy way out. Thus, the first comparative study was able to establish the general classification categories ('bands', 'chiefdoms', etc.) which would hold the cases contained in the empirical sample. Then, the cases classified in each category are submitted to a new comparative study, as without comparison no regularities can be detected and therefore neither is it possible to propose generalizations. What happens is that this second operation concludes with the definition of sub-types. In view of the proliferation of these sub-divisions and, inversely, the scarcity of reliable inter-cultural explanations, one may wonder whether this research strategy will inevitably lead to a taxonomic exercise with no foreseeable end. It will generate new abstract socio-political forms, derive from these the keys to empirical recognition that can be used to classify new discoveries or 'reappraise' cases already known and thus, prepare the way for 'dynamic' interpretations, as usually occurs, in non-archaeological disciplines (anthropology, historiography, etc.).

In spite of these critical comments, we can learn something from the identification of a certain number of inter-cultural regularities. The old nineteenth-century evolutionism postulated that, under similar material determining factors, there would also be similar human responses. This causal bond, or at least the suspicion that certain correlation exists, remains valid. This provides support to those who believe that the organization of societies is determined by factors that must be elucidated in each case. To sum up, there are reasons for not giving in to relativism and scepticism.

The explanation of change: the reasons for the rise of civilizations

To state that one of the priority aims of processual archaeology was to classify the societies represented in the archaeological record in one or another evolutionary stage is not sufficient. New Archaeology aimed to distinguish itself from traditional scepticism by reaching an understanding of the past society 'behind the artefact'. One of the reasons for the success of neo-evolutionary typologies lay in the fact that they were able to characterize, in social, economic, and political terms, the material remains found at a site or in a region being studied, as well as creating a model for the process, that is, the dynamic cultural system in its passage through different stages of change. Their application to the material remains which, until then had been thought of as silent, static, or merely aesthetic, conferred upon them the suggestive and vivid social images described by ethnography.

Therefore, to classify a European Bronze Age society as a 'chiefdom', to give an example, did not only signify 'filing' it within one of the most beloved typologies in our profession. It meant visualizing a living organism with scenarios and social actors (far more than actresses): chiefs competing among themselves for the favour of their followers, an intensification in production, the appearance of craftsmen, armed conflicts between political units, exchanges and gifts, worship, and public ceremonies... However, research did not stop there. The very name of 'processual archaeology' evokes social change as something needing an explanation, within and between cultural systems. What was the reason for the transition from egalitarian societies to the first complex societies? Why did only a few of them take the leap towards civilization? The neo-evolutionist anthropology of researchers like Fried and Service had not paid enough attention in their respective schemes to explaining the reasons for the transition from one stage to another. Perhaps they had not seen a pressing need to do so, as they were working with an ethnographic record levelled off to a 'zero' time, a present with no history. However, in archaeology, the time dimension is inherent in the observation, something that we see in every strata or level that we identify during an excavation. Hence, the question was unavoidable: what factors caused the appearance of complex societies in which places and in which times? Can any regularities be seen among the cases that are known, apart from the formal peculiarities expressed locally or regionally? What lessons can we learn from them?

Processual archaeology has proposed numerous explanatory models for the development of social complexity and the rise of civilization and the State in different parts of the world. As we have already noted above, the immense majority of the proposals made in the 1960s and 1970s, coinciding with the influence of functionalist thought, are based on the conviction that the appearance of ruling elites and the consolidation of inequality was a response to situations of need and scarcity that signified a threat to the survival of society as a whole. In this respect, the *raison d'être* of institutionalized government was, and still is, the provision of a service aimed at the common good of the group that created it. The elites solved problems by leading, and in this way made possible organizational changes by which a given society was able to deal successfully with the challenges they were posed with. If you listen carefully, you will hear the echoes resounding from Plato's time, and which the intellectual thought legitimizing states has kept going since then.

In their exact structure, the proposed explanatory models usually articulate their arguments around a materialist causal connection that combines technological, demographic, and environmental variables. It is often said that the models may be either monocausal or multivariate, depending on whether they give priority to a single variable as the causal driving force or instead the coincidence of several.

However, it is rare to find pure monocausal models, even less so when they aim to be generalized to all the cases of the emergence of a civilization. Instead, they tend to give the catalysing role to a certain variable and then bring others into play. We have already noted that in processual arguments, social complexity developed as an organizational instrument to cover basic deficiencies that brought on a crisis. Equally, everyone knows that the most decisive deficiency for human life is the lack of food. Therefore, one of the arguments that is most often put forward in order to explain the appearance of institutionalized leadership is precisely the need to ensure the provision of food in situations of population growth or risks due to environmental factors. In short, the tension between mouths to feed and subsistence resources has become the most frequently used explanatory factor.

Starting with the initial imbalance between population and resources, the process set in motion may take different paths according to the particularities of each case. In the first group of models, the need to ensure food, in this case by the direct control of the territory where it is obtained, leads to situations of competition between communities, ending in armed conflict. Under these conditions, the most decisive social activity is war and, in this way, military leadership becomes the most highly valued function. If the subsistence imbalance continues and war is inevitable, military leadership and political leadership become one and the same. In this context of war, the annexation of new territory by conquest favoured the consolidation of an elite. In recent times, the works of R. Carneiro[49] and D. Webster,[50] enlarged upon by M. Harris,[51] are the most often cited examples of this kind of argument. In these, the concepts of 'environmental circumscription' and 'social circumscription' are of fundamental importance. Both describe situations in which population pressure on resources leads to conflicts and in which the division of the group or migration are not feasible solutions. As a consequence, the defeated populations end up integrated, with a subordinate status, in political units that become increasingly hierarchical.

On other occasions, the deficiency that becomes a threat to society comes from the ecological peculiarities of the environment in which they live, supposing that the communities involved practise some form of agriculture. Several variations emerge from this basic idea. In the first of these, the conditions of the environment set a challenge that the societies try to overcome. It is the classic example of groups living on the flood plains of large rivers surrounded by an arid region, as in Mesopotamia, Egypt, and the coastal valleys of Peru. In these situations, the dryness of the climate makes it difficult to obtain regular and sufficient harvests using simple agricultural systems. The solution consisted of investing in a huge amount of social labour to start up complex irrigation systems and plan farming activity, which would permit more prosperous agriculture. If war was the crucial activity in the previous case, its place is taken here by economic management, whether it be to coordinate the building and maintenance of large hydraulic works (dams, canals, irrigation channels, etc.) or to predict the annual floods of the rivers. The explanatory model given by K. Wittfogel in his 'Eastern Despotism'[52] is the most clearly defined version, although in a certain way its main components were already present in Childe and were also emphasized by Steward. Although the paradigmatic cases are located in desert environments, there are other variations of this same model in which the coordinating role of the elites has been required in situations where the challenge to be solved was an excess of water and the subsequent need for drainage, such as in the lowlands of Central America and certain parts of Europe and Asia.

In a second main variation of the imbalance between population and environment, a given territory would have lacked a certain crucial resource for the growth of the economy. These are often raw materials for the manufacture of implements, such as metals and certain types of rocks. Faced with this situation, the society needs to organize itself to establish exchange relationships that may sometimes reach quite distant objectives.[53] Political leadership would then fall upon the people in charge of organizing trading expeditions, as regards both the accumulation of local goods suitable for exchange and the actual planning of the exchange operations.

The social organization of exchange is the source of other explanatory proposals. At a local or, at the most, regional scale, another group of models has stressed the links between the appearance and consolidation of centralized leadership and the organizational needs of economic systems based on the redistribution of goods. In Service's influential scheme, originally published in 1975, the first chiefs had their *raison d'être* in the management of exchanges maintained between communities that were becoming increasingly specialized in producing certain types of goods. This specialization was encouraged by ecological conditions, according to which local communities tended to focus on the economic activities in which they had certain advantages because of their proximity to the relevant resources. In this context of growing productive specialization, the development of an exchange network allowing the access of each community to the products of the others became a necessity. According to Service, the most successful way of carrying this out consisted of the centralized management of the exchanges following a pattern based on redistribution. Success led to the position of chief, the leader managing the transaction, becoming hereditary. With time they enlarged their functions and, together with their assistants, they formed the bureaucratic type of government, cloaked with religious authority, typical of early civilizations.

Other variations highlight the periodic, and unpredictable, insecurity that affects the acquisition of food in any society. In the case of the best illustrated studies, a large number of local factors are mentioned which might affect agricultural production in a certain year. For this reason, the communities in a region arrange a 'social storage system' aimed at alleviating the situations of scarcity that might occasionally affect one or another of them (*bad year economics*). The individuals in charge of managing this system of exchanges, loans, compensation, and food reserves fulfil an essential function for collective survival and therefore their political role will gradually increase in importance and centrality.[54]

A final variation underlines the generic difficulties associated with population growth. Thus, it is expected that the more people there are, the more difficult it is to organize any enterprise. From this viewpoint, leaders are necessary to coordinate the increasingly abundant and complex information flow between individuals and groups, and to take the appropriate decisions so that the social system can continue working efficiently.[55] Under these conditions, it is not necessary to stress any particular causal factor, but, in Flannery's words, 'socio-environmental pressures' giving rise to an increase in complexity may be of different sorts.

To sum up, over and above the precise courses taken by the explanations for many of the cases that have been studied, processual archaeology has conceived the State as an organizational, institutional mechanism enabling certain societies to adapt efficiently and survive in situations of risks derived from techno-environmental factors. Hence, its crucial function requires it and legitimizes it. Again paraphrasing Flannery, to maintain state leaders 'is expensive but necessary'.[56]

However, the fact that they might have been thought necessary is not at all the same as being considered eternal, as the history of mankind has shown over and over again. Thus, although it has not been a priority topic of study, 'New Archaeology' has paid a certain amount of attention to the collapse of complex societies.[57] Once more, Flannery marked out a large part of the script in his 1972 paper cited above. We saw that he pointed out that promotion and linearization are evolutionary mechanisms whose action had a great deal to do with the increase in complexity, as they favoured the processes of segregation and centralization within a society. However, it may happen that the institutions begin to serve their own interests rather than those of the society, or that they end up destroying the controls that ease and rectify perturbations between sub-systems.[58] In the words of R. Rappaport, taken up by Flannery, this can be the cause of 'pathologies' that increase internal tensions. One of these pathologies is *hyperintegration* or *hypercoherence*.[59] It consists of a very close relationship between small sub-systems or institutions, or very determinant central hierarchical control over them. In both cases the sub-systems lose much of their autonomy and response capacity, and the change (or perturbation) in a unit may affect them all seriously and rapidly.

Critical remarks

Processual archaeology signified a turning point in the development of our discipline. Its efforts in widening the scope of archaeological research and making it more incisive should be acknowledged. It effectively criticized the traditional consideration of archaeological objects as works of art (aesthetics) or as fodder for typologies (archiving). In this way, it put in motion projects that enlarged the scale of regional research and encouraged the development of specific fields of study of invaluable aid in understanding economic habits, environmental conditions, or the political boundaries of the territory. In addition, in what must surely be its most important contribution, it drew attention to the need for an explicit formulation of the procedures through which the knowledge of past societies was obtained, particularly as regards the problematic connection between archaeological evidence (the present) and the extinct socio-cultural reality (the past). The way chosen to make this link and reach understanding can be summed up as below:

1. Human diversity, as documented by ethnographic observation and text-based history, is classified into evolutionary categories by using the degree of centralization and institutionalization of the political leader as its basic criterion. One of these categories is the 'State', which represents the highest level of the classification scale.
2. It is necessary to summarize the defining characteristics of each evolutionary stage as regards the different aspects of human activity defined previously ('economy', 'demography', 'kinship', 'government', 'beliefs', etc.). The result takes the form of a list of discrete elements with different levels of empirical implications: from direct correlation (for example, 'writing') to those of a relational kind (for example, 'full-time specialization', 'bureaucracy'). The category 'State', like the ones supposed to precede it, is defined by addition, by the total of this series of diagnostic elements.
3. Procedure of observation and comparison among the assemblages of material elements in archaeological cultures and the cited diagnostic characteristics.
4. Construction of a 'social archaeology': the interpretation of the past in the light of the operational dynamics attributed to each of the reference evolutionary stages.

The problem with this method is that it leads to an archaeological re-understanding of what was supposedly already understood in another field of knowledge. It denies the history and the specificity resulting from unknown solutions and conflicts, as it starts with the premise that the initial sample documented by modern observation includes the whole of social variability. However, we already pointed out in the remarks on anthropological neo-evolutionism that this aspiration is only an assumption: there is no reason to believe that the ethnographic sample is all-inclusive as regards forms of social, economic, and political organization. Consequently, to accept the ethno-historical models is implicitly a confession of incompetence by archaeology. It continues to relegate the discipline to a basic task of classification: whereas historical–cultural archaeology 'filed' objects in types and cultures, processual social archaeology classifies archaeological cultures in socio-political forms situated on a higher level of abstraction. In practice, the 'rebellion' of cases whose material expression does not match the stipulated classification criteria has been the cause of the proliferation of new categories and sub-categories, without this involving any methodological variation.

This articulation of research is conditioned by the convergence of several factors. One of the most important, if not *the* most important, refers to the characteristics of the archaeological information itself. The birth and growth of archaeology has been guided mainly by the antiquarian tradition, according to which the minimum unit of meaning is the individual object. The find itself, alone or together with others by formal analogy, provenance, or function, suffices to shape the archaeological discourse. This tradition has signified that most of the archaeological data available to research on the first states and civilizations come from objects in isolation, at the best of times with a reliable chronological reference. The problem deriving from this situation is that archaeology has hardly developed its own theoretical and methodological body, able to work reliably with categories like 'specialization', 'kinship', 'territory', 'intensification' or 'leadership', which form the basis for others, such as the one concerning us here: the State. In contrast, an archaeological record classified into types and periods makes it easy and convenient to work with diagnostic traits: a tablet with signs *is* writing; a pyramid *is* a large collective public work; jewellery made from exotic metal and gems *is* a product of specialized craftsmen and long-distance trading networks. Therefore, due to a mix of scientific immaturity and factors of the empirical reality being studied, archaeology has been impelled to identify, show, or prove *indirectly* the relational categories of key economic and political traits in social research, such as the State.

Another aspect of the critique stresses the ontological concept of society defended by processual archaeology. The project of a processual 'social archaeology' is, in fact, an attempt to put a 'political archaeology' into practice. It forces archaeology to accept that its primary scientific aim is the study of political relationships, raised to the governing field of social relationships. However, not any form of political relationships, but those which, articulated around concepts like 'prestige', 'charisma', and 'status', are posed in terms of consensus, equilibrium, and the common good. For various reasons, this is once again a difficult assumption to verify. The first of these is that the notions used to apprehend politics refer to the subjective attitudes of individuals, which are impossible to demonstrate archaeologically. We cannot interview the citizens of the past to ask them if they admired one or other leader or whether they enthusiastically agreed with certain controls, such as the rules of behaviour. This is to say, if politics is defined as the result of motivated individual actions, it is placed out of the reach of archaeology. The second reason that we referred to above is the assumption that political actions are aimed at the common good. In this field, the 'bank' will always win. The very existence of archaeological remains covering a period of time is cause for arguing that the society worked, and if it worked, it worked with everyone on board. If life worked better materially for some than for others, this is justified because of their own merits, gained or consented; through their service to the community in the case of the former, or by forced moderation in the case of the latter. In the light of this reasoning, who would dare to say that Plato was *out of date*. In contrast, although we may find archaeological evidence of violence, the assumption of the common good can always turn into the assumption of a necessary 'lesser evil'. In short, the supposition of the government and leader's good faith will always come out winning, even though at the price of being unable to know any more than what we already presupposed. It is the perfect preconception, it paralyses.

ARCHAEOLOGY OF THE STATE IN POST-MODERN TIMES

Since the 1980s, criticism has increased around processual 'social archaeology'. In a certain number of cases, it might be said that this is self-criticism, as it comes from 'first generation' processual researchers who abandoned the ecological-functionalist approach to interpretation that had been in vogue in the 1960s and 1970s. However, the most forceful objections have been put forward by a new generation of archaeologists whose points of view usually lie in that constellation of philosophical postures, emotional attitudes, and artistic sensibilities that are often designated as 'post-modernity'. Once again, these are approaches rooted basically in English-language archaeology, just as processualism had been. Their sources are so diverse as to include structuralist and post-structuralist philosophies, neo-marxism (above all critical theory and structuralist Marxism), or action and game theories. With so many and so varied reference points, it is not appropriate to refer to these initiatives as part of a 'school' championing a single programme or manifesto. We would be nearer the truth if we said they consist of a series of positions that are often very different from one another, but which have in common their rejection of most of the premises that defined 'New Archaeology'. This 'post-processualism', or at times belligerent 'anti-processualism', shares a series of proposals that we can summarize as below:

1. Societies are *not* organic wholes organizing themselves to achieve an internal balance and adaptation to the surrounding environment. Societies are collections of individuals and interest groups who pursue their own respective goals. They have no limits marked out and do not form uniform blocks; instead they allude to a changing and diffuse network of relationships among individuals and groups.

2. Societies are *not* necessarily founded on the consensus among their members in favour of the common good. Individuals' behaviour is *not* programmed by the system, because no such monolithic-like system exists. Individuals, even though they have been brought up according to the dominant social rules of behaviour, are able to change them, to subvert them through their actions in the situations where they lead their lives. The new decalogue to understand life in society should include new and old concepts like power, competition, conflict, strategy, ideology, identity, action/agency, and decision-taking, all framed within a social ontology that distrusts teleologies such as 'adaptation' and 'homeostasis'. Instability and conflict are the general rule, and not a 'pathological' exception.

3. The way of approaching research should also be different. The classification approach of processual social archaeology is considered exhausted and insufficient to capture the multiple dimensions of social aspects of historical reality. The insistence on establishing generalizations is considered counterproductive, as it hides beneath a cover of uniformity, a wealth of nuances and relationships taking place in the multiple contexts of action. Beginning with the consideration that archaeologists are ideologically oriented interpreters, attempting to influence the

modern political context, they will try in the same way to narrate how individuals and groups in the past actively built their world.

Critical approaches to processual archaeology have also shown a great interest in dealing with topics connected with the origin and consolidation of inequalities, as well as with the functioning of early states and civilizations.[60] Without wanting to simplify too much, we can point out that many of the recent contributions tend to pay less attention to the discussion on the appropriateness of classifying different societies in one or other of the stages proposed by neo-evolutionist anthropology (bands, tribes, chiefdoms, states, etc.) and instead focus on concrete historical trajectories which are able to show the play among relationships of power, the mechanisms through which some sectors gain control over others, the role of ideology, competition and tension among positions, and the transforming action of individuals and groups. In fact, the category of 'State' (and its specific adjectives, like pristine, archaic, early...) has even been questioned, and it has been suggested that it should be abandoned as a way of designating a subject of archaeological research, and be substituted by more lax expressions, such as 'early complex polities'[61] or 'generalized structure of authority'.[62] In this way, it is possible to avoid the reification of the State and the implicit consideration of it as an all-inclusive organizing centre, and at the same time, re-orientate research through more flexible concepts like 'constitution of authority', 'governance', 'power', or 'legitimacy' which enable the dynamic character attributed to political relationships to be expressed more correctly and precisely.

In fact, in the new contributions, politics is still positioned in the centre of the theoretical baggage and on the agenda of research (the slogan might now be 'Death to the State! Long live Politics!'). The way of approaching it and defining it has changed, however, as 'instability' and 'conflict' have replaced 'stability' and 'conformity'. Now, politics is understood as the dynamic and decisive scenario in human relationships where the course of history or histories is played out. It is more important to narrate the *political process* than to be content with identifying the political forms which this produces with greater or lesser consistency and permanence. In this context, the main interest lies in the figure of the individual or rather in groups of individuals united by a particular similarity or interest, whether it is called a faction, class, lobby, or any similar term. The ruler loses his central position as other personalities forgotten by history make their appearance: slaves, peasants, craftsmen, and prostitutes. They are all attributed the capability of making decisions and taking action; they are agents who act strategically depending on the dictates of their subjectivity. The actors of neo-evolutionist and functionalist politics: generous *big men*, efficient manager-chiefs, and majestic kings are abandoned or questioned, and instead the aim is to visualize the strategies followed by aggrandizers, accumulators, emergent leaders, great men, head men, and entrepreneurs and their success depending on the number of followers they take with them. Leaders are no longer thought of automatically as 'social servants' and instead research supposes that their behaviour is influenced by selfishness, ambition, and the wish to increase their quota of power at the expense of others. The aim is to show how certain positions of power become consolidated while others are undermined at their base and finally collapse. New concepts like 'heterarchy' and 'transegalitarian societies'[63] supported by a critical reinterpretation of the ethnographical data once used by functionalism and neo-evolutionism, are proposed to explain these dynamic scenarios. Finally, it is no longer so important to demonstrate when the threshold of the state and civilized life was crossed as to indicate the points where power was exercised in a regular, which is to say institutionalized, way.

Despite taking these new directions, archaeology continues to depend upon anthropology, possibly conditioned by the academic structure existing in the United States of America, the country where most research is carried out. It is true that the functionalist and adaptationist approaches to understanding have lost importance, but in their place there has appeared a proliferation of interpretations inspired by post-structuralist thought and game theory and structuring, often after these have been applied in anthropology. In its internal structure, the inferential mechanism tends to be analogous with the one put in practice by 'New Archaeology': denomination of modern (ethnographic) phenomena corresponding to the field of politics (power, authority, conflict), derivation of a list of material correlates, archaeological comparison and acceptance for the past of the anthropological interpretation made from ethnographic documentation. 'Political action' and, above all, the category 'power' now cover a large part of the ontological field of social life. Political action is supposed to be guided by will or, what is the same, by the particular subjective interests of each individual or each group, where groups are understood as the aggregate of individuals linked through sharing an egoistic interest. As the satisfaction of these interests requires the exploitation (subordination) of other individuals, political action is inseparably connected to the attainment and exercise of power. Political action is coupled with the strategic choice among several possibilities, although always with the objective of obtaining or preserving positions of power. If you listen, you will hear echoes of Machiavelli, resonances of Hobbes and, in reference to more modern literature, louder messages from M. Foucault, A. Giddens, and A. Mann.

However, in a scenario dominated by subjective will, there are other possible forms of expression and ways of understanding politics apart from a straight race for power. From other viewpoints it is stressed that certain societies organize themselves precisely to ward off the consolidation of any kind of authority that might lead to the State. In this case, the most direct reference is the anthropology of P. Clastres.[64] The same discipline offers other diametrically opposite ways of tackling the question, although they are all guided by the concept of subjective decision. Thus, for example, A. Testart has recently emphasized the role of 'voluntary servitude' in the birth of the State. The State would then be understood as the creation of a man who was supported by loyal friends in order to ensure power:[65] 'authority', 'loyalty', 'power' are variations and facets of the interpersonal relationships that subsume all social life. These and other proposals have received a warm welcome in modern archaeology studying the formation of the first states.

Recent proposals for the study of inequalities display several positive aspects. One of these is that they displace the task of classification from the leading role which it has held in research until now. At the same time, this contributes to taking significance away from the fact of placing a society on one side or another of the threshold that leads to civilization and the State. In other words, it tries to avoid the main criterion being to distinguish between human societies, depending on whether or not their political organization is articulated by state institutions. Leaving behind the powerful connotations of the state and focusing research into archaeological materiality on certain trajectories and developments is, in principle, a guarantee for achieving a more detailed understanding that is surely closer to reality. Otherwise, we might think that no substantial changes have occurred to human societies from the appearance of Sumerian city-states to the consolidation of capitalist states: after all, they are all states, even though the modern ones are clearly larger and more 'complex'.

Thus, for example, in accordance with greater attention to the specificity of state developments, some research on Mesopotamian city-states in the primitive Dynastic period has questioned the role of the temples and palaces as centres from where social activities were ruled according to a unitary way of thinking.[66] The attribution of this role owes much to the importance that traditional research granted to the texts preserved on the clay tablets used by the centres of power themselves. Based on such partial sources, it is not surprising that it was believed palaces and temples monopolized life in the first cities. However, the study of new types of evidence furnish arguments suggesting that both institutions were simply two participants, together with several others who until then had remained invisible to research. In this way, while temples and palaces tried to exercise a growing control over economic, political, and administrative aspects, forming centripetal forces, other social sectors, such as private landowners, independent craftsmen, and slaves, put up resistance and supported centrifugal trends. All this, on a game-board with diffuse, ever-changing boundaries.

In a similar way, the reappraisal of archaeological evidence from Minoan Crete has also involved questioning the traditional view according to which a small number of palatial centres controlled the economic, political, and ritual activities of the population across a territory.[67] Instead, a more flexible, diffuse, and less hierarchical relationship structure has been proposed, characterized by the competition between factions of political interest, where the palaces were places of consumption and ceremonial activity in the framework of open competition in pursuit of power.

If in these two cases the new interpretations take away rigidity, authoritarianism, and centralism, other studies imagine greater complexity than was traditionally acknowledged. Until recently, North America was a large region where the appearance of civilization was an unknown phenomenon and where, at the most, light sporadic echoes of Central American civilizations might be heard. However, new research at the site of Cahokia (Illinois), other nearby sites, and in the region around them (Greater Cahokia), together with a new reading of previously known evidence, suggest changes in the state of the question. In this respect, the size of the residential areas, and the numerous monumental structures like squares, mounds, and pyramids, show that Cahokia, and the nearby complex of settlements, would have been a centre of political-administrative and ceremonial attraction comparable with a true city. There, the leaders of the corporative groups presiding over a stratified society competed for power, although none of them may necessarily have held it in a centralized and permanent way over the others (heterarchy). Cahokia did not develop some of the characteristics of typical states, such as writing or the conquest of new lands, but it does show a case of *statemaking*, in the light of its impressive building projects, funerary rites, and festivals.[68]

In these and other examples, the centrality granted to politics as a privileged agency to explain society and history, pushes determinations of a material kind into the background. Thus, in the dawn of complexity, the *big man*, an ambitious and charismatic entrepreneur, transforms or 'dynamizes' the economy by making more people produce more things (by his charisma, his seduction, his 'gift of the gab': the weapons of his ambition). Politics 'leads' the economy. Politics uses it for its own ends, such as when a chief displays great generosity by arranging huge feasts or when he destroys large amounts of goods in public. Political action demands public consumption and the economy is that obliging, and almost always invisible (implicit), dimension that supplies consumables to the political wills in play.

We should be aware where these approaches are taking us. To be sure, it may be said that a certain margin of individual choice is given in many human actions, although it is also true that in many others this margin is nearly reduced to zero.[69] In any case, the range of possibilities depends on whether these possibilities are feasible, that is to say, that they have occurred or the material conditions for doing so exist (today, deciding to spend your holidays on Pluto instead of on Neptune is the same as not deciding anything). We may discuss whether will is conditioned by the reality of what has occurred or, on the contrary, the extent to which will influences what is produced. However, the fact is that no choice can be put into practice if it is not about real or achievable things; that is, that have been produced or could be produced under the given conditions.

The variable range of choices in political action and in individual use or consumption is reduced drastically when we consider the individuals imagined by post-processual archaeology at the time when they are taken; that is, when the scenario and conditions allowing one or another of them to think of taking any option actually has to be constructed. In this situation, individuals lose all freedom to act according to their own wishes, because production always *depends* on others in the context of any division of labour. At the time of producing, individuals lack the 'freedom' to decide what to produce, how much, how, and even with whom. Production is an everyday and unavoidable act, and it is collective in its realization. The position of each person in the organization of production also determines the possibilities of consuming after the production has been distributed. It therefore determines the person's life and the conditions of their 'freedom'.[70] A servant of common people will work and consume as such; a king will consume according to his majesty because the menial work permits it. To consider the capability of political action of one or the other, ignoring the necessary relationship established between both, is to forget reality. In conclusion, when the productive cycle, essential for social life, is examined, the individual person loses all centrality, in the same way that political action is moved off-centre as the driving force behind all.

To give greater importance to the political dimension above all others in research on the working of societies, involves, as we have seen, assigning individuals a capability of action determined by subjective will: an 'agency'. It means giving them a central role in their future, with no more limits than the will of the other actors and actresses on the stage. However, this ontology is based on a fiction: a society made up of individuals who do politics but do not produce the material conditions that any politics needs to come into effect. Aristotle did not believe in this type of fiction and knew that only the citizens 'sufficiently provided with resources' could take part in the government of the *polis*. In other words, only men maintained by the labour of women and slaves could be 'free', true political individuals. The objection should be made of post-processual archaeologies that the individual ontology they propose is only credible in worlds like that of (Greek) mythology; worlds where gods and heroes, unconcerned with eating or dressing, or producing so that others might eat and dress, put their desires and passions in play, fight, and scheme, making politics their sole and eternal *raison d'être*.

NOTES

1. The Uruk period in Low Mesopotamia holds the title of the oldest 'home' of civilization in the world. Its precedents and development unceasingly provoke new perspectives and debates. For an up-to-date review of these, consult Redman (1978); Algaze (1993, 2001); Forest (1996); Frangipane (1996); Pollock (1999); Rothman (2001, 2004); Postgate (2002); Butterlin (2003); Huot (2004); and Yoffee (2005).
2. The latest research at key sites like Hieracompolis and, above all, Abidos (Dreyer, 1998; Hartung, 2002) raises the possibility that at least in upper Egypt, the first states may have emerged in the proto-dynastic period (beginning of the Naqada III period) if not before (Naqada IIc–d), together with the so-called 'Dynasties 0 and 00'. This scenario places us a minimum of two centuries before Menes-Narmer, the first monarch in the First Dynasty, who ruled over a unified valley at about 3000 BC. However, other scholars delay the birth of the State until the start of the Ancient Empire, well inside the third millennium BC. For an overview of the state of the question, see Hassan (1988); Kemp (1989); Wilkinson (1996, 1999, 2003); Bard (2000); Compagno (2002); and Midant-Reynes (2003).
3. Critics have recently claimed that the Indus civilization, whose best known centres are Mohenjo-Daro and Harappa, did not develop state political institutions (Possehl, 2002).
4. The Shang dynasty has traditionally been considered the earliest Chinese civilization, appearing in the second millennium BC. However, the possibility that the State arose several centuries before, at least in the light of the new discoveries about the Erlitou period, cannot be ruled out (see Liu, 1996, 2004; Bagley, 1999; Maisels, 1999; Liu and Chen, 2003; Liu et al., 2004).
5. The consideration of the Olmec society (lowlands of the Gulf of Mexico; end of the second millennium–mid-first millennium BC) as a state is a point of controversy. Although the monumentality of the architectonic structures documented at sites like San Lorenzo and La Venta or the refinement of the stone statues, has been evaluated by some scholars as symptoms of a true Central American 'mother civilization', for other researchers these elements are not enough to raise the Olmec society above the level of chiefdoms (see Demarest, 1989; Grove, 1997; Clark, 1997; Flannery and Marcus, 2000; Spencer and Redmond, 2004). Fewer doubts are held about the consideration of Monte Alban as the capital of the first Zapotec state (Oaxaca) at the end of the first millennium BC (Marcus and Flannery, 1996; Blanton et al., 1999; Spencer and Redmond, 2004). And of course, even less so, the later civilizations centred on Teotihuacan and the Mayan cities from the early first millennium AD.

6. In truth, a clear line drawn between 'chiefdom' and 'State' has never been unanimously accepted in Peruvian archaeology. The different proposals have placed the threshold of the state at different times between the so-called Initial Period (between the second and first millennia BC) with developments like the one documented by Chavín de Huántar (Lumbreras, 1981 and 1989) and the Moche, Nazca, Wari, and Tiwanaku societies in the first millennium AD (Stanish, 2001; Billman, 2002). In recent years, however, research at different settlements provided with monumental architectural structures in the North Chico region has given rise to the debate about the possibility that the first states might have arisen in certain coastal valleys as early as the third millennium BC (see Shady and Levya, eds., 2003). For an up-to-date discussion with the intervention of opposing points of view, also consult Haas and Creamer (2006).
7. V. G. Childe, *Man Makes Himself* (1936).
8. Childe (1951) says that diffusion is not an automatic process, like the spread of a contagious disease. A society can copy an idea, such as a technical invention, a political institution, a superstitious rite, or an artistic motif, only when it fits within the general structure of that society's culture; in other words, only when that society has evolved to a stage which will accept the idea.
9. The page numbers given here refer to the edition published by Penguin Books in 1964.
10. *What happened in History*, 107.
11. *What happened in History*, 108. This is a quotation taken from *The Origin of the Family, Private Property and the State*, by F. Engels (chapter IX).
12. *What happened in History*, 138.
13. V. G. Childe (1950).
14. C. Maisels has enlarged Childe's list to twelve points, by noting that point number ten in fact includes three different aspects and that the first two are even contradictory: functional complementariness among peasants, artisans, and rulers; ideological means to maintain organic solidarity and state organization (Maisels, 1999: 26).
15. R. Mc. Adams (1966: 10–12).
16. C. Redman (1978).
17. Childe (1950: 16).
18. Childe (1950: 13).
19. G. Daniel (1968).
20. S. Piggott (1961; with our italics).
21. As we shall see, the satisfaction of these needs requires different solutions in each case, which are conceptualized as the 'driving-force' behind change. Thus, depending on the place and time, factors such as trade,

war, the need to coordinate or widen the reach of agricultural work, the struggle against uncertainty in the annual provision of food through 'social storage', or the need to regulate the flow of information are often used as the basis of explanations about the evolution of mankind.

22. The sociological theories adopted by processual archaeology presuppose that social life was founded through an agreement or community of individual interests, a premise referring back to the *ius naturale* idea of a social contract.
23. K. Flannery (1972) 'The Cultural Evolution of Civilizations', *Annual Review of Ecology and Systematics*, 3, pp. 399–426.
24. Flannery (1972).
25. ibid.
26. Lamotta and Schiffer (2001: 50–1)
27. Adams (1966: 14)
28. With his division between egalitarian, chiefdom, and stratified societies (Flannery, 1972).
29. In this case, they divided between Family-level Group, Local Group, which included both headless groups and collectives with a *big man* system, and Regional Polity, which grouped together chiefdoms and states. See A. W. Johnson and T. Earle (1987).
30. Flannery (1972) and Redman (1978).
31. Of all the possible traits, writing has usually taken the leading role.
32. C. Renfrew (1973).
33. See, for example, the essays contained in T. K. Earle, ed. (1993).
34. C. Renfrew and P. Bahn (1991).
35. J. Marcus and G. Feinman (1998: 6–7).
36. Adams (1966: 12).
37. M. Harris (1974).
38. Egypt, Mesopotamia, North China, Mexican Highlands, and Peru. See J. Steward (1949).
39. Egypt, Mesopotamia, Indus Valley, and the Mayas (Childe, 1950).
40. Mesopotamia and pre-Hispanic Mexico (Adams, 1966).
41. Central America, Peru, Mesopotamia, Egypt, Indus Valley, and China (Service, 1975).
42. Ancient Egypt, Mesopotamia, Shang China, the Aztecs, and their neighbours in Mexico Valley, the classic Maya period, the Incas, and the Yoruba. See B. Trigger (2003). Other studies, of more popular informative kind, increase the sample to include at least ten cases (see, for example, R. Whitehouse and J. Wilkins, 1993).
43. Steward (1949: 22–3).
44. Trigger (2003: 662).
45. A good example is the severity of the opinion expressed recently by Trigger about Steward's proposal (1949). After criticizing empirical

inconsistencies, he finally does not hesitate to claim that it was 'not only the most influential cross-cultural study of early civilizations ever published but also the most pernicious' (Trigger, 2003: 26).

46. F. Nietzsche, *On Truth and Lies in a Nonmoral Sense* (1873).
47. Marcus and Feinman (1998: 10).
48. It might be appropriate to add 'Archaic State' to this list, to judge from the title of the book these authors were editing.
49. R. Carneiro (1970).
50. D. Webster (1975).
51. M. Harris (1974).
52. K. Wittfogel (1957).
53. W. Rathje (1971).
54. P. Halstead (1981); J. O'Shea (1981); F. Hassan (1988).
55. Flannery (1972); H. T. Wright and G. A. Johnson (1975).
56. Flannery (1972).
57. See J. A. Tainter (1988); and Yoffee and Cowgill, eds. (1988).
58. Flannery (1972).
59. ibid.
60. In the last two decades, a myriad of approaches have tried to overcome (or 'revisit') the main deficiencies of processualist social archaeology, sometimes 'from within' and other times declaring their frontal opposition. For a review of the most significant contributions, see: Patterson and Gailey, eds. (1987); Gledhill et al., eds. (1988); Wason (1994); Price and Feinman, eds. (1995); Earle (1997); Feinman and Marcus, eds. (1998); Haas, ed. (2001); Chapman (2003); Smith (2003); Yoffee (2005).
61. Smith (2003).
62. Yoffee (2005: 17).
63. See Crumley (1987) and Hayden (2001).
64. Clastres (1974). See also Blanton (1998: 152).
65. Testart (2004: 7).
66. Stein (2001).
67. Hamilakis, ed. (2002).
68. See Pauketat (2004: 75, 167–74). For a less extreme view of Cahokia in the context of the Mississippian period, you can consult Milner (2004: 124–68).
69. The possibility of suicide reminds us that the margin for individual decision is never equal to zero.
70. Because, paradoxically, freedom is always less conditioned.

10

Towards a Marxist Archaeology of the State

Marxism encompasses many varied lines of thought, knowledge, and social change inspired by Marx's writings. Marxism questions and combats the foundations supporting capitalism, so it is logical that this system disowns those who try to undermine and discredit it. To say that the essence of liberalism is to encourage tolerance, or that 'open societies' are characterized by their acceptance of freedom of thought and action is no more than a myth: propaganda put forward by capitalist States. They are myths similar to those sponsored by rulers in classical times (and others chronologically much nearer to us) when they justified their government by alluding to divine right. For whatever reason, and despite being in the background of some of the most influential theories explaining humankind's past (Childe), Marxism has played a marginal role in the archaeology developed by research institutions in capitalist States. On the few occasions that it has been able to 'gatecrash' archaeological research, to approach through prehistory the development of social inequality and the formation of the State, the most outstanding contributions have often been made outside the Anglo-Saxon academic world, in Spain,[1] Italy,[2] and Latin America.[3] Its role has been comparatively smaller in countries like Great Britain and the United States.[4]

The fact that research based on Marxism has been infrequent has not prevented the proposals and results from being heterogeneous. On many occasions, great similarities can be seen with processual archaeology in the methods used to approach the topic, above all in the observation and testing procedures. In these cases, the difference from the processual tradition is the replacement of Fried or Service's typologies of socio-political evolution with others devised according to Marxist evolutionism, as proposed by Engels in *The Origin of the Family, Private Property and the State*. Terms such as 'tribal socio-economic formation' or 'initial classist society' substitute others like 'tribe', 'chiefdom', or 'civilization' in the same methodological structure. The keys for interpretation also change; where before it said consensus, now it says imposition; where before it said prestige, now it says power and exploitation. In any case, these keys to understanding still come from outside archaeology. Whole scenarios are imported mainly from neo-Marxist anthropology (M. Godelier, C. Meillassoux, E. Terray) and these come into service after the operations of empirical comparison and inference. In consequence, the critiques that have been made for processual archaeology could be applied to part of the archaeology inspired by Marxism.

However, if we are agreed on the pertinence of approaching research into the formation of States and their functioning and dynamics on new foundations, it is necessary to establish which precise aspects should be overcome and at least sketch out possible ways to achieve this.

1. The identification of the first States and civilizations according to a methodology anchored in philological–historiographical designation and in the comparison with a list of empirical correlates derived from this imposes great restrictions upon research. It defines a threshold suggesting a transcendental before and an after in the history of human groups. In practice, this transcendence imposes a general classification of societies into civilized and uncivilized, favours the academic division between prehistory and ancient history, and conditions, in an implicit and acritical way, how archaeological research into prehistoric societies can be approached. Therefore, the agreement on which the first States should be, unavoidably relegates to pre-State categories of political evolution those societies dated in earlier periods and/or those located beyond their frontiers, as well as prejudging the nature of the socio-political interpretation they should be assigned. In the case of European prehistory, a quite successful consensus reserves the designation 'State' for only a few archaeological groups prior to the Roman expansion at the end of the first millennium BC. To be specific, this convention affirms that the first States on European soil developed by the shores of the Aegean during the middle and late Bronze Age (Minoan and Mycenaean civilizations). It is not until the Iron Age that the qualification of State or State-like

society reaches other Mediterranean regions and their areas of influence (Etruria, Hallstatt principalities, Western pre-Roman aristocracies), while many other societies only became States when they were absorbed by the Roman expansion. This has led, in the first place, to the proliferation and consequent 'piling up' of chiefdom societies of greater or lesser complexity in 'barbarian' Europe between the fifth and first millennia, as research rules out any of these societies possessing the rank of State. And, in second place, it tends to assume that the formation of the first European States was always a result of secondary or derived processes, so that the main causes are attributed to commercial, military or colonial activities of a restricted number of classical civilizations.

2. The observation and comparison methodology propitiates that archaeological research follows a classification according to scales of socio-political organization derived from neo-evolutionism.

3. The classification in socio-political terms brings with it interpretations on social dynamics drawn mainly from anthropology (whether they are of the functionalist, structuralist, or neo-Marxist kind). This interpretative method is often confused with explanation. To go on in this way condemns archaeology to continue holding a marginal position within the production of knowledge. It condemns us to know no more about the past than what a part of the academic community think they know about the ethno-historical present. It assigns to the past interpretations drawn from other data, for other times and furthermore, based on reasoning accepted unconsciously or uncritically. Interpretative dependence is a symptom of a more profound methodological poverty. If we do not try to overcome it, we will have to continue accepting that the only thing archaeological materials can achieve is to evoke more or less fortunate interpretations in the minds of ideologically (in)formed archaeologists.

4. The cross-cultural comparative method is based on classifications of societies, whose very premises condition the results to an indeterminate but doubtlessly important extent. As usually happens in practice, this method leads to the proliferation of new classifications or to the possibly sterile debate about the

correctness or pertinence of the subdivisions that have been proposed for them.

5. To situate the driving-force of politics and therefore of social life in the sphere of the will, decision, and action of individuals or groups of individuals, implies the acceptance of an idealist ontology. With this approach, archaeological materials are the remains of the physical resources that the threads of ancient decision moved at their will. This way of seeing things may satisfy human vanity in our times, as it maintains human beings in the role of the measure of all things. However, if we distrust humanist theologies as much as divine ones, it is time to concentrate on knowing ourselves from everything that produces us and we produce, instead of comforting ourselves and feeling satisfied with imagining what we supposedly are. With this aim in mind, archaeology has much to offer.

NOTES FOR ARCHAEOLOGICAL RESEARCH ON THE STATE: THEORY

Our objective in the following pages is to suggest lines of research on the State based on the social materiality that produces it. We will first note a definition of the category in the relational field in which it arises, and leave for a later section an outline of what could be the most appropriate procedure in the field of empirical inquiry.

In the opinion of many, the State is the maximum political institution, the most rational, and as if it were a living creature, the most astute and intelligent. No matter whether it appears under coercive or beneficent forms, few would dissent if they heard that politics nowadays is politics of State or it is nothing; that it is only worthy of its own name when it is of the State, from the State or through the channels that the State establishes. Indeed, if we decided to enlarge its semantic field to include within it everything, from relationships by marriage to ethical considerations in which politics is understood as a parody of everything affable, adequate, or opportune, politics of State would then be called 'high politics' and would subsume other kinds from a position of authority.

However, politics is much more than this. It is found in any type of relationship in which human beings are immersed. Whether these be economic, social, or ideological, the touch that politics brings in social relationships, what comprises it exclusively is no more than the *dealings* we have with our fellow humans about people and objects that we find in our joint wanderings amongst things. These *dealings* among one and another, as we *regularly* move in situations of concurrence, will fix, in time, the ways we behave with everything around us. Political entity is said to be reached fully when these dealings become rules for *good deeds* or the *good life*.

After a prolonged period of trials at coexistence that entangled the community instinct of social life and which led to the construction of different identities, some societies *became* States. They then instituted the opportune foundational pretexts as a kind of excuse to impede internal dissensions and to appropriate what after then was sanctioned as out of bounds. The State as an institution of coexistence, with its regulations and conditions to support it, *was produced*; it was materialized in forms of relationships that a certain production of social life demarcated historically.

The production of social life

Social life occurs as a material fact. Men, women, and objects of which male and females are cause and consequence, constitute the indispensable objective material conditions for social life. These conditions (men, women, and objects) must be produced continuously in the framework of a certain natural environment. This production is, therefore, the first social act.

In several collective publications,[5] we proposed widening the reach of the classic paradigm of production, which was focused exclusively on the production of objects (food and artefacts), in order to make room for other aspects. In this way, together with the production of objects, we designated the generation of men and women as 'basic production'. The explicit recognition of this production implies the consideration that biological reproduction constitutes the primordial activity of every society and its *basic* material support. There is no doubt that the production of new men and women is a primordial social task. However, it is still being discussed whether the gestation process belongs strictly to the biological realm or is a concern of labour affairs. If we incline for this latter option, we would have to justify why this would be the only work activity determined by biological factors (only women can gestate and suckle) and independent of previously accumulated social work. It appears hard to overcome this dilemma, especially when the frequency of pregnancies and the question whether these end in childbirth or not, depend to a large extent on unmistakeably social requirements.

In those publications we also proposed the so-called 'maintenance production'. This is aimed at preserving, caring for, and maintaining the objects and social subjects operative, in some cases until they fall into disuse or are cancelled, and in others until they die, parting them from their social life. The maintenance production does not involve modifying qualitatively the value of the initial use of its object, but rather to update it when it is reduced for one reason or another. To sum up, we could note that the objective of the production and maintenance of objects is to provide for a collective of women and men, whereas the objective of basic production and the maintenance of individuals is the provision of the men and women who make up any society.

Division of tasks and the social division of production[6]

Not everyone takes part in an identical way in the activities involved in the three productions of social life. This implies certain division within the collective, which can be expressed in various dimensions and depend on several reasons. One of these dimensions concerns the distribution of certain missions, so we refer to it as the *division of tasks*. In the human species, gender and age are two highly important factors with regards to the assignation of tasks. The sexual factor derives from the fact that only women are able to engender new individuals and to suckle them. As regards age, its influence extends to both sexes and all forms of production, as the effective participation in these depends on the ability of the organism to carry out certain actions and mechanical and intellectual operations satisfactorily. This ability varies notoriously depending on age. In addition to sex and/or age, other physico-biological characteristics such as agility, memory, keenness of hearing and sight, physical strength, etc. have also been important factors for the performance of one or other kind of task, particularly in the past. However, as well as these factors that might be called universal, the development of the division of tasks in every society has depended on other aspects and has taken different forms throughout history. Occasionally, a group may have promoted a greater division of tasks as the means of increasing production; that is, tending towards a simplification of certain missions that would redound to obtaining as many or more products while investing less effort in overall terms. In other cases, as Marx stressed,[7] the adoption of technological innovations in the production of manufactured goods or food could bring with it a new and deeper distribution of tasks within a community.

Any division of productive tasks involves a certain fragmentation of the group, which is expressed in the formation of various relational contexts of different distances. However, another dimension exists in social division, probably of greater transcendence than the distribution of tasks. In the 'Introduction' to the *Gundrisse* and later in *Capital I*, Marx put forward a key distinction. Production, in the abstract sense, is articulated in a cycle that includes differentiated *moments*: production itself, distribution or exchange, and consumption. Production and consumption form a unit for Marx, as any production process is meaningless if the final product is not consumed or used; besides, all production processes involve the consumption of raw materials, resources, and labour force. However, unity is not the same as identity (the production of something is not its consumption), as the time of the production and the consumption of a thing are deferred in time and, as we shall see, in space. Between the production and the consumption is situated the distribution, mainly responsible for this deferment. The exact mechanisms adopted by distribution vary according to the historical circumstances, from reciprocity or bartering to taxation.

Among humans, it very rarely happens that an individual consumes what he or she has been entirely responsible for producing. In fact, perhaps the most distinctive feature of the development of mankind, which has taken place in the evolutionary history of life, is the *'dislocation' between production and consumption, between the agents and the place involved in production and the agents and place involved in consumption.* In view of this, we designate as social division of production the expression adopted by the *'dislocation' between the places of production, places of distribution, and places of use and consumption in a society.* This dislocation expresses a social division which adds to and, in turn, goes beyond the division of tasks we have made reference to above. The social division of production generates as many or more particular contexts of relationship as the division of tasks. Women and/or men recognize each other socially not only through their respective participation in the different tasks performed in the framework of the three productions, but also, and perhaps much more, through their participation, different or not, in the various contexts of production and consumption. The particular relationships embarked upon within all the contexts will contribute to the generation of individual subjective qualities (the particular 'I's') which can finally manifest themselves or come together socially as ideologies: ideologies that will end up as conflicting views if material disagreements arise among the groups involved in social life.

General production and the 'place' of politics

One of the main problems for any materialist research is to determine the 'place' and the contents of politics in the general framework of social life. As it traditionally refers to decision-taking by individuals and groups, the study of politics has favoured the use of volitional or intentional arguments of an idealist or psychological kind, which normally contradicts any materialist approach. We can find numerous examples in modern archaeology when, after describing an initial social situation created around technological, demographic, and ecological variables, the 'ambition of power' of a sector of society, or the 'competition' to obtain prestige among certain individuals, are introduced as factors that influenced decisively in the culmination of the processes forming the State. With the series of arguments that we will explain below, we will attempt to avoid this contradiction, situating the 'place' of politics in the field of material conditions making up all human collectives.

Given certain conditions of the division of tasks and the social division of production, the members of a community participate in and from the result of the three productions. However, in the course of the production cycle, there is a consideration of vital interest which has rarely been expressed: *the real development of production requires an up-to-date knowledge of the limits and make-up of the group involved, and also the variety and amount of the other materialist conditions that may be accessed.* In which of the three *moments* of the general production cycle proposed by Marx can these considerations be located? In our opinion, the answer is that the *distribution of objects and subjects* 'knows' the limits of the community, *where this is understood as the group directly committed to participating in the production and the consumption*. Faced with this statement, it is however necessary to clarify the meaning of the term 'distribution' that we have adopted here, as in fact Marx considered two definitions. In his own words:

> In the shallowest conception, distribution appears as the distribution of products, and hence as further removed from and quasi-independent of production. But before distribution can be the distribution of products, it is: (1) the distribution of the instruments of production, and (2), which is a further specification of the same relation, the distribution of the members of the society among the different kinds of production. (Subsumption of the individuals under specific relations of production.) The distribution of products is evidently only a result of this distribution, which is comprised within the process of production itself and determines the structure of production. To examine production while disregarding this internal distribution within it is obviously an empty abstraction; while conversely, *the distribution of products follows by itself from this distribution which forms an original moment of production.*[8]

Based on this quotation, it is clear that the factor that best contributes to delimit the social group is the distribution of objects and subjects in social production and not strictly that of products made for consumption. Even so, to remove this possible source of ambiguity or confusion it could be preferable to use different terms such as 'assignation' or 'delivery' in reference to the meaning that we are interested in highlighting.

Distribution–allocation should not be understood as a previous starting point, foreign to production, as a kind of rational decision guided by thought. Every assignation always comes after a material event. The two meanings of 'distribution' that Marx referred to, already accompany a certain social division of production, however small it might be. It is precisely this effective dislocation which in practice gives rise to ignorance and uncertainty, leading to questions such as: Who will participate in this or that task? (Who can we count on?) What material means are available to carry it out? (What can we count on?) What is the range of *producible* goods and in what amounts should they be produced? Who are they aimed at, and in what amount? Are there too few of us, enough, or too many in relation with all this? Through being involved in relationships that produce them individually and as a social group, everyone has something to say in reply. However, because of the dislocation involved in the social division of production and also in the division of tasks, the answers need not necessarily be unanimous, and neither will the verbal or material arguments, wielded in favour of one or other answer, be of equal weight. The multiplication of the kinds of individual and group experiences and existence propitiated by productive division is the cause of new objective and subjective relationships. The subjects provide different opinions and contrasting assessments about how social life is produced and/or how it *should* be produced.[9] The discussion will be accompanied by strategies which could divide the relational fields even more if they involve alliances that cross the divisions defined by production. The final decisions will give way to cooperation or will end in grievances. Politics has entered social life.

We affirm that politics is connected to the distribution–allocation of individuals, groups, and objects in relation with production and consumption. Its 'place' lies in the management of social dependencies which it forces to the cancellation or satisfaction of the needs of particular collectives, in the framework of a certain conjunction between division of tasks and social division of production.[10] The essential social knowledge to guarantee economic objectives can be called the 'raw material' of political relationships. The members which this assignation reaches will be considered members of the community. *Politics arises out of the relationship and is designed to reach a decision*, in this case about the limits of the group and the permissible degrees and forms of affinity in its interior and towards the exterior, always within the framework of a certain historical organization of the production of social life.

With this approach, 'domestic unit' and 'community' gain meaning as different expressions of the organization of assignation–distribution, understood as part of social production. Domestic units are usually the result of experiences regulated by basic production and the maintenance of individuals. As well as this task, they can acquire a more or less significant role as units of production of food and artefacts. Politics also takes charge of settling the relationships between domestic units, communities, and groups of communities, which arise from the possibility of exchanging products and people at different geographical scales. The original reference of politics is always what is common, not individual people, as they are (we are) nothing without the social and economic relationship which allows us to exist.

Political practice, in its contents of meeting, deliberation, and decision, can develop according to a wide range of relational expressions, from assemblies to single person despotism. Its continued functioning is often sanctioned by the introduction of offices and institutions. In turn, the rules and regulations generated and applied in these contexts can manifest themselves in power relationships and, on the other hand, favour the formation of ideologies of identity or exclusiveness, which we currently refer to with terms such as 'ethnicity', 'nationalism', or 'patriotism'. These ideologies often take on discourses with metaphysical contents and adopt distinctive symbols for the group, which is represented by them. In conclusion, politics establishes the degrees of affinity within and among communities and is provided with the informative and coercive means to guarantee this distribution order in social relationships.

It should be highlighted that politics is not located outside production, nor does it guide it or structure it from a metaphysical authority, in the style of 'tradition', 'culture', the 'self-aware individual', or the 'spirit of the times'. It finds its meaning as one more tool in the organization of production, and extracts its criteria in accumulated social know-how after multiple experiences of trial and error in the organization and development of the production of the previous social life. And thus backwards in time, ever since mankind was identified by the dislocation of production and consumption. The division of tasks and the social division of production, developed in the framework of the production of social life, by themselves result in the need for politics, understood in the first place as an aspect of the management or administration of the production–consumption cycle.

The formation of the State

The key factor in the explanation of the formation of States is the development of the division of tasks and the social division of production. The compartmentalization, the dividing-up of production and social life in general, places people in situations of greater dependence on others. Think of a group of individuals specialized in a certain occupation, such as cutting down trees or knapping flint.

Their world revolves around these activities and many of their worries and expectations too. However, their life depends on the consumption of other things, apart from wood or stone, and also on entering into relationships with other people different from those they work with on a certain job. Therefore, in the course of the development of the division of tasks and the social division of production, distribution–allocation becomes increasingly important and, at the same time, the place of politics is enlarged.

Distribution, in societies where the division of tasks and the social division of production has become more extensive, runs the risk of turning into *unequal distribution*. Once again, although in somewhat different terms from the ones used here, Marx set the guidelines:

> The division of labour implies the possibility, nay the fact that intellectual and material activity—enjoyment and labour, production and consumption—devolve on different individuals, and that the only possibility of their not coming into contradiction lies in the negation in its turn of the division of labour.... With the division of labour, in which all these contradictions are implicit, and which in its turn is based on the natural division of labour in the family and the separation of society into individual families opposed to one another, is given simultaneously the distribution, and indeed the unequal distribution, both quantitative and qualitative, of labour and its products, hence property: the nucleus, the first form, of which lies in the family, where wife and children are the slaves of the husband.[11]

States arise to preserve and establish certain dissymmetrical economic distribution systems. Their appearance was not led by will, but by the lack of coincidence between social production and consumption. The viewpoint we are suggesting here also affects the classic problem about the causes for the rise of States. In general, the causal models in use presuppose a starting point in equilibrium, which was altered by one or several destabilizing factors (a cause or causes such as, for example, population increase or climate change) until society reaches a new situation of equilibrium in the form of a civilization or State. In a certain way, this approach situates the origin of the causality in the exterior of social relationships, which only react to something coming from outside. In addition, it is always complicated to justify why in certain situations these causes propitiate the rise of a civilization and the State, whereas in other apparently similar cases their incidence is imperceptible or seems to favour completely

Towards a Marxist Archaeology of the State 239

different courses. Thus, not all the agricultural societies in arid countries with rivers have produced civilizations, and nor have all the endemic wars terminated in the rise of military States.

From our point of view, it is preferable to face the problem of the formation of State organizations by considering what *conditions* made them possible, instead of assuming the action of one or other causal factor of general application. Among the *necessary*, but not *sufficient*, *conditions*, is the development of the social division of production and unequal distribution–allocation. This, nonetheless, has to conclude as an *essential condition* in a relationship of social exploitation in benefit of a few. It is a route which respects a necessary itinerary.

1. In the first place, society obtains regular material output for its reproduction and security. The productive forms, in all the activities they consist of, establish channels from which it is usually fatuous or risky to leave, as they are based on the tranquility provided by the reiteration of experiences and uses being chosen.

2. The community establishes rules of coexistence which it sanctions outside private contexts and which situate collective relationships beyond subjective interests. The birth of politics.

3. The contexts fomented by the division of tasks and the social division of production are the scenario of routine experiences. From these arise particular inter-subjectivities, producing shades of differences in social life. The recognition of these differences within a common life constructs 'ceremonies' of identities. First, each group can describe themselves as different. But also the groups of subjects recognize each other by the things they do, with, because of and for others, although *not any other*. The scope of *us-all*[12] expresses both the real collective in which everyone takes part *de facto* and an entity in which everyone can *identify themselves* ideally.

4. Despite social relationships stagnating in habitual ('traditional') forms, some of the differences noted in their interior can lead to material asymmetries. In this case, certain private collectives take advantage of their position in the production–consumption cycle, although this advantage may go unnoticed for those traditional ways, stuck in the past. The new material reality now threatens to reduce them to pure formalisms. This

difference between material reality and old ways demands an update, which is not necessarily the same as consensus. The division of society into classes appears as a possible scenario.
5. The asymmetries have become more acute, exploitation has been established, and private material interests have crystallized in classes. Political relationships may, under certain circumstances, consolidate in States. With them, the aim is for the asymmetries to be maintained in order, at the same time as identities of compulsory membership are constructed from an Order. Ideology becomes specialized.

The main objective of the State will consist of safeguarding, through the use of force, the relationships of economic exploitation between classes, at the time and place in which antagonism derived from these relationships goes beyond certain limits.[13] The State is therefore a historical product, arising in the context of certain socio-economic conditions. We may digress, in order to clarify the categories involved in this definition. We talk of 'exploitation' when a producing collective is deprived of the consumption of part of the social product that would be their right according to their contribution. This part that is taken away, generated by mechanisms of 'added value' and which can be called more properly 'surplus',[14] is consumed by another collective, who do not provide any comparable compensatory material. This appropriation is then called 'property', which is always 'private' because it deprives others of it. The different collectives then make up 'social classes' occupying antagonistic places in social production. The classes are made up of individuals of both sexes and the same age groups, but while some cooperate economically to produce, others cooperate politically to continue being produced (maintained), consuming what others have produced, consuming them. For this reason, any discussion on liberty and action which does not take into account this relational reality will never leave the field of speculation. The final guarantor of the maintenance and also the extension of exploitation relationships within a State are rooted in the use of force by a sector specialized in this task. The exercise of physical violence with these aims may also be given the name of coercion. The other forms of violence that are used or selectively tolerated from the State (duress, alienation) are based on coercion.

It is important to specify an aspect of the relationship between exploitation and violence. Societies can function aggressively and even cruelly without any exploitation in their midst. Inequalities between sexes and between age groups, for example, are circumstances which do not always involve contexts of exploitation, although they contribute to unleashing episodes of physical violence. In the same way, there is no doubt that some wars, murders, and robberies enable gain with nothing given in return, but the term 'booty' cannot be confused with the notion of 'surplus'. A surplus is obtained through mechanisms extracting added value which are eventually brought together in laws and title deeds. It must be remembered that although exploitation requires violence to maintain itself (coercion), not all violence denotes contexts of exploitation, and nor does this take place at the rate and as the consequence of each violent event.

In addition, private property should not be confused with the particular property of any object or product. The private property which we are referring to is that of production factors (objects and means of production and labour force) susceptible of engaging mechanisms of added value that will provide surpluses for the exclusive benefit of a few. A toothbrush or a car may be exclusively mine, but because of that I am not included among the ranks of the owner class. To be allowed into this, I should hold deeds for land, slaves, machinery, or capital, depending on the period of time. The property that the State safeguards refers to the factors of social production alienated in a few hands; that is, the source of their material privileges. The surplus obtained by mechanisms of added value express the differential materialization of social benefit. *Exploitation, private property, added value, and surplus go hand in hand only in State societies and are usually co-responsible for the fact of the State.*

The politics of State

'State' should not be confused with 'society'. It would be more correct to use the expressions 'society with State' and 'society in a State' than 'State society', as the latter term connotes an entity whose essential property is that of being a State. The State tries to make us believe that it is the soul of social relationships, its substance and its sustenance. For Plato and Aristotle, life in the *polis* and its government were inseparable; for the Christian tradition, kings and emperors followed on Earth a model inspired in eternal divine order; for the modern, enlightened philosopher, the political contract that the State established inaugurated true social life; for contemporary idealists, the reason of State (Hegel) or the collective sentiment incarnate in this (nationalist romanticism) overwhelms any social logic or expression. However, the real process is exactly the opposite. One thing is social relationships, previous and contemporary with any State, and a very different thing is the self-interested control that the State imposes on more or less extensive portions of them. The State takes over areas of coexistence, regulates them, prescribes and forces so that, in the end, it appears as their creator. Obviously, it does not achieve its goals acting like a spectre, without a body or place, but requires certain material conditions. This is the reason for the bureaucracy in all its expressions (administrative, informative, legislative, military, or police), provided with personnel, equipment, and installations. However, as a mechanism for control and obligation, the State does appear something like a spectre, as it moves in directions marked ideologically, at the service of a project that will never belong to everyone although it ends up affecting all of us.

The economic and ideological regularization installed inside society forms the necessary fabric for the advent of the State, but the net that catches society is not materialized until one segment of it sets itself up as a ruling body and appropriates the sense of order. Politics acquires a definitive sense of State when it aims to link social reality to certain ethical–moral principles, whose material entailment only benefits a sector of society. In this divided society that Marx describes for us, the State sets itself up as the patron of the very control of social dynamics and, with the excuse of improving it, weaves in a general interest, in reality adapted to privileged interests.

Once exploitation is regulated and its profits are controlled, time becomes a determining factor of production in State societies. With its variables of efficiency and productivity, social production acquires the character of an institution: rule-typified, preordained, and decided. On the one hand, it attempts to force the social collective to invest more time in producing than in living together. On the other, those two variables help to construct a space-time universe of obligation which in turn captures time and space for mutual enjoyment. When this point is reached, the State regulates social meetings and holidays, separating them from the economic–social background they come from more or less distantly. As it adopts them and sponsors them, it only keeps alive the ideas of their interest. This

Towards a Marxist Archaeology of the State 243

regulated behaviour results little by little in the problem of ideologies, a term that has already appeared several times in the above discussion.

A social collective gradually includes within its closed or fluid process of development ideologies and institutions that sanction it and oblige it. In both cases, society nourishes with its labour myths of ignorance constructed out of the desire of understanding, together with tales of survival which embellish coexistence and communication. Societies turn them into ideological resources that preserve their effectiveness as long as they remain together with economic forms, but which usually accelerate their alienating role when they are separated from them.

Ideologies are inseparable from the State when they are established as compulsory mediation for social coexistence. We know of no State societies that remain apart from this mediating ideological component, but neither can we assure that societies which possess it always form States. When this mediating component establishes rules of duties, typifies sanctions, regulates the 'good life', and constructs exclusive forms of ethics, it is located at the gates of a State society. However, the State institution will not consolidate if the control of the means of alienation, its symbols, and artefacts does not imply its controllers having the differential accumulation and benefit of social resources. The main ideological consequence of exploitation is the establishment of an unavoidable ideological nexus between religion or, if you prefer, moral and affective beliefs, and the political–economic realm as an effective place to be preserved.

Once it is in function, the State proclaims the virtues of coexistence, and hides the vices that provide benefits to only a few citizens. When it *becomes* a State, a society aborts its own freedom of movements and ingenuity, abandons the search for alternative ways of living, and living together, and is forced institutionally to devote itself to exclusive activities that respect and obey *self-interested normality*. The type-rules that ensure a common, but not shared, existence facilitate the generation of a monochrome façade for the State and in this way fossilize the supposed collective identity that is now seen as full of aggressive gestures against the *others*, all of whom are enemies from that moment.

All States exclude internally and externally. In the exterior they exclude all other human collectives *against* whom they were established. They identify themselves as such in opposition with them, and they continue developing until the others also differentiate them. Without that exclusion, States would not have their *raison d'être*. In the interior they display a clear division, as the exclusion reaches the segments of the population who had no interest in its development; an itinerary that established social division of production and which only became possible when socio-economic dissymmetry was institutionalized.

History has no record of a harmonious State. All known Constitutions linked their origin to the proclamation of a rational agreement with self-professed objectives of avoiding internal conflicts and providing security against the exterior. All those Constitutions recognized *de facto* the exclusive context which supported the idea of State. However, the fact maintaining that supposed agreement is the opposite. Its starting point lies in the economic–social dissymmetries found within itself and only later does it need to proclaim itself to ensure ideologically what materially was already a reality.

The State, in its desire to maintain its private binomial 'law equals justice', foresees conflicts between what belongs to one and what is of another. State sovereignty *decides* that what characterizes its subjects does not lie in a shared and collective labour, but in the dictates of the State itself; an entity structurally alienated as it is located *outside* and *above* everything; an institution that rules the world exclusively and according to its own disposition. Finally, the State, as the definitive *protector* of good sense and morality, establishes the *morality* of good sense and constructs the moral *good sense* appropriate to its *control*.

The state-of-the-world

Since its first appearance, the State has prescribed policies of coexistence. A *decision-making* politics that corresponds to certain social groups. The social idea that it defends is incarnated in representatives who are established around *decisive* mafias. Before the triumph of bourgeois revolutions, Rousseau warned that representation lethally attacks what he called the general will of the people, the place where sovereignty lies: 'the moment a people allows itself to be represented, it is no longer free: it no longer exists'.[15] It seems that warnings like this fell on deaf ears, because bourgeois parliamentarism declared the virtue of representatives and their parties deciding about other people's things. With the full development of capitalist democracy, representatives and parties very often appear to be the employees and departments, respectively, of the private businesses that sponsor them.

The politics of State transmits the will of a few people with the means and opportune conditions to impose their self-interest.[16] From domestic and municipal politics to the politics of State and between States, decisions are taken in certain closed shops by *decisive* people, loaded with material conditions, who move the world as they please; clearly an unmistakeable demonstration of free will and the triumph of freedom, even if really only applicable to them. The power groups in the solidly *united*, powerful *States* decide the high politics of subsidiary States and in the same way determine the route that social life should take. In opposition to them, groups of resistance rebel and little by little undermine the credibility of that political system or die in the attempt.

In the background of this *state-of-the-world*, politics dilutes its primitive meaning anchored in distribution, and shapes a simulation, in the hands of the powerful, that upholds the *meaning* of politics within a supposed freedom of ideas. They insist that politics is politics of ideas or is nothing. Active politics, of effective participation, is being substituted by politics as a shared ideology. This politics of ideological affinities, in which empathy is its empirical parody, shelters behind the claim that thinking alike builds community, but forgets that if politics were to be made by people who are materially and ideologically equal, it would not exist as unnecessary. Arising from this confusion, politics 'in the first person' is the subjective dictatorship, that of people who believe their ideas are reality, who live in a confused parallel world with the idea as incarnation of reality, red with shame because they have no link with it.

We have travelled from high politics to the depths of reality. And now we wonder, what is worth researching in politics? Labour politics, the politics of social relationships, the politics of political relationships as social relationships of decision, the politics of what relationships should be and are not but should come to be, or simply research the past of politics, its archaeology? The starting point is evident. Politics always was archaeological: *we live in a used world, decided by what came before us*. Thus, politics, despite what it might seem, has little to do with future aspirations. As the supposed link between social reality and moral principles, it should be pointed out that it usually respects obsolete principles anchored in out-of-date realities which object to the material progress of society through ideologies full of punitive-legal resources.

NOTES FOR ARCHAEOLOGICAL RESEARCH ON THE STATE: METHOD

Theory is one thing, and the (pre)historic research which it should help to articulate is another. There are theories and premises about this which turn into prejudice and inhibit research. Thus, if one thought that the State is inseparable from human life in society, there would be no point for archaeology to inquire into its origins, as this topic would possibly receive the attention of the disciplines that study human ontogenics (palaeontology, genetics, ethology). In the same way, if it is thought that only certain symbolic objects denote the appearance of the State, it would be impossible to determine whether the relationships that produce States and those that they establish, are compatible with other objects. We might say the same of both situations: if we already know so much at the outset, the incentive for initiating research is so small as to be almost inexistent.

In the case of the theoretical notes we have given above, we have attempted to get round this objection. It is true that we offer a definition of State in which several categories converge, but in itself it does not predetermine the result of the empirical research it might help to inspire. To summarize, we have shown that the State safeguards the relationships of economic exploitation between classes by the use of force (coercively), and it arises at the time and place where the antagonism derived from these relationships goes beyond a certain limit.

The proposed definition does not need the prerequisite that the first States had to arise in scenarios acknowledged as 'pristine' or that any form of exploitation necessarily assumes the existence of a State, or, for sure, that exploitation is inherent in human societies. As we have shown, it is a guide with which questions can be posed, for which there are no answers before tackling empirical research. Adopting this attitude produces a series of effects in the methodological field. Perhaps the most important is distrusting approaches that identify or reject the existence of States based on the comparison between certain archaeological materials and a list of characteristics

Towards a Marxist Archaeology of the State 247

denoting types of socio-political development. Why should writing be taken as an unmistakeable metonymy of civilization and State? Why should it be an unmistakeable symptom of power and inequality? Do exploitation and coercion need to be put down in writing? In the same respect, why is it usually assumed that every large architectural or engineering construction is the result of coercion and command, exercised from a position of power, preferably of a single person? Have our hierarchic societies made us forget that productive collaboration and coordination need not depend on the threat of the whip? The situation does not improve epistemologically even if we add discrete features, such as 'irrigation', 'monumental public works', or 'specialized craftsmen'. In the last resort, as we saw, this methodology rests on a double initial assumption, which is 1) a State will only be identified as such if it complies with the standard developed according to the evidence of a *few determinate States*, and 2) it has not been archaeology (not even anthropology) which has granted the statute of State to this small reference group, but it was themselves, by putting the names of their rulers down in *writing*.

Unlike a methodology based on the identification of diagnostic elements, we suggest that research should be oriented at looking in the archaeological record for the relationships designated in the key categories that define the fact of State, such as 'economic exploitation', 'social classes', and 'coercive force', which in turn are based on others like 'added value', 'surplus', and 'property'. All these categories should be used as tools to interrogate the social materiality studied by archaeology, and never to supplant its answers in our name. It should be emphasized that what all the above categories have in common is that they refer to realities of a relational kind. Consequently, the questions they raise cannot be answered by a single empirical element or type of material remains (whether it be 'writing', 'throne', or 'pyramid') but require the prior identification of the agents or terms in relationship and, later, a reasoned proposal of their meaning.

'Economic exploitation' is without doubt the central category, the *necessary condition* for the rise of the State, although not sufficient for its demonstration. Determining whether a society fuelled forms of exploitation and, if the answer is affirmative, delimiting its range, forces archaeological research to inquire, in the first place, how exactly the production, distribution, and consumption cycle was articulated, and discover the extent reached by the division of tasks and the social division of production: what subjects and objects a society produces, how and where, how objects and subjects are distributed, and how soon; who consumed what had been produced, to what extent, and where. Answering these questions involves attending to the place of social practices in their exact manifestation and activity.[17] The materiality of every archaeological deposit, divided up into the different activity areas, identified in structural spaces, is able to provide the necessary answers (production x in areas a and b with the means c and d; storage of x_1 in area e: consumption of x_2 in area z, etc). The objects that have lost their context and which populate large parts of archaeological territory for various reasons are not barren for research, even though their orphanhood has forced them to be less loquacious.

The existence of exploitation relationships could be proposed if significant and lasting material dissymmetries between two or more collectives are recognized. These dissymmetries are seen when their respective contributions to social production are inversely proportional to the profits made with the products obtained from it, qualitatively and/or quantitatively. A collective 'A' exploits another collective 'B', both consisting of individuals of both sexes and similar age groups, when 'A' consumes what 'B' produces over and above what 'A' provides for 'B's' consumption. This consumption without compensation should result in significant differences in the material living conditions of each one. If this occurs, it is possible to refer to each group with the term 'social class'. What is consumed differentially by the privileged class is given the name 'surplus', and ultimately as 'alienated labour', appropriated by mechanisms of added value, and consequently denoting relationships of 'property'.

Difference is not necessarily the same as dissymmetry or exploitation. Differences express an enhancing degree of heterogeneity in terms of social production, although, as we have shown, they can also lead to an effective and affective gap among the various segments making up the collective. The development of social tasks and functions dissociates the entity of coexistence and builds complementary or alternative worlds. The former usually provide open and fluid societies and the latter, closed and conflictive ones. Social differences bring more successes than obstacles. Diversity in skills, tasks, dedication, considerations, and ideas does not necessarily lead to exclusion, but on the contrary may nourish the desire to share and coexist, as it deposits social satisfaction in one and another, in those without whom society would not exist. Differences are a meeting place if they do not happen strictly *for themselves*. In contrast, when they materialize in economic–social dissymmetries they manifest the exclusion and exploitation we are referring to. Therefore, dialogue changes to conflict if the dissymmetries are of the material kind. The differences corresponding to the various bodies and forms of thought are then materialized as weapons of goods in property which avoids distribution and sharing *appropriately*.

Archaeology, as it often deals with contexts of amortization or consumption, especially funerary types, tends to observe dissymmetries precisely on the consumer level (if they existed, obviously). Based on this, it is licit to propose the hypothesis that the dissymmetries observed in the consumption correspond to others in production. However, being licit does not mean that it is true. Therefore, these hypotheses should be regarded as incentives to orientate future investigation towards productive aspects, in order to appraise them affirmatively or negatively.

It is worth taking into account several points when analysing archaeological materials in relation with the category 'exploitation'.

1. *Not all the material differences we are able to detect can be explained by a situation of economic exploitation.* These differences can be observed in the raw material used to manufacture artefacts, in certain stylistic elements of these, and in terms of their frequency in one place or another. Not all differences between groups of objects which do not affect the character of the *productive activity* carried out with them can be considered an unequivocal sign of dissymmetry.

The qualitative differences expressed in the differential deposit of certain objects classified as symbols is not evidence in itself for the operation of exploitation relationships. A sceptre or a crown is not equivalent to a king, even though many kings have owned them. To interpret such items as 'prestigious objects' or as 'emblems of power' is to make gratuitous attributions if we are unable to prove whether their owners received public admiration ('prestige') or whether, in contrast, it was the public who suffered the scourge of their will ('power'). To interpret them directly as a reflection of exploitation relationships would be, as in the above cases, to impose a preconception over and above what the objects display.

2. *The increase in production and/or the centralization of what is produced does not necessarily imply exploitation relationships.*

Obtaining a larger amount of products and/or their centralization, far from being necessarily a response to the generation and control of surpluses, could also be the result of communitarian policies of foresight that do not involve exploitation relationships. Because of this, the evidence of elements such as supra-domestic storage, or tools and installations with a larger productive capacity, should not be assessed as unequivocal indications with which to identify exploitation relationships, and much less, State institutions. Remember that surpluses, the material expression of obtaining added value and, therefore, of exploitation, are identified in those goods alienated from the people who produced them and finally consumed by another collective in their exclusive benefit and with no compensation. Thus, the products destined for a later collective consumption do not enter this category, and neither do the resources for obtaining supplementary products for collective use. In order to propose the existence of surpluses, other kinds of evidence must be invoked to show that the products were obtained and enjoyed privately by privileged sectors. In the same way, the division of tasks and the social division among direct and indirect workers, and the dislocation of society in the various ways of obtaining resources, need not imply exploitation even though they may facilitate it, as we have seen.

3. *Not all the economic exploitation relationships we may propose presuppose or imply a State structure.* According to the definition of State that has been given, not all the economic exploitation relationships generate State politics. It is possible to detect situations of dissymmetry but whose reach does not cause permanent tension among the groups involved. Exploitation is the necessary and sufficient condition of the existence of a State only when it reaches a certain level and redounds to it until it is institutionalized as proper and natural for the social life it claims to comprise. This threshold is not strictly visible in economic exploitation relationships, but in the new social division it gives rise to: that which occupies those who take charge of safeguarding the economic exploitation relationships through the exercise of physical violence.

A certain level and extent of economic exploitation gave birth to the conditions for the appearance of specialists in the exercise of physical violence, armies, and police, detachments equipped with objects also specialized in the business of destruction and which we more properly know as weapons. The appearance of specialists in the exercise of

Towards a Marxist Archaeology of the State 251

physical violence in class societies is a sign of the extent to which it is justified to classify as State the order that governs its political relationships.[18] We should point out that we are referring to *detachments armed because of social exploitation* and not warriors armed through community connections who are unrelated to exploitation mechanisms. It little matters that these specialized detachments are exclusively recruited among the ranks of the exploiting class, or among the exploited, or even if they come from different sources, even other countries. It little matters that they occasionally claim to defend the whole collective in inter-State conflicts, as this fallacy hides the fact that they are defending others. Their *raison d'être* will remain anchored in the struggle between classes, without which history would have followed different courses. Physical violence associated with exploitation is the first institution of the State.

Physical violence exercised by the State will be the basis for the use of other forms of violence (psychological, symbolic) and the support of the compulsory regulations with which the State submits the social relationships it takes under its aegis. In order to regulate and force, the State may promote further social divisions. Bureaucrats, specialists in law, morals, or education will colonize areas of social relationships which until that point had lacked decisive and decision-making intermediaries. In their activity, they will endow themselves with the opportune materials, often unique portable objects and outstanding monumental buildings. This network of new rules and obligations, historically of diverse reach, may be fixed in laws, although physical violence is the means which, in the first and last instance, guarantees or suspends any rule or legal system.

The methodological approaches that we have noted suggest a relational proximity among the groups of evidence making up the archaeological record. It is no longer a case of comparing individual finds with a list of features representing the standard traits of a State. In the first place, it involves working with reasonably full and abundant archaeological documentation referring to structured contexts of different kinds. The areas of activity identified in the contexts will justify the characterization of social units and will provide the extent of their involvement in parts of social production. Next, an assessment will have to be made of the contribution of each group to production as a whole and, at the same time, the sharing-out of products for their consumption. Then we will be in a position to discover whether or not economic exploitation relationships were in operation.

The reach and form of physical violence in social relationships will still have to be evaluated. Effects (the material expression of suffering), means (objects used to produce it), and representation (the symbolic and ideological recreation of effects and means) of the violence will enable a decision to be made about whether armed conflict was installed in politics and whether the exploiting class was in a position to arbitrate it for their benefit with specialized personnel and means. Archaeological research into the State could finally be completed with other evidence of its intermediary and regulating role in other areas of social relationships ('worship', 'administration of justice', etc.).

Among the most crucial policies of the State are those oriented at regulating consciences. Perhaps for this reason, archaeology has traditionally considered that ideological systems and the myriad objects that help to materialize them are some of the most revealing manifestations of States. It is however true that these objects used for communication are found in many other societies. When a material form specifies an ideological function and 'materializes' an abstraction, it acquires a normal character which fixes the symbol within the desired exclusiveness of obedience, respect, and devotion, if it is necessary. In addition, the specialization of distinctive emblems, such as tattoos, marks, hairstyles, or various objects may serve to characterize a social group or segment of a different class or condition, sex, age, or consideration. As we have stated above, we should avoid considering these symbols as denoting the existence of a State, if they do not accompany the fore-mentioned dissymmetrical material accumulation. In the last analysis, it will always be necessary to take into account which groups controlled and enjoyed the goods and resources, and *against* whom.

In the light of the proposals expressed here, perhaps certain societies which archaeology has classified as chiefdoms should be included in the group of those that fostered States. And in contrast, maybe others that are comfortably installed in the select group of the first civilizations do not denote the exploitation of classes that is characteristic of States. Diversity exists, and in its knowledge it is worth continuing to work.

NOTES

1. Lull and Estévez (1986); Nocete (1989); Lull and Risch (1995); Castro et al. (1998); Lull (2000); Nocete (2001).
2. Tosi (1976).
3. Lumbreras (1974, 1989, 2005 (this edition includes several papers published since the 1980s)); Montané (1980); Bate (1984); Vargas (1987 and 1990).
4. Gilman (1976 and 1981); Gailey and Patterson (1988); McGuire (1992); Patterson (2005).
5. Castro et al. (1998, 1999).
6. For a preliminary treatment of the questions developed in this section and the following, see Castro et al. (1998) and, above all, Lull (2005).
7. Marx used the term 'division of labour' instead of 'division of tasks', which we prefer here: 'How far the productive forces of a nation are developed is shown most manifestly by the degree to which the division of labour has been carried. Each new productive force, insofar as it is not merely a quantitative extension of productive forces already known (for instance the bringing into cultivation of fresh land), causes a further development of the division of labour' (*German Ideology*, part 1A).
8. Marx, K., *Introduction to the Grundrisse*, translated by Martin Nicolaus (our italics).
9. Lull (2005: 22).
10. For more information about this, see Lull et al. (2006).
11. *German Ideology*, part 1A.
12. An 'Us' that integrates all the particular 'us'.
13. See an enlargement of this definition rooted in Marxism in Lull and Risch (1995).
14. In prehistoric archaeology, the term 'surplus' is usually applied at the time of the formation of peasant societies. The underlying reason is that agriculture is basically attributed the capacity to increase the production of food above normal demands or requirements. However, it should not be forgotten that these productive systems need a surplus in order to start a new cycle of production with them, so that this necessary overproduction should not be considered a surplus, as is often wrongly done, even in Marxist circles (see Mandel, 1969: 27 and following). In the wake of other publications (Castro et al., 1998, 1999), we identify surplus as that which is taken away from the people who produce it and ends up being consumed by another collective for its exclusive benefit and with nothing given in return. Therefore, we do not define as surplus the products saved for a later collective consumption (such as storing

seeds for the next crops) or the resources needed to obtain goods or supplementary food for collective use.
15. *Social Contract*, book III, chapter 15.
16. 'In U.S. electoral politics, for just one example, the richest one-quarter of one percent of Americans make 80 percent of all individual political donations and corporations outspend labor by a margin of 10–11 ... with contributions being equated with investments.' It is not necessary to add any comments to the conclusiveness of the data given by R. W. McChesney (1998: 10–11).
17. Castro et al. (1996).
18. For a more complete account of physical violence, the motives causing it and its material expressions, see Lull et al. (2006).

11

Epilogue. Theories on the State and the Archaeology of the State: Continuities and Complicity

It is sometimes said that what we usually call 'the past' has gone, never to return, and an insurmountable discontinuity separates us from past human life, which we attempt to discover through archaeology. It would be hard to disagree if this statement referred strictly to the irretrievable nature of the experiences each person has lived through. However, it would be less easy to justify it after a careful look around ourselves, surrounded as we are by material conditions, all of them the living past, without which our reflection would not even be possible.[1] Nor would it be easy to justify the remark if we review the history of Western thought on the State and its applications in archaeology. Today we still accept old arguments and premises, and confront one another in debates that are no less old, which bring problems and dead weights that usually leave few alternatives to scientific inertia.

One of the objectives we set ourselves when we wrote this book was precisely to make clear the continuities that link, explicitly or implicitly, contemporary archaeological approaches and the main trends of Western political thought on the rise and functioning of the first States. In case these continuities have gone unnoticed or been explained incompletely or ambiguously, we shall summarize below those that, in our opinion, are the most significant.

INDIVIDUAL AND...SOCIETY?

The concept 'individual' is so important and omnipresent in the dominant liberal-bourgeois thought that today we can even afford not to take it into account. It is one of the premises of the *commonest* sense of our times, and has become internalized as something that is so much a part of human life that its importance is beyond all discussion. In fact, the individual is imagined as a kind of small god: the *starting point* of what is called 'society', an artificial entity that did not appear until he (they) decided to create it, and the finish line, because the only purpose of the social artifice is to serve him, satisfy his needs, aspirations, wishes, and interests.

The image of the individual as the alpha and omega of social life can first be traced in Machiavelli, although only since its truly modern version was formulated, with the seventeenth- and eighteenth-century believers in *ius naturale* (Hobbes, Locke, and Rousseau, among the philosophers studied in this book), has it occupied the central role that it is currently granted. Previously, Greco-Latin thought had revolved around the political community, for whose happiness and well-being philosophers like Plato and Aristotle had required virtuous citizens, either in the art of ruling or in the temperance of being ruled. Later, Christianity saw the individual as a soul endowed with freedom; however, the soul was always subedited to divine Providence and, as its instruments, to kings, who had been chosen by Him to lead the *community of believers* on the straight and narrow path to eternal salvation. Unlike Greek and Christian tradition, and to a large extent contemporary idealism in relation to Hegelian philosophy and nationalist romanticism, modern liberal thought began to weave a concept of the autonomous individual as the first and foremost reality of a world that could then be called 'social'. From this viewpoint, the association of individuals that we identify as 'society' is defined as the result of the *coincident will* of many who sought solutions for their problems or the satisfaction of their private interests. In other words, the result of a certain agreement between selfish individuals who experienced the same problems or desires. In this way, the foundation of society involved, at the same time, the establishment of the law and its supreme guarantor, the State.

In recent times, the role of the individual as the unifying force of the social world has intensified even more. Modern thought had been responsible for giving a leading role to the *rational* individual. Reason, as a generic human faculty in the service of private interests, was able to foresee the advantages of the association of individuals and the consequent foundation of common relationships. However, a more recent contribution to the image of the rational individual is precisely its apparent opposite: the irrational individual, someone who does not need to justify his or her actions by means of plans, conditions, or agreements, but who surrenders to the impulses of his or her feelings, emotions, or desires. Contemporary individuals, according to this ultra-liberal (or, rather, ultra-liberated) image, dream not of being accountable to the State, but rather of being accountable only to their *states* of mind.

For a long time, archaeology did not feel too comfortable with such pre-eminence of the individual. Unlike historiography, archaeology does not usually work with evidence bearing proper names (never in the case of prehistoric archaeology), and less so with private biographies and epic tales, but with anonymous material remains which often are so fragmented that it becomes even more impossible to identify in them the unity that is attributed to any 'individual', whether or not they are animate. Only in rare and fortunate occasions, the skeletons preserved in tombs allow professions, posts, or political conditions to be glimpsed, and even so, these suggest a succinct portrayal of 'personage' rather than a gloss of decisions, actions, and achievements. Historical–cultural approaches, ubiquitously dominant in the history of the science, were more than aware of this deficiency and were content with subliming the invisibility of the individuals by resorting to the 'artefact', the whole or fragmentary pseudo-individual capable of shedding light on past cultures. Processual archaeology also failed to situate individuals in the place that dominant liberal thought required, although the theoretical decalogues of 'new archaeology' always bore their importance in mind. We should recall that functionalist sociology, the model for the 'social archaeology' in New Archaeology, gave a key role to the individual, so that their achievements, crystallized in the form of power or public recognition (prestige), formed the basis for the institutionalization of political and social relationships and, therefore, the framework of cohabitation. Even so, the totalizing counterweight of the notion of 'socio-cultural system' and, of course, the fore-mentioned difficulties in distinguishing individuals with names and surnames in the archaeological record (identifiable, in the best of cases, after detecting subtle particularities in an object—'signatures', always within the framework of a previously and clearly established artefact style as the social norm) can explain the little importance given to the notion of 'individual' in processual research.

In recent decades, however, things seem to be changing. Through contemporary Anglo-Saxon archaeology, we are witness to the appearance of the individual in its purest state: as subjectivity in action, as agency. In a certain way, this has been a surprise, as one of the main sources for post-processual approaches, post-structuralist critique, provided reasons for undermining every belief system or thought in general constructed from the pre-eminence of the human subject, either from Reason or Will. Nonetheless, instead of exploring Derridian *dissemination* or in the *death of the author* yearned for by Foucault, post-processual and post-modern archaeologies have reaffirmed the centrality of the individual subject, granted by modern liberal philosophy. Through the opportune citations to sociological theoreticians like Bourdieu and Giddens, individuals reappear as less sufficient entities than in modern thought, actors often misinformed of their environment, imperfect and unreliable in their decisions and actions, and even ignorant of the consequences, sometimes unexpected, that these might have, but once more, omnipresent, motivated and creator of relationships and social structures. An important detail: the archaeological visualization of the past individual continues as opaque as ever; the new aspect resides in the licence granted to the other individual, the archaeologist-interpreter, to speak of the past individual as a way to make himself or herself visible in the academic and/or political present. With no more basis than the subjectivity of the interpreter, archaeological elucidations are as changeable and voluble as they assure the relationships among people have been and are.

In consonance with this 'flexibility' of the individual, research into the formation of the State now seeks to avoid rigid or fixed institutional categories (even proposing to drop the category of 'State' itself) and aims to adopt other categories with a dynamic sense ('networks', 'factionalism', 'State-making'). These are, however, set in motion, or rather, in action, by the old subject conceived by Hobbes and Locke which has survived both the death announced by post-modern thought and the reluctance of Marxist tradition to regard the individual as a historical subject. It is true that in Anglo-Saxon post-modernity, the collective of subjects has lost that unanimity that the modern idea of a social contract upheld, and now it is postulated that the individual agency is a source of diversity and conflicts to achieve and hold on to power. It might be said that the image now transmitted of human groups shows them full of applicants to the post of 'New Prince', in Machiavelli's words. However, and what is more important, the same characteristically modern ontology underlies them, according to which the 'I' is the prerequisite for the creation of any 'Us'.

The expansion of post-processual archaeologies shows a trend towards self-absorption among certain influential circles in our profession. Archaeological remains attend unmoved (like true 'guests of stone'[2]) to this new *re-* (and not *de-*) construction of the individual, now more subjective than before and as powerful as his or her academic and political position allows.

SOCIAL RELATIONSHIPS

To state that human beings are social animals by nature, is to say all without saying hardly anything. For Aristotle, the persistence and ubiquity of human community, whether or not it is in the form of the much-praised *polis*, makes any additional consideration about this fact unnecessary. Or almost. The Stagirite added at the start of *Politics* that no one is self-sufficing unless he is either a beast or a god,[3] which is to say, he does not belong to the human race. In this way, he situated the crux of the social matter in the attainment of the material conditions that enable life. In our eyes, Aristotle may be called elitist or sexist, but at least he never lost sight of the fact that the enjoyment of political rights and, if appropriate, the exercise of government, is based on material and relational reality, and not solely or primarily on the moral condition of some individuals. Citizens, the true community of political actors, could act as such because they were maintained by the people who lived in the *polis* without being citizens. Citizens belonged to an empirical, physical community, embodied in the city, its rural surroundings and its properties and buildings, and from it, only those men gifted with the art of ruling were distinguished, those capable of benefiting that restricted collective. Citizens in antiquity acquired and enjoyed that status because their properties (land, wives, slaves) guaranteed them the necessary leisure time to lead a virtuous life. We should be thankful for the frankness: the State is the joint work of leisurely land-owners who wish to continue being such; their true happiness consists of it.

Marx and, later, a part of Marxist tradition, have translated the original idea of the importance of the material support of social life with the central category of 'production'. Production of the material conditions for life, that is, new men and women, and all kinds of artefacts, food, and other raw materials, is the primary social, everyday, and unavoidable fact for any human collective. Production takes place in certain physical situations involving social objects and subjects; contexts that, through the demands of the division of production, will continue to diversify historically; contexts where human groups will forge differences that will sometimes end in conflicts, as the relationships of property and economic exploitation become established. Thought is also produced within those parameters, even that thought which has forgotten its material source and claims it is the origin of everything, either through the mouth of a god, a native spirit, or sovereign and autonomous individuals.

In Chapter 10, we have explained some of the foundations for the development of archaeology that is consistent with an emphasis on production as the driving-force of all social life. As regards archaeological research into the State, the Marxist approach[4] sidesteps several of the ideological premises that compromise other kinds. One of these premises, especially widespread among processual archaeologies, assumes that the holders of political leadership and government act in good faith—that is, their actions are oriented towards the achievement of the common good, either by aiding the redistribution of goods or, to give another example, by organizing the population to construct and maintain large infrastructures. One way or another, the rulers enable the survival of the governed population and increase its well-being, and in return they receive public recognition of their role. Rulers and ruled make up a solid unit, guaranteed by mutual coexistence and supported by benefits for all. These contemporary readings still echo strongly with Plato's words, as when in *Republic* he compares the efforts of a ruler towards his subjects with those of a steersman who longs to guide his ship to a good port, and with the shepherd who protects and leads his flock. Not too distant from this idea, we would find the importance Hegel gave to the great men, those who know the spirit of their people and lead them along the way of the universal spirit. The more recent voices of evolutionism and cultural ecology sound equally familiar, when they understand political leadership as part of an adaptive mechanism put into practice by human groups in their continuous struggle to survive. In short, numerous classical and contemporary theories share the idea that leaders are people who are stirred to live and act by the desire to benefit their community.

Another ideologically filled premise that influences contemporary research states exactly the opposite: political leaders are selfish individuals who act in their own benefit, which with a greater or lesser frequency is detrimental for their followers or their subjects. Many post-processual proposals assume that viewpoint. In this case, we can find the first modern echoes in Machiavelli and, by extension, in all those philosophical positions that are based on the desire for power as an intrinsic part of human nature, from the Thrasymachus sketched out by Plato to the contemporary *Homo politicus*. In this case, the most ambitious, astute, and manipulating individuals succeeded in placing themselves at the head of the first complex societies and, later, of civilizations and States. Subordinated to them would be the people who, through bad luck, ignorance, ingenuity, or pusillanimity, fell into debt with the more powerful or directly beneath their yolk. We can recognize in them that silent majority, blind to the future, who allowed others to raise the first fences on the earth and enclose their pieces of ground, as Rousseau described in his *Discours sur l'inégalité*.

Both positions, supported by supposed characteristics of 'human nature', are, however, influenced by ideology because they introduce an ethical–moral assumption to the research method: the goodness-virtue or the evilness-corruption of the rulers or, in other terms, the 'strength' of these in comparison with the 'weakness' of the rest of the population. In contrast with these approaches, Marxism in archaeology is primarily interested in the organization of economic production in a society and on the distribution and use of what is produced among the members of that society. The result of the diagnosis reached by an empirical investigation does not aim to uncover virtuous leaders or audacious villains but, if there are any, the reach and extent of the relationships of exploitation; that is, relationships of objective material imbalance between groups made up of men and women: relationships that can be identified in the archaeological record, independently of the ideology of the researcher and of who might have held it in the past. Therefore, we should leave behind that concept of politics which is judged according to the moral quality of the ruler (often attributed by the person who describes it) and substitute it with the materialistic analysis of the conditions that propitiate the circumstances of political forces in each historical moment. If archaeology is unable to discover what the material basis was for the power and hereditary privileges that arose with the appearance of the first States, we shall remain prisoners of the moral Manichaeism that has characterized Western political thought so much.

MORALITY, IDENTITY, AND STATE

As we have just seen, for many processual and post-processual approaches, individual morality is a basic component in the wickerwork of social relationships. In contrast, for historical–cultural archaeology and sectors of contemporary archaeologies, the social cement is provided by the Idea with a capital I; that is, an abstract principle that is established in the collective teleology (when people should aspire to carry it out) or in powerful regulation for behaviour (when, having been carried out, it rigidly shapes the social being). In traditional approaches, each 'culture' is defined as a symbolic network which differentiates some ways of being from others. Prescriptive by definition, the culture demands devotion and obedience from the humans, so political consensus is given as taken. At the same time, the vindication of the notion of 'identity' by some contemporary archaeologies presupposes that human conduct takes shape, above all, according to an idea, or in pursuit of an idea whose origin cannot be explained by strictly material causes.

In idealist political conceptions, *morality* and *identity* are synonymous terms which nourish the same *Idea*. The precepts of what we should be (morality) guide individuals' behaviour and thought in a certain way; whatever they might do, their thought will not stray from a universe of exacting commandments in the form of apparent rights and definite duties. These commandments will determine what is right and wrong, and from this, will question what is appropriate or not, creating guilty or innocent people. *Proper* identity, shaped in the haze of individual conscience, and *ex-propriated* identity (the feeling of belonging to a nation, a people, a caste, a class, etc.) participate in a same ethical body that sanctions whether we deserve to belong to that group, chosen by no one knows who (a group with a *firm* tradition, which is to say, abandoned to its own alienation). Otherwise, we move, if life allows us to do so, among the ranks of eccentrics, outsiders, illegal immigrants, the subversive, or expendables, depending on the severity of those who claim to be the holders of the Idea of common Good, a *common sense* that is no more than the *only* sense of what Good is believed to be.

As one of us has suggested,[5] the *what should be* that morality aspires to, questions above all being itself, as it declares itself *opposed* to it and it encourages it to follow the path determined by what is thought to be correct and good. Morality nourishes a *system of presuppositions* which, as a kind of 'social soul', moves contradictorily between what is intimate, instinct and what, in reality, *is done*. The identifying *what should be* forces us to move in a direction, precisely that which is supposed to constitute being itself. The modification of a person's conscience through teaching *alternative* moral principles can make us vary the concept we hold of the world, but it is insufficient, although necessary, to alter our usual behaviour and to transform the world itself. Behaviour is not an exclusive consequence of our will, but pivots between what we *want, can,* and *should* do, three factors that fluctuate inside and outside volition and condition it until behaviour has been channelled along different paths.

To advocate the autonomous nature of the ethics of the individual claiming an intimate, interior, and aprioristic morality, like Kant in his *Critique of Practical Reason*, or to stand side by side with those who defend a heteronymous morality typical of socio-environmental determinisms, does not distance us from the same idealistic field, where the thought-conscience binomial is the driving-force behind human acts. We could give numerous examples of this idealistic tradition: in the consideration of *Good* (Plato) or the *Salvation* of souls (Christianity) as the main guidelines for the actions of rulers; in the affirmation that conformity to the laws of a State is the highest *ethical–rational duty* of its members (Hegel); in the doctrine that believes belonging to a State is a profound aspiration of vernacular feelings or the greatest expression of their reaffirmation (Nationalism); also, and finally, in theories claiming that social systems display an intrinsic tendency to equilibrium (homeostasis) and the search for adaptation to the environment (cultural ecology). However, if the Idea, in singular, has inspired these and other great doctrines throughout Western history, the situation is somewhat different today owing to the appearance of the *plurality of ideas*. Here is perhaps where contemporary archaeologies that move around different 'identities' feel most at home, as in fact, the human condition is conceived as a particular set of related identities. According to this plural conception, social life would not be adequately described by the image of a single Idea that guides or hovers over a united collective, but rather that of multiple collectives holding their own ideas; collectives that, by pursuing their fulfilment or private affirmation, often clash in the struggle for power and hegemony. It would be normal to find numerous identities in a society, sometimes contradictory and even ephemeral, each one of which would vindicate ethnic, religious, and nationalist principles, of gender, age, class, etc. For this reason, instead of ideas, we usually speak of ideologies *sensu lato*, where these are defined as interested and partial ideas, or to be more rigorous, as preconceptions which are impossible to avoid. All pretensions of universality therefore disappear, and this is substituted by a much more local and assignable notion: success, the social pre-eminence of one or other group identity.

All these classical and contemporary approaches are the opposite of Marxism because they pay more attention to what people think than what they do. They are also the opposite of so-called ordinary materialism, which deals more with what is done and with what means (technology) than to how the arrangement and social benefit of means and products are organized. For Marxism, the contexts of social practice are the breeding ground of ideas, of the representations of groups of human beings concerning the world in which they live. Ideas can be as varied as the many living contexts that are connected in a society. Out of all these, only some will finish as ideologies, precisely at the instant in which social life, far from occurring in unison, has given rise to groups with imbalanced material realities. Ideologies, like ideas in general, last and are brought up to date as long as they maintain that link with material reality. Otherwise, they will end up as a burden that sooner or later will be cast off. Therefore, the ontological process of ideas begins with a productive material connection, is diversified in time with the social division of production, and, in classist societies, the dominant ideas or, to be precise, ideologies, will end up being drafted, inculcated, and administered by those who also hold the ownership of other material conditions for social production. However, as these conditions are not homogeneous nor shared out equally, there always remain spaces for the gestation of new ideas, some of which will be set up as combative ideologies against hegemonic representations.

By accepting the diversity and even confrontation between ideologies, one might wonder whether archaeology based on materialist Marxism is compatible with archaeology of identities. It is clear the

Marxism and thought on identities (in plural) are the opposite of doctrines that are articulated around the primacy of a single guiding idea ('identity', now in singular). However, they differ profoundly in the representation of the formation process of ideas. To answer fully, it is necessary to clear up some ambiguities in the use of the concept 'identity'. In philosophy and logic, 'identity' refers to the property of a single object ('A' is identical to 'A', that is to say, a tautology) or to the property that can be described after comparing absolutely equal objects ('A' is identical to 'B'). As we cannot make archaeology about isolated objects 'identical to themselves' or be restricted to groups of objects whose members are 'totally identical to each other' (total identity between two archaeological objects does not exist), it is clear that the use of the expression 'archaeology of identity or identities' can be the cause of confusion.

In reality, 'identity' is given meanings that are nearer to 'identification'. References to 'identity', or rather 'group identity', allude to a collective whose members are *distinguished* because they share a condition or an aspiration that has some kind of socio-political repercussion, whether it be directly or indirectly. The declaration of identity takes place 'from inside' when the members of a group admit they share a feeling of adhesion or affection for some abstraction (for instance, 'We, the Tikopia'); that is to say, they 'identify themselves' with this.[6] In contrast, it is assigned 'from the outside' when the individuals included in a group are given the name by others ('They, the Barbarians'; the babies). In addition to these identity groups, modern studies on the subject also accept identity on an individual level, in which case the focus of attention is placed on the way a person perceives and reworks his or her relationship with other individuals, groups, or surroundings (landscape), how their own bodies feel and assimilate the effects of the practices in which they take part (embodiment), and in addition, they become objects and media in the process of building individual (self) and social subjectivity. The role of 'material culture' in the production of individual and social identities is basically mediatory: it provides lasting symbols, images, and emblems that can be read metaphorically and metonymically by the agents involved in the identity processes.

In any case, 'identity/identification' is above all a classifying, categorizing concept and its use always takes place in the framework of social relationships. It is obvious that the internal categorization of social collectives varies according to the criterion being applied, and at the same time, it is also easy to imagine that there are numerous criteria susceptible to being used. Therefore, the problem for social research would be of a theoretical kind (what relationships are held among the possible different groups existing in a society? Are all these groups of comparable importance, or are some more decisive than others?—in other words, are all the classification criteria of equal weight?) or methodological (how to *identify* group identities recognized as such in the past, in the empirical record?).

It is precisely in the theoretical–methodological aspect of modern archaeologies of identities where we find problems. These studies are based on precise empirical realities, whether these are generic and therefore presumably universal (such as to be born a woman or a man; to be going through adolescence or entering in the third age) or are specific to some societies and groups (for example, to have dark skin, go hungry, or worship the sun). However, these realities, which are always empirical and some of them can easily be proven by prehistoric archaeology, are essential conditions but never sufficient. To be so, they always need the *decision* of the archaeologist-interpreter in two ways. First, he or she decides which of the theoretically countless empirical peculiarities denotes a politically active social group. Secondly, the archaeologist-interpreter attributes to this supposed active group an ethical–moral assessment and the kind of personal feelings that must correspond to it. At this point when, for example, to have been born a woman becomes significant as 'woman' is associated with 'inferiority' (morality) and consequently with 'privation or absence of political rights' (ethics). In this example, in principle, several possibilities exist for the formation of group identities, although it will suffice to mention two of them as examples: some women may be content in that role of inferiority and even be recognized through their own actions, apart from rights of political participation; in contrast, other women may share the harm that the privation of rights causes them and as a result, form an identity group whose activity is aimed at reversing the negative evaluation that justifies their subordination, and in that way, come up against the opposition of those who were happy with the status quo. In this second example, the existence of the initial identity (subordinated women) could only advance by negating it and progressing towards its dissolution (a social horizon in which women enjoy political rights).

Which of the two possibilities described in the example would we opt for as the conclusion of a hypothetical research project in prehistoric archaeology? At this point, aspects of method must be taken into account. If the interpreter rejects the application of an objectively guaranteed method that links social materiality and the characteristics of the chosen social groups, the archaeology of identities will be no more than another version of the subjective projections of professional archaeologists. Otherwise, where does that ethical–moral assessment come from, to rank the plurality of empirical differences in a society and, at the same time, choose the tone of the individual feelings that foster adhesion to the chosen group identity? In this respect, we very much suspect that the frequent reluctance in published works to tackle these questions makes us fear the fore-mentioned pre-eminence of the interpreter.

In short, the archaeologies of identities are removed from Marxism as regards ontological and epistemological questions. When we research State societies, it would not be strange to come across a swarm of group differences, many of them indicated by their corresponding material emblems, susceptible of being interpreted in terms of identity. The reason is that, by definition, State societies are divided societies. To the differential characteristics derived from the division of tasks and the social division of production, we can now add the socioeconomic classes with antagonistic interests, and in addition, other groups and subgroups with common interests, tolerated or encouraged by the State apparatus itself (for example, religious beliefs, sport clubs, or folk music groups) which cut across the previous divisions. *Group identities are formed and consolidated based on inclinations produced by the interpretation of material effects—that is, the result of* affection *for the* effects. What we know of as identity belongs to the world of feelings and, thus, it seems to push individuals internally towards one form of behaviour and not another. They are committing feelings that incorporate and equalize those with whom we have things in common, as well as differentiating us from other collectives. These feelings are nourished, may change if the situations that caused them do so, and even be unwilling to change, at least for a time. These possibilities of feeling decisive individually, united to the capability of acting, contribute to creating the air of freedom that is granted to will.

We would not like to be blind to these possible polymorphous realities, nor be opposed to them being the subject of research for archaeology. However, we insist that such research should depend less on the subjectivity of the interpreter and more on what the archaeological objects are objectively able to show. We also wish that this research could show how State societies have favoured the creation of groups 'following ideas' or 'swept away by ideas', and why these ideas fill us with feelings in turmoil until we lose awareness of the real material conditions in which we live. In this respect at least, an archaeology of identities, instead of celebrating them acritically, could help to rid us of many of those which nowadays colonize us.

MODERN ARCHAEOLOGY AND STATE

At the start of the twenty-first century, it may seem unnecessary to recall that a long time has gone by since archaeology succeeded in separating itself from art history and the mere aesthetic contemplation of ancient objects. However, it is very necessary to remember that this autonomy was won by vindicating its own space within historical, sociological, and anthropological sciences. Therefore, if we are going to move in those fields, it is vital to be able to work with the same categories as they use, in the same way we know when to use a pick or a brush during an excavation, or how to position a potsherd when we draw it. To pretend that 'theory' is not part of the task of archaeology is to mutilate that task, reduce its objectives to making inventories and catalogues, and, with luck, be content once more with the contemplation of these old things. At the same time, to vindicate the importance of 'theory' does not need to imply censuring the excitement of discovery or the fetishism of the find, which are perhaps too deeply rooted in our primate curiosity. However, neither the strict description and classification of objects nor the emotions felt when they are uncovered and seen, should stand as the only interests or attractions of archaeology. To know the origin and the use of the concepts and categories of social analysis is necessary for archaeology to become one day a fully autonomous scientific discipline. In this respect, to delve into the contents of classic works, like the ones discussed in this book, is fundamental to discover the premises of the theoretical and methodological approaches that each archaeologist tries to put into practice in his or her research. We hope to have shown that, for example, Plato and Hobbes are not only a living part of the present, but that modern research on the formation of the first States is still entangled in the same questions that they were able to synthesize. The same can be said for many other 'classics' who, precisely because that is what they are, should be present much more than they are in the training of professional archaeologists. If they were, it would be possible to make substantial progress in our knowledge of the past and, at the same time, avoid misunderstandings, ambiguities, and pseudo-problems that currently take up much of the effort spent in research.

The topic of the second part of the book has dealt with something called 'Archaeology of the State'. We would not like the name to end up creating the thing, that is, that with our text we might support or foster a specialized field of study. Archaeology does not work with evidence of a political nature, and much less of an ethical or moral kind, even though archaeologists might be prone to understand them as the direct result of these regulations. Archaeology is interested above all in objects produced, used, and discarded, and therefore its information is directly socioeconomic data. If we aim to discover something about the politics that these objects enabled, we should not ignore that primary condition of objects as social materiality, unless we simply wish to impose the self-complacent blindness of our own personal politics. The role of the category 'State' should be strictly synthetic; it should only be used after the application of an explicit method and a rigorous empirical investigation to determine whether the finds match the guidelines of the initial definition (see the methodological discussion in the second part of this book). The main thing is not to classify in order to recognize, but to learn how the production of social life occasionally ended up adopting political forms of State.

At the present time, most archaeological work is undertaken by State institutions or is carried out under their supervision. This fact alone should cause us to ponder to what extent this surveillance conditions the perspectives and results of research into the first societies that developed into States. It is surely no coincidence that the vast majority of works that have been published not only avoid questioning the nature and functioning of both past and present States, but also openly try to give reasons for their inevitability and/ or advisability. Whether this is the product of State control in the training of archaeological staff in the pay of the institution, or instead the effect of more or less covert editorial censorship, is a matter worthy of being studied in greater depth.

Contemporary States, like any other in the history of humankind, function to guarantee and increase the profits and privileges of the owners of the means with which social life is produced. In any case, it is (still) an exaggeration to describe the present situation with the image of a 'Big Brother', able to move all the threads of social relationships in a single direction. The members of the owner class only behave 'fraternally' among themselves when they need to defend their private interests with the strength of a united class (echoes of Aristotle and Locke). These 'big brothers', however mighty they are, are not all-powerful. This is because social life is produced every day, because at the start of the day everything still remains to be done, and they cannot do this task on their own. In the disunity of the powerful, in daily collective production, cracks appear, gaps for unity, criticism, and generation of alternatives.

We would be prepared to doubt the Marxist position expounded in this book, and to grant all the credit to contemporary idealism that believes modern society (at least, Western society, which is the one that carries out most archaeology and writes that thing we call history) is a freely moving scenario, open to individual initiatives, to the plurality of opinions and 'identities', and the free expression of emotions and feelings. We would be delighted to second that view of society, as long as alternative thoughts and life experiments had a real chance of being carried out in practice. Otherwise, it would have to be admitted that the State represses or eliminates anyone who goes against the *status quo* of the owners of capital, those who trust that the State will ensure their happy existence as citizens, those who are the only ones materially, and therefore truly, free.

What is the role of archaeology in all this? The breadth of the perspective given by the timescales we work with, above all in prehistoric archaeology, combined with the 'sincerity' of the material evidence that we research, comprise highly suitable scenarios for the critique, questioning, and demythologizing of the 'common sense' imposed by modern States. In this respect, archaeology can provide elements of political and socioeconomic debate in general. However, this critical potential would lose its effectiveness if we admit that any interpretation can be acceptable, even by resorting to the well-worn phrases of 'everything is valid' and 'because I validate it' (I, who made it). For this reason, archaeology needs to go a long way to define a coherent and explicit method that can extract all the information contained within archaeological objects. Perhaps, after all, that is the main aspiration underlying this book.

NOTES

1. Lull (2007a), *Los objetos distinguidos. La arqueología como excusa.* Bellaterra, Barcelona.
2. In the Spanish 'convidado de piedra', a reference to the original title of the work 'Don Juan' by Tirso de Molina. It is used to refer to a guest at a meeting who takes no part in it and is ignored by the hosts. (Translator's Note.)
3. *Politics*, book I, part II.
4. We are not referring here to neo-Marxist approaches of subjectivist undertones.
5. Lull (2007b), Ética y Moral. Política y (di)sentimiento, *Jornadas Marx en el Siglo XXI*, Universidad de la Rioja, Logroño 12–14 de diciembre.
6. In this case, 'identification' makes full sense, as it combines the meanings of the distinction of the group and of the adhesion of the members of the group to an idea.

References

Adams, R. McC. (1966), *The Evolution of Urban Society: Early Mesopotamia and Prehispanic Mexico*, Aldine, Chicago.
Algaze, G. (2001), Initial Social Complexity in Southwestern Asia: The Mesopotamian Advantage, *Current Anthropology*, 42, pp. 199–233.
—— (1993), *The Uruk World System: The Dynamics of Expansion of Early Mesopotamian Civilization*, University of Chicago Press, Chicago.
Aristotle, *Politics* (trans. B. Jowett, available online at <http://socserv.mcmaster.ca/econ/ugcm/3ll3/aristotle/Politics.pdf>).
Bagley, R. (1999), Shang Archaeology, in M. Loewe and E. L. Shaughnessy, eds., *The Cambridge History of Ancient China: From the Origins of Civilization to 221 BC*, Cambridge University Press, Cambridge, pp. 124–231.
Bard, K. (2000), The Emergence of the Egyptian State (c. 3200–2686 BC), in I. Shaw, ed., *The Oxford History of Ancient Egypt*, Oxford University Press, Oxford, pp. 61–88.
Bate, L. F. (1984), Hipótesis sobre la sociedad clasista inicial, *Boletín de Antropología Americana*, 9, pp. 47–86.
Billman, B. (2002), Irrigation and the Origins of the Southern Moche State on the North Coast of Peru, *Latin American Antiquity*, 13, pp. 371–400.
Blanton, R. E. (1998), Beyond Centralization: Steps Towards a Theory of Egalitarian Behavior in Archaic States, in G. Feinman and J. Marcus, eds., *Archaic States*, School of American Research, Santa Fe, pp. 135–72.
Blanton, R. E., G. Feinman, S. Kowalewski, and L. Nicholas (1999), *Ancient Oaxaca*, Cambridge University Press, Cambridge.
Bobbio, N. (1987), *La teoría de las formas de gobierno en la historia del pensamiento político*, Fondo de Cultura Económica, Mexico.
Butterlin, P. (2003), *Les Temps Proto-Urbains de Mésopotamie. Contacts et acculturation à l'époque d'Uruk au Moyen-Orient*, CNRS Éditions, Paris.
Carneiro, R. (1970), A Theory of the Origins of the State, *Science*, 169, pp. 733–8.
Castro, P. V., R. W. Chapman, S. Gili, V. Lull, R. Micó, C. Rihuete, R. Risch, and M. E. Sanahuja Yll (1996), Teoría de las prácticas sociales, *Complutum Extra 6. Homenaje a Manuel Fernández-Miranda*, 6, pp. 35–48.
—— —— —— —— —— —— —— (1999), *Proyecto Gatas 2. La dinámica arqueoecológica de la ocupación prehistórica*, Monografías Arqueológicas, Consejería de Cultura de la Junta de Andalucía, Sevilla.
—— S. Gili, V. Lull, R. Micó, C. Rihuete, R. Risch and M. E. Sanahuja Yll (1998), Teoría de la producción de la vida social. Mecanismos de

explotación en el Sudeste ibérico, *Boletín de Antropología Americana*, 33, pp. 25–77.
Chapman, R. W. (2003), *Archaeologies of Complexity*, Routledge, London.
Childe, V. G. (1934), *New Light on the Most Ancient East*, Paul, Trench, Trubner & Co., London.
—— (1936), *Man Makes Himself*, Oxford University Press, Oxford.
—— (1942), *What Happened in History*, Pelican, Harmondsworth.
—— (1950), The Urban Revolution, *Town Planning Review*, 21 (1), pp. 3–17.
—— (1951), *Social Evolution*, Watts & Co., London.
Clark, J. E. (1997), The Arts of Government in Early Mesoamerica, *Annual Review of Anthropology*, 26, pp. 211–34.
Clastres, P. (1974), *La société contre l'État*. Les Éditions du Minuit, Paris.
Compagno, M. (2002), *De los jefes-parientes a los reyes-dioses. Surgimiento y consolidación del Estado en el antiguo Egipto*, Aula Aegyptiaca, Barcelona.
Crumley, C. (1987), A Dialectical Critique of Hierarchy, in T. C. Patterson and C. W. Gailey, eds., *Power Relations and State Formation*, American Anthropological Association, Washington DC, pp. 155–69.
Daniel, G. (1968), *The First Civilizations*, Thames and London, London.
Demarest, A. (1989), The Olmec and the Rise of Civilization in Eastern Mesoamerica, in R. J. Sharer and D. C. Grove, eds., *Regional Perspectives on the Olmec*, Cambridge University Press, Cambridge, pp. 303–44.
D'Hont, J. (2002), *Hegel*, Tusquets Editores, Barcelona.
Earle, T. K., ed. (1993), *Chiefdoms: Power, Economy, and Ideology*, School of American Research, Advanced Seminar Series, Cambridge University Press, Cambridge.
—— (1997), *How Chiefs come to Power. The Political Economy in Prehistory*, Stanford University Press, Stanford.
Dreyer, G. (1998), *Umm el Qaab I: Das prädynastische Könisgrab U-j und seine frühen Schriftzeugnisse*, Deutschen Archäologischen Instituts, Abteilung Kairo, 86, Philipp von Zabern, Maguncia, Mainz.
Engels, F. (1869), *Biography of Karl Marx* (trans. Joan Walmsley and Trevor Walmsley at <www.marxists.org>).
—— (1875), *Letter from Engels to Bebel* (18–28 March 1875)
—— (1884), *The Origin of the Family, Private Property and the State*, London.
Feinman, G. and J. Marcus, eds. (1998), *Archaic States*, School of American Research, Santa Fe.
Feuerbach, L. (1974 [1839]), *Aportes para la Crítica de Hegel*, La Pléyade, Buenos Aires.
Flannery, K. (1972), The Cultural Evolution of Civilizations, *Annual Review of Ecology and Systematics*, 3, pp. 399–426.

Flannery, K. and J. Marcus (2000) Formative Mexican Chiefdoms and the Myth of the 'Mother Culture', *Journal of Anthropological Archaeology*, 19 (1), pp. 1–38.

Forest, J.-D. (1996), *Mésopotamie. L'apparition de l'etat (VIIe–IIIe millénaires)*, Méditerranée, Paris.

Frangipane, M. (1996), *La nascita dello Stato nel Vicino Oriente*, Laterza, Rome.

Fried, M. H. (1960), On the Evolution of Social Stratification and the State, in S. Diamond, ed., *Culture in History: Essays in Honor of Paul Radin*, Columbia University Press, New York.

—— (1967), *The Evolution of Political Society. An Essay in Political Anthropology*, Random House, New York.

Gailey, C. W. and T. C. Patterson (1988), State Formation and Uneven Development, in J. Gledhill, B. Bender and M. T. Larsen, eds., *State and Society. The Emergence and Development of Social Hierarchy and Political Centralisation*, Unwyn Hyman, London, pp. 77–90.

Gilman, A. (1976), Bronze Age Dynamics in Southeast Spain, *Dialectical Anthropology*, I, pp. 307–19.

—— (1981), The Development of Social Stratification in Bronze Age Europe, *Current Anthropology*, 22 (1), pp. 1–23.

Gledhill, J., B. Bender, and M. T. Larsen, eds. (1988), *State and Society. The Emergence and Development of Social Hierarchy and Political Centralisation*, Unwyn Hyman, London.

Grove, D. C. (1997), Olmec Archaeology: A Half Century of Research and its Accomplishments, *Journal of World Prehistory*, 11, pp. 51–101.

Haas, J. ed. (2001), *From Leaders to Rulers*, Kluwer Aademic/Plenum Publishers, New York.

Haas, J. and W. Creamer (2006), Crucible of Andean Civilisation. The Peruvian Coast from 3000 to 1800 BC, *Current Anthropology*, 47 (5), pp. 745–75.

Halstead, P. (1981), From Determinism to Uncertainty: Social Storage and the Rise of the Minoan Palace, in A. Sheridan and G. Bailey, eds., *Economic Archaeology. Towards an Integration of Ecological and Social Approaches*, British Archaeological Reports, International Series, 96, Oxford, pp. 187–213.

Hamilakis, Y., ed. (2002), *Labyrinth Revisited: Rethinking Minoan Archaeology*, Oxbow Books, Oxford.

Harris, M. (1974), *Cows, Pigs, Wars and Witches: The Riddles of Culture*, Random House, London.

Hartung, U. (2002), Imported Jars from Cemetery U at Abydos and the Relations between Egypt and Canaan in Predynastic Times, in E. C. M. Van den Brink and T. E. Levy, eds., *Egypt and the Levant: Interrelations* from the 4th through the Early 3rd Millennium BCE, Leicester University Press, London, pp. 437–49.

Hassan, F. (1988), The Predynastic of Egypt, *Journal of World Prehistory*, 2 (2), pp. 135–85.

Hayden, B. (2001), Pathways to Power. Principles for Creating Socioeconomic Inequalities, in T. D. Price and G. M. Feinman, eds., *Foundations of Social Inequality*, Plenum Press, New York/London, pp. 15–86.

Hegel, G. W. F. (1807), *Phenomenology of the Spirit*.

—— (1821), *The Philosophy of Right* (trans. S. W. Dyde 1896, online at <libcom.org/files/Philosophy_of_Right.pdf>).

Hobbes, T. (1651), *Leviathan, The Matter, Forme and Power of a Common Wealth Ecclesiasticall and Civil*, Oxford World's Classics, Oxford.

Huot, J.-L. (2004), *Une archéologie des peoples du Proche-Orient (vol. I). Des premiers villageois aux peoples des cités-Etats (X–III millénaire av. J.-C.)*, Errance, Paris.

Johnson, A. W. and T. Earle (1987), *The Evolution of Human Societies. From Foraging Group to Agrarian State*, Stanford University Press, Stanford, pp. 18–22 and 314–20.

Kemp, B. J. (1989), *Ancient Egypt. Anatomy of a Civilization*, Routledge, London.

Lamotta, V. M. and M. Schiffer (2001), Behavioral Archaeology. Toward a New Synthesis, in I. Hodder, ed., *Archaeological Theory Today*, Polity Press, Cambridge, pp. 14–64.

Lenin, V. I. (1917), *The State and Revolution*, Moscow.

Lisón, C. (1975), Prólogo to L. H. Morgan, *La sociedad primitiva*, Ayuso, Madrid, pp. 9–68.

Liu, L. (1996), Settlement patterns, chiefdom variability and the development of early states in north China, *Journal of Anthropological Archaeology*, 15, pp. 237–88.

—— (2004), *The Chinese Neolithic. Trajectories to Early States*, Cambridge University Press, Cambridge.

Liu, L. and X. Chen (2003), *State Formation in Early China*, Duckworth, London.

Liu, L., X. Chen, Y. K. Lee, H. T. Wright, and A. Rosen (2004), Settlement Patterns and Development of Social Complexity in the YiLuo Region, North China, *Journal of Field Archaeology*, 29 (1–2), pp. 75–100.

Locke, J. (1690), *Second Treatise of Government. An Essay Concerning the True Original Extent and End of Civil Government*, London.

Lull, V. (2000), El Argar: Death at Home, *Antiquity*, 74, pp. 581–90.

—— (2005), Marx, Production, Society and Archaeology, *Trabajos de Prehistoria*, 62 (1), pp. 7–26.

—— (2007a), *Los objetos distinguidos. La arqueología como excusa*. Bellaterra, Barcelona.

—— (2007b), Ética y Moral. Política y (di)sentimiento, *Jornadas Marx en el Siglo XXI*, Universidad de la Rioja, Logroño 12-14 de diciembre.

—— and J. Estévez (1986), Propuesta metodológica para el estudio de las necrópolis argáricas, *Homenaje a Luis Siret (1934-1984)*, Consejería de Cultura de la Junta de Andalucía, Seville, pp. 441-52.

—— R. Micó, C. Rihuete, and R. Risch (2006), La investigación de la violencia: una aproximación desde la arqueología, *Cypsela*, 16, pp. 91-112.

Lull, V. and R. Risch (1995), El Estado Argárico, *Verdolay*, 7, pp. 97-109.

Lumbreras, L. G. (1974), *La arqueología como ciencia social*, Histar, Lima.

—— (1981), *Los orígenes de la civilización en el Perú*, Milla Batres, Lima.

—— (1989), *Chapín de Huántar en el nacimiento de la civilización andina*, INDEA, Lima.

—— (2005), Estudios arqueológicos sobre el Estado, in E. González Carré and C. Del Águila, eds., *Arqueología y sociedad. Luis Guillermo Lumbreras*, Instituto de Estudios Peruanos, Lima, pp. 187-276.

Machiavelli, N. (1513), *The Prince* (trans. P. Bondanella, Oxford World's Classics, Oxford, 2005).

Maisels, C. K. (1999), *Early Civilizations of the Old World. The Formative Histories of Egypt, The Levant, Mesopotamia, India and China*, Routledge, London.

Mandel, E. (1969), *Introducción a la economía marxista*, Ediciones Era, Mexico.

Marcus, J. and G. Feinman (1998), Introduction, in G. Feinman and J. Marcus eds., *Archaic States*, School of American Research, Santa Fe, pp. 3-13.

Marcus, J. and K. Flannery (1996), *Zapotec Civilization: How Urban Society Evolved in Mexico's Oaxaca Valley*, Thames and Hudson, London.

Marx, K. (1842a), Leading Article in Number 179 in the Cologne Gazette (*Kölnische Zeitung*), *Rheinische Zeitung* (Rhineland Gazette), 10, 12, and 14 July.

—— (1842b), Proceedings of the Sixth Rhine Province Assembly, *Rheinische Zeitung*, October-November.

—— (1843a), Letter to Ruge (Cologne, March).

—— (1843b), *Critique of Hegel's Philosophy of Right* (trans. J. O'Malley, available online at <www.marxists.org>).

—— (1844a), *The Economic and Philosophic Manuscripts* (trans. G. Benton, available online at <www.marxists.org>).

—— (1844b), *On the Jewish Question*, Paris.

—— (1844c), Critical Notes to the Article: 'The King of Prussia and Social Reform'. By a Prussian, Paris.

—— (1859), Preface, A Contribution to the Critique of Political Economy (trans. S. W. Ryazanskaya, available online at <www.marxists.org>).

—— (1857), *The Grundrisse* (trans. available online at <www.marxists.org>).

—— (1871), *The Civil War in France*, Paris.

—— (1875), *Critical Marginal Notes on the Unity Programme of the German Social-Democratic Worker's Party* (trans. available online at <www.marxists.org>).

Marx, K. and F. Engels (1846), *The German Ideology* (trans. available online at <www.marxists.org>).

Marx, K. and Krader, L. (1988), *Los apuntes etnológicos de Karl Marx* (transcritos, anotados e introducidos por Lawrence Krader), Pablo Iglesis/Siglo XXI, Madrid.

McChesney, R. W. (1998), Introduction, in N. Chomsky, ed., *Profit Over People: Neoliberalism and Global Order*, Seven Stories Press, New York.

McGuire, R. H. (1992), *A Marxist Archaeology*, Academic Press, San Diego.

Meek, R. (1976), *Social Science and the Ignoble Savage*, Cambridge University Press, Cambridge.

Midant-Reynes, B. (2003), *Aux origins de l'Égipte. Du Néolithique à l'emergence de l'État*, Fayard, Paris.

Milner, G. R. (2004), *The Moundbuilders. Ancient Peoples of Eastern North America*, Thames and Hudson, London.

Montané, J. (1980), *Marxismo y arqueología*, Ediciones de Cultura Popular, México.

Morgan, L. H. (1877), *Primitive Society*, London.

Nietzsche, F. (1873), *On Truth and Lies in a Nonmoral Sense*.

Nocete, F. (1989), *El espacio de la coerción. La transición al estado de las campiñas del Alto Guadalquivir (España) 3000-1500 a.C.*, British Archaeological Reports, International Series 492, Oxford.

—— (2001), *Tercer milenio antes de nuestra era. Relaciones centro/periferia en el Valle del Guadalquivir*, Bellaterra, Barcelona.

O'Shea, J. (1981), Coping with Scarcity: Exchange and Social Storage, in A. Sheridan and G. Bailey, eds., *Economic Archaeology. Towards an Integration of Ecological and Social Approaches*, British Archaeological Reports, International Series 96, Oxford, pp. 167-83.

Patterson, T. C. (2005), Craft Specialization, the Reorganization of Production Relations and State Formation, *Journal of Social Archaeology*, 5 (3), pp. 307-37.

Patterson, T. C. and C. W. Gailey, eds. (1987), *Power Relations and State Formation*, American Anthropological Association, Washington DC.

Pauketat, T. R. (2004), *Ancient Cahokia and the Mississippians*, Cambridge University Press, Cambridge.

Piggott, S. (1961), *The Dawn Of Civilization*, Thames and Hudson, London.

Plato, [*c.*380 BC] *Republic* (trans. R. Waterfield, Oxford World's Classics, Oxford, 1998).

——, [360 BC] *Crito*.
——, [360 BC] *The Statesman*.
Pollock, S. (1999), *Ancient Mesopotamia: The Eden that Never Was*, Cambridge University Press, Cambridge.
Possehl, G. (2002), *The Indus Civilization: A Contemporary Perspective*. Altamira, Walnut Creek.
Postgate, N., ed. (2002), *Artefacts of Complexity: Tracking the Uruk in the Near East*, British School of Archaeology in Iraq, Aras & Phillips, Warminster.
Price, T. D. and G. M. Feinman, eds. (1995), *Foundations of Social Inequality*, Plenum Press, New York/London.
Rathje, W. (1971), The Origin and Development of Lowland Classic Maya Civilization, *American Antiquity*, 36 (3), pp. 275–85.
Redman, C. L. (1978), *The Rise of Civilization: From Early Farmers to Urban Society in the Ancient Near East*, W. H. Freeman and Co., San Francisco.
Renfrew, C. (1973), Monuments, Mobilization and Social Organization in Neolithic Wessex, in C. Renfrew, ed., *The Explanation of Culture Change: Models in Prehistory*, Duckworth, London, pp. 539–58.
Renfrew, C. and P. Bahn (1991), *Archaeology. Theories, Methods and Practice*, Thames and Hudson, London. (More recent editions are available.)
Ripalda, J. M. (1978), Note 18, *Crítica de la filosofía del Estado de Hegel*, Crítica, Barcelona.
Robles, L. and A. Chueca (1995), Estudio Preliminar, in *La Monarquía* de Tomás de Aquino, Tecnos, Madrid.
Rothman, M. S. (2004), Studying the Development of Complex Society: Mesopotamia in the Late Fifth and Fourth Millennia BC, *Journal of Archaeological Research*, 12 (1), pp. 75–119.
—— ed. (2001), *Uruk Mesopotamia and its Neighbors. Cross-Cultural Interactions in the Era of State Formation*, School of American Research, Advanced Seminar Series, Santa Fe.
Rousseau, J.-J. (1755), *Discourse on the Origin and Foundation of the Inequality of Mankind* (trans. G. D. H. Cole online at <http://www.constitution.org>).
—— (1762), *The Social Contract* (trans. G. D. H. Cole online at <http://www.constitution.org>).
Sabine, G. H. (1937), *A History of Political Theory*, Holt, Rinehart and Winston Inc, New York.
Service, E. R. (1962), *Primitive Social Organization: An Evolutionary Perspective*, Random House, New York.
—— (1975), *Origins of the State and Civilization: The Process of Cultural Evolution*, W.W. Norton & Company, London.

Shady, R. and C. Levya, eds. (2003), *La ciudad sagrada de Caral-Supe: Los orígenes de la civilización andina y la formación del estado prístino en el antiguo Perú*, Instituto Nacional de Cultura, Lima.

Smith, A. T. (2003), *The Political Landscape. Constellations of Authority in Early Complex Polities*, University of California Press, Berkeley/Los Angeles.

Spencer, C. S. and E. M. Redmond (2004), Primary State Formation in Mesoamerica, *Annual Review of Anthropology*, 33, pp. 173–99.

Stanish, C. (2001), The Origin of State Societies in South America, *Annual Review of Anthropology*, 30, pp. 40–64.

Stein, G. (2001), 'Who Was King? Who Was Not King?' Social Group Composition and Competition in Early Mesopotamian State Societies, in J. Haas, ed., *From Leaders to Rulers*, Kluwer Academic/Plenum Publishers, New York, pp. 205–31.

Steward, J. (1949), Cultural Causality and Law: A Trial Formulation of the Development of Early Civilizations, *American Anthropologist*, 51, pp. 1–27.

St Thomas Aquinas (1265–7), *On Kingship* (trans. G. B. Phelan, revised by I. Th. Eschmann, Pontifical Institute of Mediaeval Studies, Canada, 2000).

—— [1265–74] *Summa Theologica* (trans. online at <www.sacred-texts.com/chr/aquinas/summa/index.htm>).

Tainter, J. A. (1988), *The Collapse of Complex Societies*, Cambridge University Press, Cambridge.

Testart, A. (2004), *L'origine de l'État. La servitude volontaire II*, Errante, Paris.

Thomson, D., ed. (1966), *Political Ideas*, Watts, London.

Tierno, E. (1991), Estudio preliminar, in T. Hobbes, *Del ciudadano y Leviatán*, Tecnos, Madrid, pp. ix–xvi.

Tosi, M. (1976), The Dialectics of State formation in Mesopotamia, Iran and Central Asia, *Dialectical Anthropology*, 1, pp. 173–80.

Touchard, J. (1996), *Historia de las ideas políticas*, 5th edn., Tecnos, Madrid.

Trigger, B. (2003), *Understanding Early Civilizations. A Comparative Study*, Cambridge University Press, Cambridge.

Vallespín, F., ed. (1990), *Historia de la teoría política*, Alianza Editorial, Madrid.

Vargas, I. (1987), La formación económico social tribal, *Boletín de Antropología Americana*, 5, pp. 15–26.

—— (1990), *Arqueología, ciencia y sociedad*, Abre Brecha, Caracas.

Wason, P. K. (1994), *The Archaeology of Rank*, Cambridge University Press, Cambridge.

Webster, D. (1975), Warfare and the Evolution of the State: A Reconsideration, *American Antiquity*, 40, pp. 464–70.

Whitehouse, R. and J. Wilkins (1993), *Los orígenes de las civilizaciones. Arqueología e historia*, Folio, Barcelona.

Wilkinson, T. A. H. (1996), *State Formation in Egypt: Chronology and Society*, Cambridge Monographs in African Archaeology, 40—British Archaeological Reports, International Series 651, Tempus Reparatum, Oxford.

—— (1999), *Early Dynastic Egypt*, Routledge, London.

—— (2003), *Genesis of the Pharaohs*, Thames and Hudson, London.

Wittfogel, K. (1957), *Oriental Despotism. A Comparative Study of Total Power*. Yale University Press, Yale, CT.

Wright, H. T. and G. A. Johnson (1975), Population, Exchange, and Early State-formation in Southwestern Iran, *American Anthropologist*, 77, pp. 267–89.

Yoffee, N. (2005), *Myths of the Archaic State. Evolution of the Earliest Cities, States and Civilizations*, Cambridge University Press, Cambridge.

Yoffee, N. and G. L. Cowgill, eds. (1988), *The Collapse of Ancient States and Civilizations*, University of Arizona Press, Tucson.

Index

absolutism 44, 48, 49, 52, 53
  Locke on 57
  Rousseau on 74–5
abstract right 87–8, 91–4
Adams, R. McC. 187, 203, 204
agriculture 72, 74, 183
  environmental challenges 209–10
  Fried on 158
anarchy 5, 27, 76
  Hobbes on 48
  medieval view 29
ancient Greece
  citizenship 3, 13, 14, 17, 24
  education of guardian-warriors 6–7
  the good 4–6
  government 9–10, 15
  happiness 9–10, 13, 16, 17, 18, 256, 259
  idealism 19
  inheritance 8
  justice 4, 13
  leadership 12
  leisure 14–15
  property 7, 13
  see also Aristotle; Plato
Ancient Society or Researches in the Lines of Human Progress from Savagery through Barbarism to Civilisation (Morgan) 137–47
anthropology 136–7, 147, 165, 166–7, 218–19: *see also* Fried, Morton H.; Morgan, Lewis Henry; Service, Elman R.
Aquinas, Thomas 28–33
  anarchy 29
  on laws 32
  on monarchy 30–1, 33
  societies, structure of 29–30
  on tyranny 30–2
archaeology 147
  and evolutionism 148–9
  modern 268–71
  and origins of State/ancient civilizations 175–9
  post-modern 215–22, 258

post-processual 258, 259, 260
  see also processual archaeology
archaic civilizations (Service) 152, 153, 155–6
aristocracy
  ancient Greece 9, 15
  medieval view 30
  Rousseau on 77–8
Aristotle 12–17, 18–19, 80, 222, 259
  on aristocracy 15
  citizenship 13, 14, 17
  community 12
  democracy 15
  government, forms of 15
  idealism 19
  marriage and reproduction 16
  polis, model of 16
  relationships 16
  society, structure of 12–15
  women, status of 12
art 186
Augustine of Hippo 27

Bahn, P. 200–2
bands (Service) 151
barbarism (ethnical period) 141–2
bartering 154
biblical quotations 26
bourgeois society
  Marx on 111, 112, 125
  and property 112–13
bureaucracy 128–9, 242
  Fried on 160
  Service on 155, 156

Cahokia, North America 220–1
calendars 186
Capital (Marx) 117
capitalism 44
Carneiro, R. 209
centralization 195, 201–2
chiefdoms 200
  and exchange 152, 154–5, 207–8
  Service on 152, 154–6, 158, 210–11
Childe, V. G. 169, 199

Childe, V. G. (*cont.*)
  and archaeological cultures 189
  comparative studies 204
  diffusion 181
  and evolutionism 188
  and functionalism 188, 189
  impact of 180-9
  and Marxism 188, 189
  on State as mediator 185
  technology 183-4
  on urban revolutions 182, 185-9
Christian political thought 95
  happiness 29, 30, 31, 33
  medieval 28-33
  precedents 25-8
  21st-century 34
circumscription, environmental/
  social 209
citizens and citizenship 259
  ancient Greece 3, 13, 14, 17, 24
  Hegel on 88
City of God, The (Augustine of
  Hippo) 27
civil society 66, 130 n. 21
  effects of 68
  family and 58
  Locke on 55-7
  Rousseau on 68, 74-5
civilization (ethnical period) 142-3
civilizations 190-1
  archaic (Service) 152, 153, 155-6
  comparison of 203-7
  origins of 175-9
  processual archaeology and evolution
    of 197-9
  rise of 207-12
  similarities between 190
Clastres, P. 219
coercion 92, 240, 247
communism 125-7: *see also* Marx,
  Karl; Marxism
communities
  Aquinas on 29-30
  Aristotle on 12
  Hegel on 88-9, 97-8
  Marx on 118-20
comparative studies 204
compassion 70-1
complexity 194-6
confederacies 141
Constantine the Great 27
consumption

  production and 233-4, 238, 247-8
  surpluses and 250
contracts, *see* covenants
councils of chiefs 141-2
covenants 50
  Hegel on 92, 93
  Hobbes 47-8
  Locke 55-6, 59
  Rousseau 75-81
crime 38, 73, 77, 92, 94
Critique of Hegel's Philosophy of Right,
  see Kreuznach Manuscript (Marx)
'Critique of the Gotha Programme'
  (Marx) 124-7
Crito (Plato) 84 n. 59
cultural particularism 169
culture 148, 149, 180

death penalty 77
demagogy: medieval view 30-1
democracy 244-5
  ancient Greece 9, 15
  Hobbes and 45
  medieval view 30-1
  Rousseau on 76-7, 79-80
differences 248-9
diffusion 181, 190
Discourse on the Origin of the Inequality
  of Man (Rousseau) 67-75, 78, 261
distribution 238
  production and 235, 236, 239
  unequal distribution 238, 239
divine laws 49
duty: Hegel on 95, 96, 99, 100

Earle, T. 198
Economic and Philosophic Manuscripts,
  see Paris Manuscripts (Marx)
education: in ancient Greece 6-7, 14
egalitarian societies 153-4, 157-8
Elements of the Philosophy of Right, The
  (Hegel) 98-102
  abstract right 91-4
  ethical system 96-8
  morality 94-6
employment 14, 55, 117-18
Engels, Friedrich 123-4, 128, 129 n. 9,
  133 n. 54, 169, 180, 227
  on property 114-15
Enlightenment 65-6
epistemology 192
equality

Fried on 157
Rousseau on 68–9, 77, 80
ethnical periods (Morgan)
  barbarism 141–2
  civilization 142–3
  savagery 140–1
Evolution of Political Society. An Essay in Political Anthropology, The (Fried) 157–60
evolutionism 121–2, 136, 163–4, 168–9
  archaeology and 148–9
  Childe and 188
  and political relationships 164
  society and 192
  see also neo-evolutionism
exchange 161, 168, 181, 183, 184, 185, 186, 198
  chiefdoms and 152, 154–5, 207–8
  Locke on 55
  Marx on 115–16, 117, 118, 233
  political leadership and 210–11
  Service on 152, 154–6, 158
exploitation 243, 247–51, 261
  violence and 240–1, 250–2

family
  and civil society 58
  Engels on 123
  Fried on 158
  Hegel on 88, 96–7
  Locke on 58, 60
  Marx on 111, 115–16, 123, 238
  Morgan on 140, 141, 142
  Rousseau on 71–2, 130 n. 12
Feinman, G. 206
Feuerbach, L. 110
Flannery, K. 198, 211
  complex societies 195–6, 212
food supplies
  food surpluses 183–4, 185–6, 188
  and leadership 208–9
Formen, The (Marx) 117–20
Frederick II of Prussia 43 n. 17
Frederick William I of Prussia 35 n. 1
freedom 11, 222, 245
  Hegel on 90–1
  Rousseau on 244
Fried, Morton H. 157–60
functionalism
  Childe and 188, 189
  society and 192

gentes 140, 141
German Ideology, The (Marx) 114–17, 122–4
good 10
  ancient Greece 4–6
  Hegel on 95
government
  ancient Greece 9–10, 15
  Morgan on 140, 141–3
  Rousseau on 77–8, 81, 82
  Service on 152–3
group identity 267
Grundrisse der Kritik der Politischen Ökonomie (Marx) 117, 233

happiness 53, 65
  ancient Greece 9–10, 13, 16, 17, 18, 256, 259
  Christianity and 29, 30, 31, 33
  Hegel 95, 97
  Locke 54, 61
  Marx 114
  Rousseau 68
Harris, M. 204, 209
Hegel, Georg Wilhelm Friedrich 86–104
  abstract right 91–4
  citizenship 88
  civic community 88–9, 97–8
  covenants 92, 93
  crime and punishment 94
  critiques of 102–4, 106 n. 90
  division of labour 94, 98
  duty 95, 96, 99, 100
  ethical system 88, 96–8
  family 88, 96–7
  freedom 90–1
  good 95
  happiness 95, 97
  on inequality 93–4, 98
  on inheritance 97
  on institutions 100
  on intention 95
  on internal polity (constitution) 99–101
  on laws 89, 96, 98, 101
  on marriage 96–7
  on monarchy 100–1
  on morality 88, 94–6
  philosophy of right 87–98
  on property 88, 92–3, 97
  on reason 90, 99
  on revenge 94
  on sovereignty 100–1

Hegel, Georg Wilhelm Friedrich (*cont.*)
    on State 89, 98–102
    triads 87–9
    on violence 93–4
    on will 88, 90–1, 94–5
    on world history 101–2
    on wrong 92
hierarchized (rank) societies (Fried) 158–9
historical-cultural archaeologies 190–1
historical materialism, *see* Marx, Karl
historical particularism 101, 148, 180, 181
Hobbes, Thomas 45–53, 66, 79
    on anarchy 48
    on covenants 47–8
    on democracy 45
    on individuals/society 49–52
    on laws 46–7, 49
    on violence 45–6
human rights 59
humanism 36–7
hypercoherence 212
hyperintegration 212

idealism 19, 121–2
identity
    group identity 267
    morality and 262–8
ideologies 10–11, 156, 234, 237, 240, 242–3, 261, 264
individualism 50–1, 58
individuals
    autonomy of 3
    Hobbes on 49–52
    and society 49–52, 255–9
inequality
    and division of labour 94
    Hegel on 93–4, 98
    Marx on 126
    and nature 93–4
    Rousseau on 68–9, 73–4
inheritance
    ancient Greece 8
    Hegel on 97
    Locke on 58–9, 60
international law 101
Introduction to A Contribution to the Critique of Hegel's Philosophy of Right (Marx) 130 n. 21
irrationality 256–7
ius naturale, *see* natural law

Johnson, A. W. 198
justice: ancient Greece 4, 13

kingship, *see* monarchy
kinship relationships 128, 140, 151, 159, 196
Kossinna, G. 180
Kreuznach Manuscript (Marx) 110–12

labour, division of
    Fried on 158, 159–60
    Hegel on 94, 98
    inequality and 94
    Marx on 114, 233, 238
    see also tasks, division of
Lamotta, V. M. 196
laws
    Aquinas on 32
    divine 49
    Hegel on 89, 96, 98, 101
    Hobbes on 46–7, 49
    international 101
    laws of nature 46–7, 48
    Locke 53–4, 57–8, 59–60
    medieval view 30, 32
    Rousseau on 70–1, 73–4, 76–7, 79, 80, 82
leadership 192–3, 221
    ancient Greece 12
    and common good of society 208–9
    and environmental challenges to society 208–10
    and exchange 210–11
    food supplies and 208–9
    Fried on 157
    institutionalization of 197
    Locke on 56
    military 209
    neo-evolutionism and 150, 162–3
    Service on 151, 152–5, 162
    see also monarchy
leisure: ancient Greece 14–15
Leviathan (Hobbes) 45–51
linearization 195
Locke, John 53–62, 66, 79
    on absolute power 57
    on civil society 55–7
    on covenants 55–6, 59
    on family 58, 60
    on happiness 54, 61
    on inheritance 58–9, 60
    on laws 53–4, 57–8, 59–60

on leadership 56
on political liberalism 59
on poverty 61
on private property 54-5, 59, 60-1
on wealth 61-2
love: Rousseau on 71

McChesney, R. W. 254 n. 16
Machiavelli, Niccolò 37-42
 on violence 39
 on virtue 38, 40
Maisels, C. 224 n. 14
Man Makes Himself (Childe) 182
Marcus, J. 206
marriage
 Aristotle on 16
 Hegel on 96-7
 Service on 154
Marx, Karl 103, 106 n. 90, 107 n. 103, 108-29
 on bourgeois society 111, 112, 125
 on communism 125-7
 on communities 118-20
 on distribution 235
 on employment 117-18
 on exchange 115-16, 117, 118, 233
 on family 111, 115-16, 123, 238
 on happiness 114
 on inequality 126
 on labour, division of 114, 233, 238
 on production 108-9, 113-15, 118, 121, 233
 on property 111-13, 114-16, 118-24
 on slavery 238
 on social reality 108, 110
 on State 109-12, 114-15, 122-3, 124-7
 on thought 108-9
 on violence 125
Marxism 227-52, 261
 archaeological research: method 246-52
 archaeological research: theory 230-46
 Childe and 188, 189
 and classification 228-30
 and identities 264-5
 and power 20 n. 4
 and production 259-60
 and State 127-9
mercantilism 44
Mesopotamian city-states 220
metallurgy 72, 74, 148, 183
Milan Edict 27

military leadership 209
Minoan Crete 220
monarchy 107 n. 103
 absolute 44, 48, 49
 Aquinas on 30-1, 33
 Aristotle on 15
 Hegel on 100-1
 medieval view 30-1, 33, 36
money: introduction of 55
morality 4-5
 Hegel on 88, 94-6
 and identity 262-8
 Plato on 11
 Rousseau on 71
 State and 244
Morgan, Lewis Henry 137-47, 169
 ethnical periods 138, 140-3
 evolutionary plan 143-7
 on family 140, 141, 142
 on government 140, 141-3
 on property 139, 142, 143
 on slavery 139, 142
 on social institutions 138-9
 on technology 138-9, 140-1, 142, 144-5
Most Ancient East, The (Childe) 182

natural law 48
 Locke on 53-4, 57, 59-60
 Rousseau on 70-1, 82
nature
 inequality and 93-4
 laws of 46-7, 48
 state of 68-70, 71, 75-6, 78, 79
neo-evolutionism 149-51
 discussion and assessment 161-8
 and leadership 150, 162-3
 political relationships 161-2, 163, 164-5
 social types 161-2, 165-6, 167
 see also Fried, Morton H.; Service, Elman R.
Neolithic revolution 182-4
New Archaeology, *see* processual archaeology
Nietzsche, Friedrich 205-6
North American early civilizations 220-1
numerical notation 186

obscurantism, religious 34
oligarchy
 ancient Greece 9, 15

oligarchy (cont.)
  medieval view 30–1
Olmec society 223 n. 5
On Kingship (Aquinas) 29–33
On the Jewish Question (Marx) 131 nn. 22, 23 & 24
Origin of the Family, Private Property and the State, The (Engels) 128, 180, 227
Origins of the State and Civilisation. The Process of Cultural Evolution (Service) 152–6

Paris Manuscripts (Marx) 113
Paul the Apostle 26–7
peer policy interaction 193
phratries 141
Piggott, S. 190–1
Plato 3–11, 18–19, 84 n. 59, 260
  on education of guardian-warriors 6–7
  on goodness 4–6
  on government, forms of 9–10
  on idealism 19
  on morality 11
  on social classes 5–9
  on women, status of 6–7
polis 3–4
political liberalism 59
Politics (Aristotle) 12–17, 80, 259
polity
  internal 99–101
  medieval view 30
post-modern archaeology 215–22
  and politics 217–19
  societies, organization of 216–17
poverty: Locke on 61
power
  Marxism and 20 n. 4
  paternal 58–9
  Plato on 4–5
  Rousseau on 80–1
  see also absolutism; sovereignty
Preface to A Contribution to the Critique of Political Economy (Marx) 113
Primitive Social Organisation: an Evolutionary Perspective (Service) 151–2
Prince, The (Machiavelli) 16, 37–40
pristine States 160
processual archaeology 189–215, 260
  assessment of 212–15
  and categorization of societies 197–202

civilization, evolution of 197–9, 207–12
  empirical regularity 203–7
  and individuals 257–8
  leadership 192–3, 208–9
  and philosophy 191–2
  social complexity 194–6
production 166, 222
  and consumption 233–4, 238, 247–8
  and distribution 235, 236, 239
  forms of (Marx and Engels) 114–15
  Marx on 108–9, 113–15, 118, 121, 233
  Marxism and 259–60
  and politics 234–7
  social division of 232–4
  of social life 231–2
promotion 195
property 38, 58, 240
  in Age of Reason 46, 50, 51–2, 53
  ancient Greece 7, 13
  bourgeois society and 112–13
  Engels on 114–15
  and factors of social production 241
  forms of 121–4
  Hegel on 88, 92–3, 97
  and inequality 73
  Locke on 54–5, 59, 60–1
  Marx on 111–13, 114–16, 118–21
  Morgan on 139, 142, 143
  origin of 72–3
  Rousseau on 72–3, 78
proto-industrialization 44
Provisional Theses for the Reform of Philosophy (Feuerbach) 110
punishment 77, 92, 94

Rappaport, R. 212
reason 46–7, 256
  Hegel on 90, 99
Redman, C. 187
regularities 203–7
relationships
  Aristotle on 16
  kinship 128, 140, 151, 159, 196
  political 161–2, 163, 164–5
  social 259–62
religious obscurantism 34
Renaissance humanism 36–7
Renfrew, C. 200–2
Republic, The (Plato) 260
  power 4–5
  social classes 5–9
revenge 94

Index

right, philosophy of 87–98
  abstract right 87–8, 91–4
  elements of 89–91
  ethical system 88, 96–8
  morality 88, 94–6
Rousseau, Jean-Jacques 41–2, 66–82, 261
  on absolutism 74–5
  on aristocracy 77–8
  on civil society 68, 74–5
  on death penalty 77
  on democracy 76–7, 79–80
  on equality 68–9, 77, 80
  on family 71–2, 130 n. 12
  on freedom 244
  on general will 76–7, 79–81
  on government 77–8, 81, 82
  on happiness 68
  on inequality 68–9, 73–4
  on laws 70–1, 73–4, 76–7, 79, 80, 82
  on love 71
  on morality 71
  on origin of society 73–4
  and political participation 78–81
  on power 80–1
  on private property 72–3, 78
  on sociability 70–1
  on state of nature 68–70, 71, 75–6, 78, 79
  on women/equality 68–9
ruling classes: formation of 186

savagery (ethnical period) 140–1
Schiffer, M. 196
Second Treatise of Government (Locke) 53–62
secondary States 160
segmental societies 154
segregation 195
Service, Elman R. 151–6
  on archaic civilizations 152, 153, 155–6
  on bureaucracy 155, 156
  on chiefdoms 152, 154–6, 158, 210–11
  comparative studies 204
  on exchange 152, 154–6, 158
  on government 152–3
  on leadership 151, 152–5, 162
  on marriage 154
  on tribes 151–2
slavery 115–17, 123
  Marx on 238
  Morgan on 139, 142

sociability: Rousseau on 70–1
social classes 240
  Aristotle 12–15
  Plato 5–9
Social Contract, The (Rousseau) 75–81
social institutions
  Hegel 100
  Morgan 138–9
  technology and 138–9
social life: production of 231–2
social ontology: society and 191
social reality 109–10
  Marx on 108, 110
social relationships 259–62
social systems: structure of 203–4
societies
  Aquinas on 29–30
  Aristotle on 12–15
  categorization of 197–202
  complex 194–6, 212
  development of 183–4
  egalitarian 153–4, 157–8
  and epistemology 192
  and evolutionism 192
  and functionalism 192
  Hobbes on 49–52
  individuals and 49–52, 255–9
  Locke on 55–7
  organization of 216–17
  origins of 73–4
  and politics 192
  Rousseau on 73–4
  and social ontology 191
  structure of 12–15, 29–30
  technology and 183–4
sophists: and justice 4–5
sovereignty
  absolute 48–9, 50
  Hegel on 100–1
  State and 244
standing armies 128–9
State 186–7
  archaic civilizations and 155–6
  Engels on 128
  formation of 237–41
  Fried on 160
  Hegel on 89, 98–102
  Marx on 109–12, 114–15, 122–3, 124–7
  Marxist tradition and 127–9
  as mediator 185
  and modern archaeology 268–71

State (*cont.*)
  and morality 244
  origins of 175–9
  politics of 230–1, 241–5
  primitive 152
  and sovereignty 244
  transitional models 167–8
  and violence 251
Statesman, The (Plato) 23 n. 55
Steward, J. 203
  comparative studies 204
  on first civilizations 205
stratified societies (Fried) 159–60
suicide 242 n. 69
Summa Theologica (Aquinas) 32, 35 n. 12
surpluses 119, 186–7, 240–1, 248
  and consumption 250
  food surpluses 183–4, 185–6, 188
symbols 249, 252

tasks, division of 232–4, 237–8: *see also* labour, division of
technology 149–50
  Childe on 183–4
  Fried on 158, 160
  Morgan on 138–9, 140–1, 142, 144–5
  and social institutions 138–9
  and society, development of 183–4
Testart, A. 219
thought: Marx on 108–9
timocracy 9
Town Planning Review article (Childe) 188, 199
trade, *see* exchange
tribes 141–2, 151–2
Trigger, B. 204, 205, 225 n. 45
tyranny
  ancient Greece 9, 15
  Aquinas on 30–2
  medieval view 30–2

United Workers' Party, Germany 124–5
urban revolutions 184
  Childe on 182, 185–9
  conceptual core 187–8
  diagnostic traits 185–8, 199–200
urbanism 185

violence 11, 92, 126, 156, 185, 215, 240
  Aquinas on 32
  and exploitation 240–1, 250–2
  Hegel on 93–4
  Hobbes on 45–6
  Machiavelli on 39
  Marx on 125
  State and 251
virtue: Machiavelli on 38, 40

war 209
  Fried on 158, 160
  Hegel on 101
wealth: Locke 61–2
Webster, D. 209
well-being, *see* happiness
What Happened in History (Childe) 182
White, L. 149
will
  general 76–7, 79–81
  Hegel on 88, 90–1, 94–5
  Rousseau on 76–7, 79–81
Wittfogel, K. 209–10
women: status of 6–7, 12, 68–9
world history 101–2
writing 142, 178, 179, 186, 247
wrong 92

WITHDRAWN